Designing a Digital Portfolio

Second Edition

Cynthia L. Baron

New
Riders

VOICES THAT MATTER™

Designing a Digital Portfolio, Second Edition

Cynthia L. Baron

New Riders

1249 Eighth Street
Berkeley, CA 94710
510/524-2178
510/524-2221 (fax)

Find us on the Web at: www.newriders.com
To report errors, please send a note to errata@peachpit.com

New Riders is an imprint of Peachpit, a division of Pearson Education

Copyright © 2010 by Cynthia L. Baron

ISBN-13: 978-0-321-63751-2
ISBN-10: 0-321-63751-8

9 8 7 6 5 4 3 2 1

Printed and bound in the United States of America

Development Editor
Becky Morgan

Copy Editor
Scout Festa

Production Editor
Hilal Sala

Interior Design
Cynthia L. Baron

Cover Design
Aren Howell

Indexer
FireCrystal
Communicationss

Proofreader
Suzie Nasol

DEDICATION

Corny as it may seem, to my mom. Finally, this one is for you.

ABOUT THE AUTHOR

 Cynthia L. Baron is Academic Director of the Digital Media program at Northeastern University in Boston, Cynthia has been active in the creative community for most of her professional life. Previously Associate Director of the Multimedia Studies program and Technical Director and Lecturer in the Department of Art+Design, she holds an MBA with a Marketing concentration and was the executive vice president of a Boston-based graphic design studio for over a decade. She has written for many publications, been a series editor for Rockport Publishers and a contributing editor to the magazines *Critique* and *Computer Graphics World*. She has edited, authored, or co-authored over a dozen books, including *Adobe Photoshop Forensics: Sleuths, Truths and Fauxtography* and *The Little Digital Camera*. Her 1996 book, *Creating a Digital Portfolio*, was the first title ever published on the topic.

ACKNOWLEDGMENTS

I was truly blessed with great people and much support in writing and producing the second edition of this book. Although I can never say enough in thanks to all the people who helped me along the way, I can at least formally acknowledge their input and contributions.

In a project like this one, a lot depends on who you know, and who they know in turn. Nancy Bernard knows how much in her debt I am for the first edition, and therefore all subsequent ones. In addition, I owe a big thank you to my dear friend Dan Peck for playing yenta on the first edition. He led me to Roz Goldfarb, whose foreword graces the book's beginning, and to Rita Armstrong for spot-on talent searching. Thanks to both of these astute women for helping the second time around.

In this edition, two colleagues were instrumental in helping the book take its present shape. The first is Terrence Masson, whose opinions and knowledge of the animation and special effects worlds provided great quotes and inside knowledge. The other is Jay Laird, who went way beyond tech editing for Chapter 7, thereby saving me at least one week of agony—and my deadline.

A quick read of Appendix B reveals what a talented, savvy, and articulate group of creatives contributed to this book. I think it says quite a bit about the quality and creativity of my contributors that most of them were extraordinarily busy during what has been one of the worst economic downturns in recent history. Yet from the established stars to the brand new talents, they were all unstintingly free with their ideas, opinions, and time.

As you might expect, I owe a lot to the publishing team. In particular, I want to thank my friend Becky Morgan, whose career has moved well beyond that of a development editor. But nonetheless, she graciously made time for this book in her busy schedule. As always, it was a pleasure to work with her. Becky's feedback was invaluable, and permeates every chapter. In addition, many thanks to Scout Festa for her attention to all the niggling details—especially those tedious commas—and to Hilal Sala for her help and counsel in production issues.

A special thank you in memoriam to Marjorie Baer, for supporting my initial book idea, and for making the first edition happen. You are still remembered.

And, as usual, thank you Shai. After all these years of being married to a classic Type A personality, he remains the unconditional One—my very best friend. I am a most fortunate woman.

FOREWORD

I often speak to student or professional groups about career, marketplace, and workplace issues. An overwhelming number of questions relate to the structure and content of portfolios. "What should the format be? How to demonstrate different forms of work: two-dimensional and three-dimensional? How should the work be viewed? How should it be delivered? How much work should be shown? What samples should be included?" There is no other topic of such critical significance, because everyone recognizes the role portfolios play in capturing work. And thus, the importance and relevance of *Designing a Digital Portfolio*.

A digital portfolio is now the professional standard. It is without question the most important and mandatory vehicle to demonstrate an individual's skill and accomplishment. It is the first introduction to a future employer, the first foot in the proverbial door. The portfolio is also a repository of past work, a personal archive to be maintained, treasured, and properly backed-up.

In developing a presentation portfolio—and many professionals have strong opinions about their "correct" or preferred method—ultimately the portfolio is a marketing tool. To successfully function as a marketing instrument, the portfolio should be as unique as its owner. This is the most difficult challenge, and this book will help in that crucial process.

Our design and interactive culture moves forward at a lightning pace and, as always, the pressure is to keep up, be current, look cool. However, I would suggest that sometimes it is also valuable to look back, for otherwise we lose perspective. Bells and whistles are not a substitute for substance. We need to make sure, in our fixation on the latest, newest and hottest, that the fundamental emphasis on content is not lost. Portfolios were constructed of 2D or 3D printed material, or on 35-millimeter slides. At the end of the day, the actual deliverable object was important. Today, some old forms may be obsolete, but there is still a need, and a place, to experience the quality of a final printed piece, to touch and smell the final result.

Designing a Digital Portfolio is unique as it offers, with clarity and logic, the process of developing a portfolio—along with personal experiences that add first-hand information. It respects traditional values, while successfully tackling the digital challenge on all issues relating to the choices of structure, content, and delivery. I believe you will agree that it fulfills a tremendous need. And, hopefully, it will aid you in fulfilling your future potential.

Roz Goldfarb
President, Roz Goldfarb Associates
August 2009

TABLE OF CONTENTS

Part III Production

Part IV Marketing

Why you need a portfolio now

For many people, a portfolio is their collection of financial investments. For those of us who are artists or designers, *portfolio* also refers to a collection of material we've created. The two types of portfolios are not actually so different. Both represent the fruits of hard labor. Both are the result of choices made to maximize potential. And poor decisions with either one can spell the difference between long-term success and failure.

Unfortunately, when not actively job- or client-hunting, we tend to ignore our portfolios. This nasty habit can start when we're students. Although the portfolio looms as the single most important factor in their future, students often are so caught up in class projects or part-time jobs that they don't prepare their portfolio until after graduation—too late to take advantage of a portfolio seminar or faculty review. Unfortunately, when the market for creatives is inundated not only with a new crop of graduates but with seasoned pros, competition can be as intense for entry-level design and support jobs as for managerial ones.

A good portfolio is all about contrasts. It juxtaposes light versus dark, big versus small, complex versus simple, colorful versus monochrome. A good portfolio can make bad work palatable, mediocre work good, and good work breathtaking.

—David Heasty

Procrastination continues into our careers. In a busy office, client deadlines take precedence, sometimes for months or even years. "Why spend the time on a portfolio? I have a job," is the argument. But creative professionals who experience an economic bust learn that the job you have on Monday can end with a pink slip sans parachute on Friday. On the following Monday, the lack of an up-to-date portfolio becomes a serious strategic error.

If you're a freelancer, and particularly if you are a recent graduate hoping to use freelance work as a road to your own studio, you don't need just any digital portfolio. You need one filled with recent work and wrapped in a current approach. But when every billable hour counts, it's hard to justify the upkeep. Unfortunately, if a prospect checks out your site and sees the dust practically shake off the page, they won't call you with a sensitive critique. You will never know you lost a job. When you're trying to remain competitive, owning only a vintage portfolio is as useful as having none at all.

No question about it—creating and maintaining your portfolio is a serious and complex self-marketing issue. It deserves your best effort: creativity, attention to detail, planning, and sometimes time-consuming production. Knowing that a good portfolio doesn't happen overnight, you should be working on it long before your need becomes critical. No excuses! If you have time to do freelance or personal projects for fun or extra cash, you can make time for your portfolio.

With the acknowledgment that a portfolio project is overdue, it's time to figure out what that means for you.

WHAT KIND OF PORTFOLIO SHOULD YOU HAVE?

If you need a portfolio at all, you need a digital version. But what form your digital portfolio takes depends on a number of factors that center on who you are and what you want your portfolio to do for you.

A digital portfolio can be a PDF, CD or DVD demo reels, a slideshow on a laptop, or, most frequently, a web address. In fact, if there is anything a wide-ranging tour through today's portfolios shows, it's that there is no longer a standard format for a portfolio.

Portfolios come in a dizzying number of styles, concepts, purposes, and forms. Over less than a decade, the template for an online portfolio, initially based on the formal book with perishable objects in plastic sleeves, has evolved. Portfolios online range from linear slideshows in the traditional mode, to intricately cross-linked artifacts, to walks through a Wonderland-like experience. Even more exciting, creatives are escaping the single-form, single-focus portfolio through posting unique portfolios at multiple addresses that allow a reviewer to jump infinitely from one collection of work to another like stones in a stream. There is more agreement that a portfolio can grow with its creator, changing focus and gaining maturity.

Every candidate we represent must have a digital snapshot of their work accompanying their résumé. A digital portfolio introduction has become the industry standard.

—Rita Armstrong

With the expansion of form comes a democratization of digital presence. Having a digital portfolio doesn't have to be hard. Graphic design, architectural walkthroughs, video, and animation are already produced digitally, and the files can be modified for online use; some 2D traditional work can be scanned; and large 2D and 3D work can be photographed. Plus, today there are a growing number of sophisticated publishing sites, some of which specialize in serving visual creatives, that can make it easy to translate a print-based portfolio into a sleek digital entry.

Your personal expectations depend on your specific creative area. A fine artist working on canvas may need only the simplest presentation on one address. An interactive designer will definitely need a sophisticated presentation on a personal site and will likely have at least one other outlet. Most important, each version of your portfolio should have different subsets of content or modes of presentation that capture all your targeted audiences. Knowing yourself, nailing your category, and being familiar with what others in your profession are doing is crucial to fielding the right range of competitive portfolios.

SHOULD YOU MAINTAIN A PHYSICAL PORTFOLIO?

Portfolio expectations vary, depending on the nature of the work you intend to show and who you want to see it. Even in professions where digital portfolios are a standard, some employers or clients will insist on seeing printed work in addition to the digital version.

Traditional portfolios may still be required for:

- **Galleries.** A digital presence is necessary, especially as part of a first-pass weeding process. But a physical presentation or on-site visit remains the expectation before any gallery decides to show or represent your work, even if that work has a digital component.

- **Environmental or product-based design.** Industrial designers, graphic designers specializing in packaging, architects, and interior designers almost always still create a traditional portfolio first before they tackle a digital version.

- **Print designers.** A digital portfolio has become a must for making the first cut, but a traditional portfolio of printed samples may still be necessary in order to examine your decisions on typography, paper, ink, and texture.
- **School applications.** Some educators, although they may be perfectly comfortable with computers, frequently require slides, not CDs or websites, for an admissions portfolio.
- **Security.** In some cases, your contractual agreement with a client may prevent you from putting a project into a digital portfolio. If you want to show it, you might have to present it in person. See Chapter 12, "Copyright and Portfolio," for a detailed discussion of this topic.

WHY THIS BOOK IS FOR YOU

This book is a resource for the creative who needs to develop any form of digital portfolio. It examines the portfolio process from beginning to end with a fresh eye, in the context of the increasingly virtual world most art and design professionals now inhabit.

For established professionals, I offer some critical how-tos of digital portfolio development and creation. Perhaps you have been presenting your work for years and have a very good sense of your profession, your skills and talents, and your local market. But making your work competitive in digital form demands new criteria, new technical skills, and maybe a fresh look at the work you've done and your assumptions about it.

> **I was fortunate to have acclaimed design writer Ellen Lupton as one of my undergraduate professors, and one thing she said to me really hit home: "If you don't have a website, you don't exist."**
> **—Luke Williams**

For the technically adept who might be less well-versed in self-marketing and presentation, I offer digital portfolio development as part of a larger scheme. This book will give you a good overview of the portfolio process, lead you through the concepts and issues from basic to complex, and help you to develop a portfolio that is right for you.

Either way, this book should make the process of developing your new portfolio a little less painful.

ASSUMPTIONS

Although this book has plenty of useful hints and specific technical how-tos, its focus is on process and results. You're free to use your favorite tools. If you don't have any favorites yet, I've suggested some good step-by-step books in Appendix A, "Resources," to help you master the software basics. Throughout the book, I recommend specific applications for different types of presentations, offer guidelines on how to use them most effectively for different stages of your portfolio project, and help you assess which tools will help you meet your goals efficiently.

I do assume that you have artistic talent within your chosen medium of expression and that you don't need definitions for basic art terms such as scale, proportion, figure, and ground. If you do, you should consider reading the discussion on partnering in Chapter 1, "Assessment and Adaptation," before you do anything else.

I admit that I've tilted the topics in this book toward graphic designers, because their portfolios generally require the most complex preparation. Design portfolios also carry the most demanding expectations, because the people who judge them look at the thinking behind the portfolio as much as the highlighted work within it.

But, to a less strenuous degree, the same holds true for portfolios in other disciplines. Today, almost every creative professional is expected to have work online. With so many portfolios vying for attention, a portfolio that displays an understanding of basic design principles does a better job of showcasing the work within it.

A well-designed portfolio is a way for illustrators or photographers to boost their work out of the excruciatingly competitive world of clip art and stock images. It's a way for an animator or other moving-image artist to present work more accessibly and with more finesse. It raises the visibility and the stock of fine artists. Most importantly, it allows you to show the world that you value and respect your work—the first step in making sure that others do, too.

CHAPTER 1

Assessment and Adaptation

You'd be surprised at what an experienced reviewer can assume about you from looking at your portfolio. Some reviewers may react negatively to choices you've made and pass you by, even if you'd do a great job for them. You can neutralize your portfolio to prevent that, avoiding examples of chance-taking work. This decision has its own pitfalls. Many art directors use a portfolio to get a sense of who you are. If your portfolio is too dry, they'll worry that they won't enjoy working with you.

It's in your best interest, then, to evaluate yourself and your work before it's done for you. Self-evaluation is tough. Although you use some of the same skills you would if you were developing a concept for a client, applying them is much harder when the product is yourself. You carry around blind spots that might make you emphasize the wrong things in your portfolio or pursue work in an area that isn't your best. What are your strengths? What will you need to overcome? Do you have the talents that your target audience wants? Where do you need to adapt to the market? Answer these questions and you have a focus that will shape your subsequent portfolio decisions.

SOUL-SEARCHING

Even if you aren't naturally introspective, don't skip this step. In fact, it's probably most important if you tend to be impatient with self-examination. You're in a profession where personality matters because it is so frequently reflected in how you approach concepts and ideas. The self-assessment checklist that follows will help you to think clearly about your abilities, needs, and goals. Not only will this help you develop an appropriate portfolio, but it will prepare you to talk effectively about yourself and your work in an interview.

Self-assessments are subjective, not scientific. You'll find this one most useful if you collate the results of each topic and use them at major decision points in your portfolio development: determining your target market (Chapter 3, "Your Audience"), preparing your résumé, briefs, and other text (Chapter 8, "Creating Written Content"), and making the all-important concept decisions (Chapter 9, "Structure and Concept"). It is less important to rack up points than it is to have the right points.

In general, solid experience is more valuable than training and can balance some gaps in formal education. Without experience, you should be more flexible in your goals and prioritize your values. In a down economy, there's always pressure to be employed first and fulfilled second. But compromises are out there. Consider positions that offer the opportunity to learn from experienced professionals, even if those positions pay less than those that reward your technical skills. Or use the pay from a production job to finally get the formal education that will open the door to new options later.

Ideally, any portfolio reflects the taste and aesthetic of its owner. It supports the theory that dogs tend to look like their owners and vice versa. It should be a true representation of who that person is and what they're capable of doing.
—Michael Borosky

Values should overlay your goals. The more selective your values, the less likely it is that you will find happiness in a large corporation, and the harder it may be for you to make a major creative change. If you have a reasonable head for detail, you might be happier as a freelancer than as an employee.

Personality is a critical component and can, in the highly subjective world of the arts, move you closer to your goals even if some of your preparation is spotty. If you've chosen one set of words to describe your work and a completely different set to describe your "true" style, you need to reexamine your answers to the other sections and prepare for many hard choices as you mold your portfolio.

SELF-ASSESSMENT CHECKLIST

These questions have no right or wrong answers. They also have nothing to do with how talented you are. (There's no way to judge that with a checklist.)

No one has to see these results but you, so be completely honest. Refer to this assessment at many points along your portfolio process: as a reality check against your target audience, as you decide what projects to include in the portfolio, and as you choose the type of portfolio most likely to help you reach your goals.

Strengths and weaknesses

1. Educational experience in my profession:
   - ☐ Self-taught
   - ☐ Non-credit classes
   - ☐ Certificate or associate's degree
   - ☐ Bachelor's degree
   - ☐ Advanced degree

2. Educational experience in a related or supporting profession (check all that fit):
   - ☐ 2D art fundamentals
   - ☐ 3D modeling or rendering
   - ☐ Environmental design
   - ☐ Video and/or animation
   - ☐ User-interface and/or interaction
   - ☐ Marketing
   - ☐ Photography
   - ☐ Graphic design
   - ☐ Industrial or product design
   - ☐ Typography
   - ☐ Scripting or programming
   - ☐ Writing

3. Work experience within a related or supporting profession (check all that fit):
   - ☐ 2D art and illustration
   - ☐ 3D design: modeling or rendering
   - ☐ Marketing and/or advertising
   - ☐ Graphic design: print
   - ☐ Graphic design: identity and branding
   - ☐ Graphic design: packaging
   - ☐ Photography or image editing
   - ☐ Video and/or animation
   - ☐ User-interface and/or interaction
   - ☐ Scripting or programming
   - ☐ Game design
   - ☐ Journalism, editorial

4. I have software training in (check all that fit):
   - ☐ Photoshop and related imaging software (Fireworks, etc.)
   - ☐ 2D illustration and print design software (Illustrator, InDesign, etc.)
   - ☐ Production software (Acrobat, color-proofing software, etc.)
   - ☐ Flash or other animation software
   - ☐ Web programming languages like ActionScript or JavaScript
   - ☐ Web design coding and software (HTML, CSS, XML, Dreamweaver, etc.)
   - ☐ Rendering or CAD programs (AutoCad, Form-Z, etc.)
   - ☐ 3D or animation programs (Maya, 3ds Max, etc.)
   - ☐ Video editing software (After Effects, Final Cut Pro, etc.)
   - ☐ I have no software training.

5. Exclusive of school, I have been working in my chosen profession for:

☐ < 1 year   ☐ 7–10 years
☐ 1–3 years   ☐ 10+ years
☐ 3–7 years

(Don't count time spent unemployed if you didn't freelance at least part-time.)

6. Rate your skills (not your raw talent) in your primary area:

☐ A master of my craft   ☐ Better than average
☐ Have lots to teach others   ☐ About average
☐ Better than most   ☐ Still learning

Goals

7. Why are you making a digital portfolio? Check all that apply:

☐ Creative outlet   ☐ Employed, looking for a job
☐ Required for school   ☐ Client marketing tool
☐ About to graduate   ☐ Professional project record
☐ Unemployed, looking for a job ☐ Need the technical practice

8. If your portfolio needs are job-related, check the statements that apply to you:

☐ I'll take any job I can get in my profession.
☐ I want a job similar to one I have or had.
☐ I want a job at a higher responsibility level.
☐ I want to do specialized work in my profession. Name the area:

_____

☐ My previous jobs were unfulfilling. I want to do something different.
☐ What I haven't liked about my jobs:

_____

_____

☐ I want/need to change my creative profession.
☐ My current profession is _____ and I want to be
   a _____ (job title).

9. If your portfolio needs are client-related, check the statements that apply to you:

☐ I am happy with the type of clients I currently have but need more work.
☐ I want to specialize in specific industries or types of work. Name the area:

_____

☐ I want to add to or change what I've specialized in. I currently specialize in
   _____ (name of area) and want to specialize in
   _____ (name of area).

Values

10. How do you like to work?

☐ Alone

☐ Collaboration or partnership

☐ As a team member

☐ Doesn't matter

11. What's your preferred working environment?

☐ I can work anywhere.

☐ I need a private space.

☐ I like to have other people around.

☐ My colleagues must be friends.

12. Select the statement that fits you best:

☐ I will take jobs from any paying client.

☐ I won't accept some types of clients or client work.

☐ In specific, I won't accept this type of work: _____

_____

Personality

13. Check up to five of these words that best describe the work you've done:

☐ Personal	☐ Trendy	☐ Thoughtful	☐ Brash
☐ Sexy	☐ Funny	☐ Playful	☐ Sarcastic
☐ Serious	☐ Sensitive	☐ Intellectual	☐ Emotional
☐ Clever	☐ Complex	☐ Detailed	☐ Impulsive
☐ Intuitive	☐ Analytical	☐ Organized	☐ Structured
☐ Elegant	☐ Crisp	☐ Boring	☐ Cooperative
☐ Confident	☐ Challenging	☐ Issues-oriented	

You've chosen words that currently describe your work. If you feel that the words you've chosen don't reflect the style or approach you'd like your work to have, select some words from the list that do so:

_____

_____

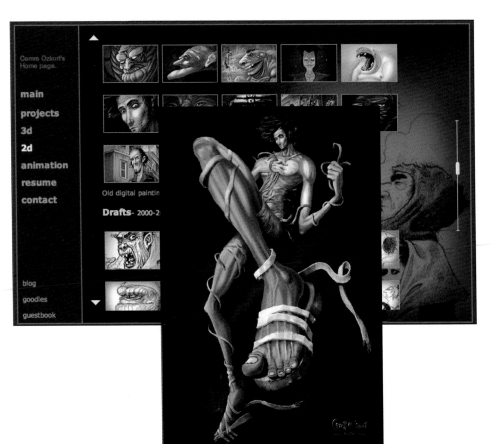

WWW.FISTIK.COM

Some 3D animators are very adept on the computer but have problems story-boarding or making detailed sketches with traditional media. Cemre Ozkurt's web portfolio has ample examples of his ability to think and draw creatively both on and off the computer screen.

Strengths and weaknesses

You have both, and you should know them well. Technical strengths and weaknesses are the most obvious and the easiest to assess. Some employers are on the prowl for specifics, like computer proficiency or knowl-edge of printing processes. They need evidence that you can handle their work.

> **The one thing I won't ignore is a lack of understanding of typogra-phy. There are lots of pieces of advertising that we can do without: photography, illustration, or even color. There is nothing that we do that is without typography. It is the single element that is omni-present. It must be understood before a person can operate at a professional level.**
>
> **—Stan Richards**

Knowledge is tougher to assess because it can be hard to recognize what you don't know. That's why the checklist differentiates between formal professional education and courses that simply cover the how-tos of an application. For example, a professional degree is most necessary in the design fields. If you don't have a degree, you'll need to balance that lack with more years of high-quality work experience. Software training is most useful in areas with very high learning curves, like 3D, while sheer skill is most important for artists, photographers, and animators.

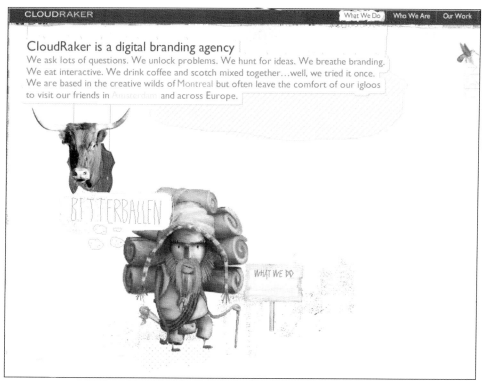

WWW.CLOUDRAKER.COM
Click Montreal and the mounted longhorn head comes down, along with a label. Click Amsterdam and the Sherpa character moves right to make room for the mounted reindeer. This interactive animation sequence has a lot of technology under the hood. How long might it take you to duplicate this combination of animation and programming? The answer to that question can mark the difference between qualifying for an interface design position and a most unpleasant learning experience.

When judging a portfolio, a key criteria for us is control. Is the designer demonstrating a sense of being in control, whatever the task? We judge our own work by this standard as well.

—David Heasty

Self-confidence is important, but it should be based on reality. Without real experience or formal education or training, you may not be qualified to tackle the challenging or sophisticated projects you crave. Or you might find that you're hired for a job that becomes a nightmare because you're behind the learning curve.

If you don't have enough training or experience to land the position you want, don't lose hope. Address the problem by focusing on a short-term goal—creating a portfolio that plays to your current strengths—while you upscale your skills and knowledge.

Goals

Begin a portfolio without understanding why you're making one, and it will fall prey to one of the classic portfolio concept errors (see the section, "What a portfolio is not"). A portfolio begun in ignorance or pure desperation telegraphs its weaknesses.

It's not enough to say, "I need a job!" A job is a financial requirement, not a goal. You could fix plumbing or drive a cab. It is equally insufficient to say, "I need clients!" You can do work for clients who aren't a perfect fit, but it would be a mistake to create a portfolio that will only bring in the wrong type of work for you. Never lose sight of the fact that you're in this because it's work you want to do—it is satisfying and it matters.

Set two goals now: your long-term career and your short-term job. The first should rule your portfolio's presentation format and the type of work you show. The second will determine the specific projects you include and how you customize the portfolio for individual needs. Perhaps you want to specialize in packaging and identity projects. Short-term, you need a job that gets you a step closer to that goal. That might mean creating a portfolio to interest companies that specialize in print, rather than those that specialize in interactive design.

What if you have started out in one direction, and your goal is to strike out in a new one? If you have been designing CD covers and want to design for the medical industry, you will be competing against people who are already "experts" in a demanding and complex field. When you make a risky and demanding change, you may have to construct your portfolio from scratch. Be sure that there is a fit between how you feel about risk and the goal you choose.

Particularly if you're still young enough to stay up all night, don't squander your energy, drive, and excitement on anything other than the people you really want to work for. You want to learn the right skills from really good people.

—Nancy Hoefig

Values

Values determine what makes you comfortable and happy. You shouldn't knowingly target situations that you'll dislike unless the wolf is scratching at the door. Even when things are tough, it might be better to take a series of freelance or temp jobs than to accept a full-time position that you know is completely wrong for you. Long term, if you subvert your taste and instincts to land a client or a job, your portfolio becomes a collection of compromises, and your self-confidence can ebb. Eventually, you've done a lot of work you don't want to show, and you will have to work extra hard to counteract it in your presentation.

> In a project, you can't really ever take yourself out of the equation. You will always be present, but the percentage changes. In an art project, you're close to 100 percent present. In a design project, that percentage is smaller, maybe 10 percent.
>
> —Yang Kim

That being said, everyone makes work compromises at some point in their careers. Some are worth making. Only you can determine where you draw the line, but you should at least know where the line is, and whether it is a realistic limitation. You can't survive without a certain amount of flexibility. Not every project is groundbreaking and edgy, and you can learn a lot from projects that make you think along unfamiliar lines.

WHAT A PORTFOLIO IS NOT

A portfolio is a marketing tool that can help you improve the amount and type of work you do, the kinds of assignments you land, and the rate of response to your presentations. Here's what it's not:

- **Your autobiography.** With very few exceptions, no one cares about artistic prehistory. They want to know who you are and what you are capable of now.

- **Your résumé.** Unlike a résumé, where time gaps stand out, your portfolio doesn't have to include examples from every job you've ever held.

- **Therapy.** You don't want people's sympathy; you want their confidence. Don't apologize and don't whine.

- **An inside joke.** Never forget that you are not Presenting Your Portfolio to your friends.

- **A grab bag.** Don't throw your work in randomly in the hopes that there'll be something for everyone.

- **A checklist.** No one reviewing a portfolio is keeping score. They don't care if you have four textbook covers, three package designs, two annual reports, and a poster in a pear tree.

Personality

Does your work display a unique flavor? This question is subjective but goes to the heart of your portfolio. If your profession is style-based, your portfolio and all the work within it should express a personality. The words you've chosen in the self-assessment profile should describe the flavor of your work. If you create images (illustrations, photographs, and so on) the words you've chosen should be strong, related descriptors. Impulsive, clever, and sarcastic might work together. Intuitive, trendy, and complex might be too far apart to provide a focused sense of who you are.

In professions, like graphic design, that emphasize variety, your personality should be less obvious in a client project. A designer works for a range of clients. A poster for a theater troupe shouldn't look like a financial firm's prospectus. The words you've chosen should describe how you approach your work, rather than describing a personal or house style. Elegant, crisp, or confident are more likely to work for you than brash, sexy, or impulsive.

I think that less happens to be more in portfolios, unless you have solid, stellar work and you've done 30 pieces that you think are great. That's unlikely. I mean, I can't even find ten in my own portfolio that I think are great.

—Bill Cahan

ADAPTING YOUR CONTENT

You've now tallied up the self-assessment and have a profile of who you are—and how the world probably sees you—as a creative professional. In creating this profile, you've defined the work you're qualified to handle, the range of work you've already done, and the type of employer or client you want. Ideally, these three areas connect elegantly. Most probably, there's an inequality somewhere that you need to address.

> **You should only select the material that you think best reflects you and your talents. I judge a person's portfolio by their worst piece, not their best piece. Because I assume that if it's in there, that could be the kind of work they could produce for me.**
>
> **—Bill Cahan**

Quality

Your portfolio is a kind of personal statement, so you want it to say what you really mean. Every time you include a project that is clearly inferior to other work you've done, you make the worst portfolio faux pas. You've said, "I am proud of this work. I think it represents the quality of material you will get from me." By saying that, you've told the savvy reviewer that you can't tell good work from bad. Or that maybe the good work you're showing is a fluke and that most of the work you do is like the inferior pieces. Either interpretation will devalue your portfolio and all of the work in it.

Some people are aghast at this idea. "This is the only piece I have that shows I can design a website! Didn't you say I needed variety?" Project variety is never served by variety of quality.

Eliminating bad work doesn't always mean eliminating work you didn't enjoy. There's no excuse for keeping in an inferior personal project because a reviewer will assume that you had creative control over it. But there is an occasional real-world piece that may not excite you but tells something important about your skills. If you have other work that shows your creativity and one piece that shows you can deliver a finely crafted but boilerplate project, you might want to leave it in. In your explanation of the project, you can briefly discuss the constraints under which you had to operate.

> **The best reel a buddy at Pixar ever saw was just a single shot of an elephant. It went through transitions from wire mesh, to solid shading, then surfacing came on and the lights hit it. It held at the very end, then came to life and walked off screen. It was so unbelievably tight, every pixel was so perfect and sweet. They leaped out of their chairs and said, "Don't let this guy leave the building!"**
>
> **—Terrence Masson**

Quantity

There are a lot of myths about how much work you should show in any type of portfolio, let alone a digital one. There's no ideal number, but whatever it might be, people overwhelmingly err on the side of too much. Minimizing the number of pieces you show is a form of self-protection. It's a lot harder to get sucked into showing an inferior project if you limit your total number of pieces.

Illustrators, artists, and photographers, who are responding to a different type of market, will almost immediately disagree. To tap the stock or clip art market, they feel that they have to carry an encyclopedic amount of work on their sites. Their error is in not making a distinction between their Flickr account or catalog site and their portfolio.

There are many outlets where you can display your oeuvre. Sites like Flickr encourage image makers to upload everything they shoot. But digital cameras and camcorders make it dangerously easy not just to shoot extensively—a blessing that photographers in the film age would have given their best lens for— but to post obsessively as well. That's fine for sharing fun ideas or trolling for facile compliments. But a portfolio should contain nothing but the artist's selects—a small fraction of your work. The person looking through a portfolio with money in her hand wants to know quickly about the artist's style and how it plays out in some example projects. This need is best served by a small, exclusive collection of highlighted images. In contrast, anyone examining work on a stock or catalog site is looking for something specific. They will treat the site like a database or search engine and search by subject.

Reworking, rethinking

Once you've trimmed your expectations of how much work to show and eliminated any work that feels off, you may discover gaps in areas that you originally thought were well covered. If you really need an example of a certain type of work, you can return to a less satisfying piece and rethink it—pushing it harder to show that you know how it should have turned out.

Reworking is almost obligatory for any piece that wasn't professionally produced, and the result can be very successful in a digital portfolio. In particular, animations and interactive projects are so comparatively easy to rework at the same level of production that you should never include a substandard one. Even with a site that was a live client project, you will boost your chances with a potential employer by showing how you would improve it.

For me, the ideal portfolio has about a dozen pieces in it. And those dozen pieces give me a clear idea of how the person thinks, how that person approaches problem-solving, and how that person understands the constraints of the craft.
—Stan Richards

You also have the prerogative of reworking projects that were OK but that suffered from built-in limitations. If your portfolio is chock-full of black-and-white line drawings and you are bored with working in black and white, why show a digital portfolio that will never get you a color illustration? Reworking an idea with fewer (or different) limitations shows versatility and enthusiasm for your work.

CREATING YOUR OWN PROJECTS

Based on your past projects, why would someone hire you? It's possible that you love the work you do and hope a revised portfolio will help you to do more of it. But if you don't have any good examples of the work you'd like to do, or any that can simply be revised, it's time to invent your own.

Invention is not a lame response, or "make work." Creative directors often look for freelancers and employees who will take initiative without losing sight of the project goals. If your portfolio shows evidence of these traits, you could very well beat out someone whose portfolio is stuffed with pedestrian color material, even though you have only one four-color piece (the one you invented). That can hold true even if the other person's portfolio contains professionally printed samples, and yours are printed on an Epson. In a digital portfolio, where all surfaces become pixels, it might be enough to get you in the door.

Not all projects are equally worthwhile as professional hole-patchers. The sidebar that follows, "Classic projects," is a starter list. Your best bet is to stick with projects that are realistic but that offer an opportunity to express your creativity. Unless you are inexplicably at a loss for structure, there will be plenty of time in your life to do product spec sheets, identity systems, and web forms. Just keep some ground rules in mind before you begin:

> **I'm looking for creativity, and for a designer's ability to be commercial when necessary. I'm looking for diversity. And for people who have worked for large corporate design firms, where they may not have had an opportunity to work on really exciting, edgy projects, I want to see some personal stuff that shows what they're able to do.**
>
> **—Cynthia Rabun**

- **Select a client first.** Having a real-world company's need to consider is much better than trying to imagine one.

- **Develop for a different audience.** Limited to the same old teen demographic? Try a company that sells to children, to retirees, or to farmers.

- **Do your research.** Take the project seriously enough to look at your client's current material, and that of some reasonable competitors. What fresh and new approach can you bring to their work?

- **Meet real design constraints.** If you are drawing poster art, produce something using real poster dimensions. If you are designing a book cover or magazine, select a standard publication size. Making an identity? Be sure to use a mailable envelope size and standard business card dimensions. Reviewers will notice immediately if you haven't done your homework.

Classic projects

Stuck for ideas? Some types of projects are dependable standards in the creative industry. They appear in many digital portfolios and for many clients. One of them could be exactly what you need.

- **Book cover and its interior layout.** Select an already-published book and reimagine it. Create new cover art, select a different typeface, regrid the pages according to your own ideas.

 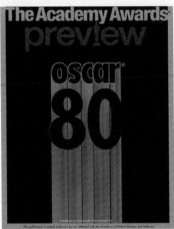

Existing 2007 cover and logo (l), Redesigned 2008 cover and logo (r)

LIONINOIL.NET
This thought project on John Locke and Jackie Caradonio's blog site takes great content and reimagines it as an opportunity for a last-minute design-happy ending.

- **Catalog.** Catalogs are the bread and butter of the consumer economy. Some of them are luscious, but most are exercises in the mundane. Select one mundane example and redesign its front and back covers and an inside spread.

- **Newsletter.** There are lots of ugly newsletters in the world. Rework one the way it should have been produced.

- **CD or DVD.** A classic opportunity is to add something edgy to an otherwise corporate portfolio. Even better—combine it with collateral work for the artist or band.

WWW.LUKELUKELUKE.COM
Posters for awareness, political campaigns, or non-profits are a great way to work with a real brief while letting your creativity off the leash.

- **Event poster.** Someone who is primarily an illustrator can shine with a few poster projects in hand. Designers love them because posters allow you to play creatively with many different elements.

- **Real estate or travel prospectus.** A stylish project provides a canvas for an elegant, understated approach. If your work has been youth oriented, this might provide a change of pace.

PARTNERING

By now, you may have skimmed forward in this book and felt a little overwhelmed by how much work your personal project will take. As a result, you might be concluding that your only option is a group portfolio website or a social networking site, at least until you've mastered some new skills. That wouldn't be the worst decision. But a lot depends on why you are making a portfolio and what your specialization is. If you belong to one of the professions that expect a unique statement online, or you feel strongly that you want to set yourself apart from others in your area, creating a personal site is still the best choice.

Instead, it might be time to ask yourself, "Do I need help?" There is no shame in concluding that you can successfully master some portions of designing and producing your digital portfolio, but not all.

Help can come in many forms. You can simply hire someone who fills the gap you see in your skills and experience. But it may be that the very reasons that you need a portfolio—short on work and cash—puts a hired gun out of reach.

If so, consider a creative partnership instead. Your partner may be a photographer who provides you with digital files of your projects. He may be a graphic designer who designs an interface for you. She may be a programmer who takes your graphic design and implements its interactive elements in Flash and JavaScript. Many times, partnerships are about bartering skills—a new business logo identity for one person, a photo shoot for another.

What you need in a partner

A partner should complement your own expertise and be someone whose work you are familiar with and respect. Ideally, he or she should be someone you have worked with on another project, so that you know what their strengths are and whether you work well together. Your portfolio is a very personal project, and the last thing you want is a partner who isn't prepared to support you and your vision.

Be prepared to give full credit for your partner's creative input. That probably means that you should not consider as a partner someone whose creative area you hope to make your own. If you are an established print designer with no desire to enter new media, it's reasonable to partner with a new media specialist to write the program, create the database, and implement the navigation. It's not reasonable to allow others to assume that you are a multimedia designer if someone else has created the concept and implemented the site for you.

Your role in the partnership

Although you should trust whomever you work with to know their own area of expertise, you should come to the table prepared to explain who you are, what type of help you need, and how much autonomy your partner will have. If the areas you need help in are areas you should ultimately know and understand, use your partnership as a learning opportunity.

Handle as much of the process as you reasonably can. Know your target market and how you want to be seen. If you're working with a photographer, take some shots yourself from the right distance and angle, with your materials arranged as you'd like them. Decide what content goes into your portfolio and how you want your work grouped. If artwork needs to be processed and you don't do it yourself, you should at least quality control (QC) every piece before it enters the portfolio to make sure it represents you well.

If you do not have Flash or programming expertise, you should at least have a hand in your portfolio's concept, look, and feel. Even better, you should come to your meetings with a proposed design. Best, you should create the static artwork and partner with someone with UI (user interface) experience to implement it.

Last but not least, you should personally test the portfolio as it develops and before you post or send it. See Chapter 13, "Presenting Your Portfolio" for a discussion of how and what to test.

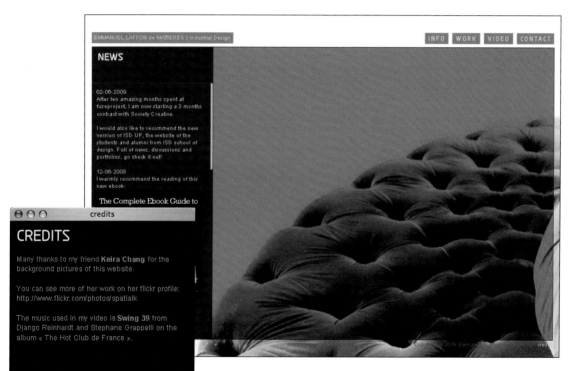

WWW.EMMANUEL-LAFFON.COM

Industrial designer Emmanuel Laffon de Mazières uses beautiful background photos as important elements on his portfolio site. He provides a credits link that not only alerts the viewer to photographer Keira Chang's contribution, but provides a link to her Flickr site.

PORTFOLIO HIGHLIGHT:
LUKE WILLIAMS WITH JONNIE HALLMAN | PARTNERING

WWW.LUKELUKELUKE.COM

By any reasonable measure, Luke Williams is a young graphic designer on the rise. On the dean's list at the prestigious Maryland Institute College of Art (MICA), a former intern at Pentagram Design, and already a junior designer at Under Armour, he could have decided to take the easy road on his portfolio. He's primarily a print designer, and for many others in this category a well-designed PDF combined with a laptop slideshow and physical portfolio might be a fine combination.

> **Jonnie and I generally have the same outlook on design: clean and simple with no excess. This made it very easy to work together.**
>
> **—Luke Williams**

But Williams doesn't ever take the line of least resistance. He not only wanted a personal website, he wanted a project that would be more like a personal presentation. It should flow beautifully, showcase the work, and crack the anonymous web wall with a peek at a real person.

Laying out the design flats in Illustrator, Williams knew exactly how he wanted his site to function, but lacked the skills to implement his ideas. He was fortunate to have as a good friend fellow student and web designer

LUKE WILLIAMS
©.09
ABOUT
ME
DESIGNER
PHOTOGRAPHER
CONTACT

SPECIALIZING IN THE PRINTED MEDIUM, I AM PRESENTLY STUDYING GRAPHIC DESIGN AND DIGITAL PHOTOGRAPHY AT THE MARYLAND INSTITUTE COLLEGE OF ART. I HAVE HAD THE PLEASURE OF COLLABORATING WITH MULTIPLE STUDIOS INCLUDING PENTAGRAM, SHAW JELVEH DESIGN AND MOST RECENTLY, UNDER ARMOUR. I HAVE WORKED WITH A WIDE VARIETY OF CLIENTS AND I ENJOY THE EXPERIENCE I SHARE WITH EACH AND EVERY ONE. THANK YOU FOR VISITING MY PORTFOLIO, I HOPE YOU ENJOY WHAT YOU SEE!

SITE PROGRAMMED BY JONNIE HALLMAN

The about and annoucement pages are very understated. With their condensed, angular type and hairline rules, they echo the design of a printed page. However, they are legibly reworked for the web—an elegant translation of a familiar aesthetic to a new venue.

Jonnie Hallman. As talented as Williams and with a shared aesthetic, he was a natural person to ask for help. Initially, Williams asked for "just" Flash tutoring. Hallman, knowing exactly what a time sinkhole that would be, secretly knocked out the initial programming as a personal challenge while they shared a movie rental.

When Luke decided to improve the site for version two, the favor for a friend evolved into a partnership, with Williams driving the concept and tweaking the design details while Hallman provided a working process that included design alternatives, feasibility feedback, and programming implementation. The result is an unqualified success, both as the embodiment of Luke's personal vision and as an example of partnering at its best.

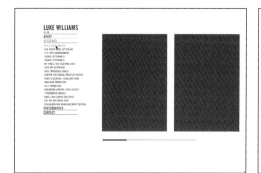

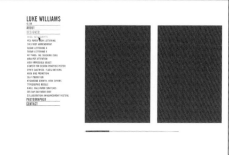

After the viewer selects a project, a set of gray windows sized to each project image builds on the screen, focusing your attention and defining the viewing area.

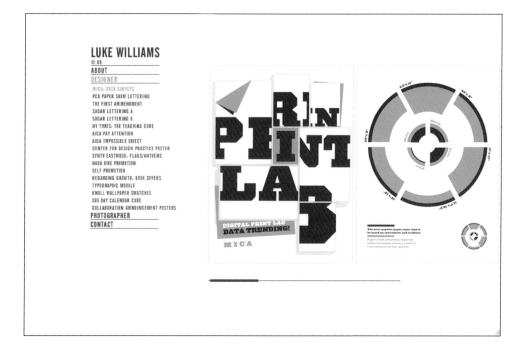

When Jonnie applied my design in Flash, the things that were influenced by him were based on user interaction. How will the images load in the browser, what will the transition look like?

—Luke Williams

Navigation and architecture

The navigation is both simple and enormously sophisticated. Although the site is obviously built with Flash technology and uses it well, it avoids busy Flash effects.

The narrow menu anchors the left vertical plane, with project titles expanding below when the main category is selected. Active categories and projects are indicated in gray, as are rollovers that "anticipate" their selection. The only other navigation element is a slender slider bar below the project images. Clicking on the bar and sliding to the right scrolls project images horizontally. Design projects are either sequential spreads or are organized visually to help the visitor explore the project. Photographs describe small narratives, and are sequenced by chronology or subject.

One of the most striking aspects of the navigation is revealed as you scroll. The menu remains firmly in place as an active element while the project work scrolls transparently behind it. This extremely usable idea is the most visible example of the Williams-Hallman creative process. As Luke says, "That was one of the things that Jonnie surprised me with. I realized that the menu wasn't going anywhere when I scrolled through the pieces. I was curious about how people would respond to it. In hindsight, I liked it and I wanted to keep it like that. It echoes the announcement text on my home page. It's all about me talking to the viewer. I'm always in the forefront, and what's behind me is my work."

Williams' design mimics the natural left-to-right motion used to present a physical portfolio. Spreads scroll across the page, allowing the viewer to have an experience similar to turning book pages.

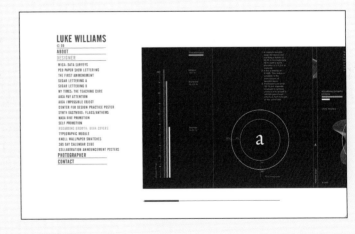

Content

Williams's content is clearly displayed in his menu, and falls into three categories: Designer, Photographer, and About. The majority of work is found under the category Designer, and is organized chronologically, with the most recent project at the top of the menu and therefore the first one a visitor sees. The projects have short, descriptive labels, but stand on their own as visual artifacts without project briefs.

Williams offers a second category of work in his photography, some of which he created for clients, and the rest of which is personal artwork. However, he never makes the mistake of confusing the viewer about his professional focus. Even his narrative photography has a strong design aesthetic.

His announcements are content as well—frequently updated ephemeral bulletins about his creative life that appear on his splash page. These updates are common on Facebook but unusual in a portfolio. Williams explains,"It's a way to speak about my work and process. I want viewers to know what I'm up to, and that I am a real person. And most importantly, I want you to feel like I am approachable. I get emails from people telling me that they saw my site and really enjoyed the experience, and I wonder if the announcement column deserves some credit." Expressive and humanizing, the announcements are great examples of portfolio text done right, and have become a signature part of his personal graphic identity.

> **My biggest goal was to demonstrate the confidence that I have in my work; for my online portfolio to be devoid of Flash animations, clever rollovers, or splashes of surprising color.**
> **—Luke Williams**

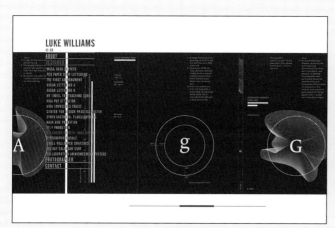
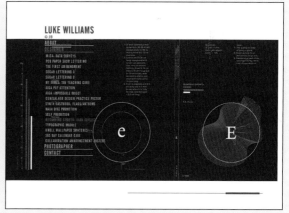

Future plans

The format, based in sophisticated Flash programming, might seem to be a future barrier. How will updates take place? Once again, a smart partnership prepared for this. Hallman created a document in XML, an easy markup language that Flash can read, then gave Williams a crash course in XML's basics. Williams can change some parameters, cut and paste text, and upload a document, allowing him to not only add individual projects and change text at will, but even add new sections to the menu.

Williams has been hired by Chicago-based advertising agency Leo Burnett, which should lead to a wide range of projects and a diversified portfolio. Although every web site eventually gets redesigned, he feels confident that the current version will stay fresh for now: "I've tried to provide an intuitive experience for the viewer. There isn't much I would want to change or add to the site, and I actually have yet to encounter a project that does not translate well in the format I've given myself."

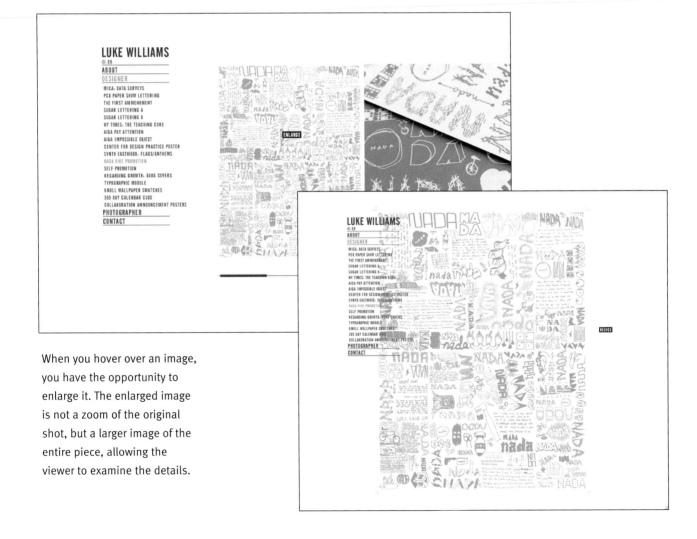

When you hover over an image, you have the opportunity to enlarge it. The enlarged image is not a zoom of the original shot, but a larger image of the entire piece, allowing the viewer to examine the details.

Williams' wry photographic essay, *Multilingual*, displays a variety of tongues in different color fields, and illustrates one of the navigational challenges Hallman solved. Given the variety of color and value in Williams' images, leaving the menu one color as the artwork scrolled behind it would impair legibility. Hallman programmed the menu so the type would respond to the individual background colors.

CHAPTER 2

Professions

Portfolios are bound together by the personality and goals of those who create them. When you define the type of work you want and identify yourself within it, you lay the first building block for your unique portfolio.

Defining your place in the world can be surprisingly complex. You might apply for several art director positions, only to find that this title means different things at different companies. Each one puts their own spin on how much experience and what talents and skills the position demands.

If you want to work on electronic media projects, do you call yourself a graphic designer? Sometimes graphic design equals print design. An interface designer? You need to know something about interface design to design a website. But interface design—the "human factors" part of design—is often handled by a person with an engineering or industrial design background. Then there's the interactive designer—the person who designs a project's look and feel. A Flash developer may play that design role, as well as do production and scripting. Some media creatives prefer the term experience designer. People in the industry will know what this means, but it will mystify most potential clients.

WWW.CREATIVEHOTLIST.COM

The Communication Arts job website has finely tuned its subject list. But many of the jobs are cross-listed, like this one for a multimedia Flash developer, which is also listed in the Advertising industry and the Design category.

Does this seem like splitting hairs? Maybe. But if you make the wrong choice as you develop your portfolio, you could end up doing work you don't like—and in the wrong industry. You should emerge from this chapter understanding the portfolio expectations for your creative niche and how to mix different types of projects to meet those expectations.

PURPOSE

The elements of a portfolio are basic, but how you mix them depends on your immediate need—the life change that is prompting you to create or update your portfolio. Are you developing and presenting it...

- For professional growth and discovery?
- For acceptance into an academic program?
- To curators or gallery owners?

- To provide elements for a larger project?
- For a full-time job?
- To gain or retain clients?

Your purpose will color the type of work you include, its format, and your presentation. It will interact with the following portfolio ingredients to create a framework that is specific to your industry.

PORTFOLIO INGREDIENTS

It's obvious that a portfolio isn't worth much unless it contains good work. But good work alone isn't always enough. Every profession has a different definition of what "good" is. What works magnificently when you present to an art director who needs an illustrator will fall flat when she needs a freelance designer—and vice versa. For each role and audience, your portfolio must contain the right kind of work, in the right format. Meet the unspoken assumptions, and you send the message that you know who you are and what you want to do.

That's good advice, you may be thinking, but not very practical. How do you know what's needed when? It's hard to answer that because every hiring situation has unique requirements, and every portfolio is individually created. But there is a short list of underlying elements that, when combined in appropriate proportions, can help to craft a portfolio that speaks effectively to its intended eyes and ears.

The following ingredients appear in different proportions in each creative profession's portfolio. A bar keyed to each category indicates their relative importance for each area. Like a great chef, use these recipes as guidelines, not laws, for finding the uniquely right proportion for your work.

Variety

You might think that variety would be a plus because it shows the full range of your work and capabilities. Sometimes it is, but you'd be surprised how often it works against you in some professions. If your pieces are too diverse, in medium, look, subject, or clientele, they can imply that you haven't yet figured out what you do best—and that you have yet to find your creative voice.

Style

As artists and designers mature, their work frequently develops a creative signature. For some professions, an identifiable style is nothing short of a requirement. For others, it's intrusive, like an out-of-tune voice in a chorus, because it gets in the way of a client's message.

Concept | creativity

There is a difference between creativity in your portfolio content and creativity in your presentation of that content. Some professsional areas expect the portfolio package in any medium to be a beautiful creative artifact. Others consider a high-concept presentation to be a nice touch, but it is not required. For a small number of portfolio types, too much attention and creative energy spent on the portfolio concept is probably a waste of time.

Process

Work in process, or work about your process, can indicate how you evolve your ideas and what it would be like to work with you. In many professional situations, how you think and problem-solve can be as important as your aesthetic decisions. For professions where production is expensive or time-consuming, process work and prototypes are so important that not showing them is suspect.

Technology and craft

Bad craft and inappropriate technology are always negative, but for some professions, they're a much bigger issue than for others. Many fine artists create personal websites that use text or navigation badly. These lacks can be painful to those in the know, but a potential curator will just go straight to the work without noticing. Weak craft in a design portfolio, on the other hand, is never forgiven.

YOUR PORTFOLIO MIX

How you approach your portfolio—digital or traditional—should depend on your purpose and the category of creative professional you are. The following descriptions define these categories. They're followed by examples of how your category interacts with a likely purpose. These templates will help you determine your ideal mix of portfolio elements, unify your portfolio, and emphasize your strengths in the context of your professional needs. Hopefully, they'll also make it clear how important it is to have a portfolio that is organized and modular, so you can reconfigure it as your situation and needs change.

As you read the following descriptions, concentrate on the one that fits you best. You're required by the way people evaluate your work to choose a category and stay consistent within it. Does your work, your chosen market, and your current portfolio seem to work within the framework of one of the descriptions below? If it works within more than one, you may be a highly versatile person, but you'll either have to make a choice, or you'll need to create more than one portfolio. (Check out Chapter 4, "Delivery and Format," for more on multiple portfolios.)

Art

This category is made up of people who have considerable control over the subject, message, media, and presentation of their creative work. That freedom usually extends to the digital portfolio. If you want to make art for commercial purposes (like an illustrator) rather than sell or exhibit art that you have made for personal expression, you should look at the other categories instead of or in addition to this section. The two portfolio purposes really shouldn't mix, as they have different audiences.

STUDENT | FOR ADMISSION

Students belong in the art category because their primary focus isn't (or shouldn't be) making a living from their artwork—although every student would much prefer to freelance for spending money than to wait on tables. Being a student is a transitional state. Because you're still on the road to your goal and able to change focus as you experience new options, you can create a portfolio that includes many facets of your creative life.

Admission portfolios are special: The people judging your work tell you exactly what they want to see. Don't take this gift for granted. Meet the requirements as closely as you can. If digital portfolios aren't mentioned as a submission medium, don't send one, even if all your artwork is computer-based. Some academic institutions are just old-fashioned, and the admissions committee isn't comfortable handling technology. Others are perfectly adept with computers but have very good reasons (see Chapter 4) why they may not welcome discs.

WHILE YOU'RE IN SCHOOL

Student portfolios should evolve constantly as you learn and complete more projects. Weed out the older work as quickly as you can. It's the rare high school project that can hold its own after a year or two of higher education.

Start a digital portfolio early. If you have a PDA, keep a few choice examples of your work stored as photos. Many students get their first experiences in their field in internships, co-ops, or as part-time or summer freelancers. You meet people at parties, at events, and even on the street. You never know when an opportunity to design a logo or shoot a CD cover might depend on your being able to show your ideas on the fly.

Keep your student portfolio wide-ranging. Even if you plan on becoming a designer, continue to include good examples of your work in other media, particularly if you are a strong illustrator or accomplished photographer. Showing that you can offer a full-service approach can be the clincher for the type of personal work that builds student portfolios, like collateral for bands or identity projects for business startups. You'll have most of your life to carry a focused portfolio, so enjoy a range of media while you can.

In general, an admissions committee is looking for variety in order to assess your strengths, weaknesses, and level of preparation. In undergraduate portfolios, craft is seen as less important than potential because technique and good habits can be taught. Don't attempt a high-concept presentation unless you are applying to graduate school in one of the design professions. Such professions also take craft issues much more seriously for graduate students, particularly if the applicant has already majored in art or design as a undergraduate.

Some college art departments help to encourage good quality student digital portfolios by developing portfolio templates. This one, developed for Art+Design students by the Educational Technology Center at Northeastern University, allows students to customize background, colors and content. It puts a clean Flash presentation within every student's reach.

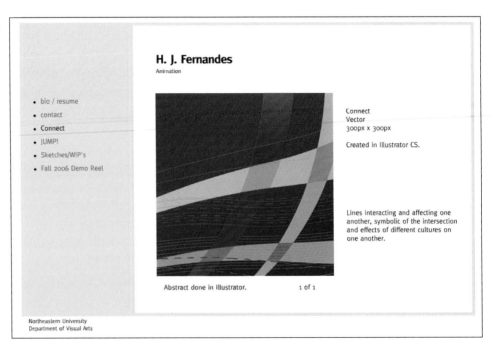

H. J. Fernandes
Animation

- bio / resume
- contact
- Connect
- JUMP!
- Sketches/WIP's
- Fall 2006 Demo Reel

Connect
Vector
300px x 300px

Created in Illustrator CS.

Lines interacting and affecting one another, symbolic of the intersection and effects of different cultures on one another.

Abstract done in Illustrator.   1 of 1

Northeastern University
Department of Visual Arts

FINE ARTIST | FOR EXHIBITION OR COMMISSION

A fine artist is someone who views his or her work solely as a means of creative, social, or philosophical expression. An artist doesn't need a digital portfolio in the same way that a designer or illustrator does. However, the benefits of personal marketing and networking outside a geographical area have persuaded many fine artists to use an online outlet for their work. You'll seldom get a show or a commission based on your digital portfolio alone, but if you're lucky it could open the door to a studio visit or an invitation to a competition.

The art world was slow to accept any merger of art and technology, including that of traditional art forms with a digital portfolio. That has changed. Curators who are sticklers for tradition still consider 35mm slides and transparencies *de rigueur*, but fortunately, their numbers are shrinking. No matter how much an artist hates technology, he should at least have a small space on one of the many group or art catalog sites for prospective clients or curators.

(art)ⁿ

contact

features

new work

ellen sandor

Virtual Photography PHSColograms

: Invisible Science : Nature Studies : Virtual Architecture : Virtual Sculpture : Virtual Portraits : Visual History :

WWW.ARTN.COM

(art)n—Art to the Nth Power—is a collective led by renowned graphic artist Ellen Sandor. (art)n highlights its virtual artwork—virtual photos on a range of topics, rendered with rich photorealistic depth—on its site. The home page is a slideshow in a minimalist but technically savvy interface, designed by Janine Fron and Jack Ludden.

As a fine artist, variety works against you. The art world looks for a unique, consistent style. Only after developing a track record of successful shows can you combine multiple interests and media in one portfolio. Unless your artwork involves technology, craft is only relevant in that bad craft can push people away. The fine art digital portfolio should keep its focus on the work, minimizing presentation concept.

2D graphics

Three groups of image-makers belong here: people who compose and/or shoot live images, those who create images through multiple forms of image capture and digital compositing, and those who draw or paint pictures—either in traditional media or on the computer. The groups can be fluid, although photographers and their clients tend to view most computer image compositing (as opposed to image enhancement) as a form of illustration. For convenience's sake, I've combined compositors and illustrators into the Graphic Artist category.

PHOTOGRAPHER | FOR LICENSE OR FREELANCE

Photographers capture images, either digitally or on film. They were among the first artists to use digital media to archive, display, and sell their work. Unfortunately, with the near-universal ownership of good digital cameras and Photoshop, more people create images that are (at least online) competitive in quality with the work of

WWW.MITCHWEISS.COM
Mitch Weiss is a prime example of a professional photographer who is comfortable with website development and has given significant thought to how he presents his work online. His site enhances and showcases his strengths in portraits and commissioned work.

established pros. By creating an enormous searchable library, Flickr has made it difficult for a photographer to justify building their own portfolio of stock images, which was a major way to drive online income for professionals only a few years ago. In this new environment, photographers' portfolios must stand out, both in the type of work they contain and the sophistication of their presentation.

GRAPHIC ARTIST | FOR LICENSE OR FREELANCE

Illustrators and fine artists often use the same tools, but to different purposes. Unlike fine artists, illustrators create artwork on assignment. Like artists, they must project a unique stylistic identity and approach. They must be not only talented and skilled in their media, but also good at interpreting and executing client ideas.

Like for fine artists, style is the most important element in this type of portfolio. But the bar is much higher in the concept and execution of a graphic artist's web portfolio than it is for a fine artist. Graphic artists should consider splitting their material between a site like Flickr, where they can post volumes of work that can range from experiments to commercial work for inexpensive licensing, and a personal site for higher-end commissioned and concept work.

A freelance illustrator's portfolio should complement the artist's style the way a good matte and frame enhance a 2D graphic. The concept is very important. In both cases, technology and craft must be fluid but largely invisible.

**WWW.FLICKR.COM/
PHOTOS/WILL_SCOBIE/**
Will Scobie takes
advantage of Flickr's great
organizing tools and
presence online. He draws
copiously, and puts the
results of loose, fun work
on envelopes, scraps of
paper, or in formal
sketchbooks where they
will be seen, but not
confused with his more
formal, developed work.

Design

The design professions share a common ground in their roles as interpreters,
integrators, and collaborators. Although there is little fluidity across the spectrum of
design professions (architects don't usually design annual reports, any more than
designers create elevations) there is quite a lot of crossover at the edges. An exhibit
or experience designer might have been trained in architecture, industrial design, or
graphic design.

ARCHITECT | FOR COMMISSION OR FULL-TIME

An architect designs buildings, interior spaces, and landscapes—the interactive
space of the real world. Because of the stakes involved, the architectural profession
has a strong commitment to apprenticeship. A new architect can expect to spend time
in a CAD support role before they are trusted to take part in the design process, so
their technical skills must be strong.

Although most young architects have some form of digital portfolio, it is often
an exact digital rendition of the traditional print-based archive of models, elevations,
plans, renderings, and photographs. Architectural firms concentrate more on photographs of finished work online, but even established professionals often show projects
that did not get built or produced in their portfolios. There will always be more
design ideas than there can be actual commissions.

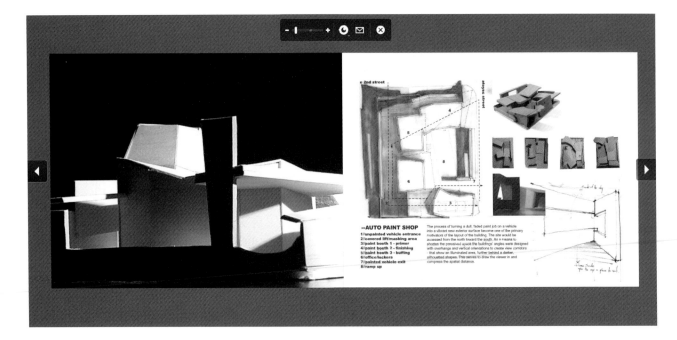

ISSUU.COM/GRACEFULSPOON/DOCS/080206_ARCH_PORTFOLIO

As this flat from architectural student John Locke's online portfolio attests, an architectural presentation should emphasize all stages of the development cycle, from first sketches to the completed project.

INDUSTRIAL DESIGNER | FOR COMMISSION OR FULL-TIME

Industrial designers design products and systems. Excellent 3D visualization talent and sketching skills are important prerequisites and play a big role in their portfolio presentations. Their strengths in usability and navigation make them naturals for careers in multimedia design. Although industrial designers overlap architects in many of the technical tools of their trade, their portfolio requirements diverge. Unlike architects, ID portfolios are frequently digital, both in web and CD form.

Young 3D designers, even ones with great creative promise, will spend their first years exercising their modeling or drafting expertise. A portfolio that doesn't display the highest possible professional craft with the widest variety of tools will go to the bottom of the pile. Process is very effective as well. In addition, usability is often a major design issue, particularly for product designers, making a great, elegantly conceived online portfolio a bonus.

GRAPHIC DESIGNER | FOR FREELANCE OR FULL-TIME

A graphic designer combines text, image, and sometimes sound to visually communicate ideas and solve strategic and marketing challenges. Graphic designers are more likely to deal with 2D projects, but many also design packaging, signage, and, of course, interactive sites. A graphic designer with a good eye for space might design a store interior as part of a client's overall branding and marketing system.

The format and design considerations of a graphic designer's digital portfolio will almost certainly be affected by the type of work in which the designer specializes. A package designer may have a portfolio that is formatted more like that of an industrial designer because so much of the work is 3D. Corporate identity designers will often show more process and speculative work.

Pieces that display good visual thinking will be more effective than pedestrian desktop publishing, even if one piece is a student project, and the desktop work is professionally printed. The graphic designer's portfolio concept will be looked at very carefully by any prospective employer, even if that designer only does print work.

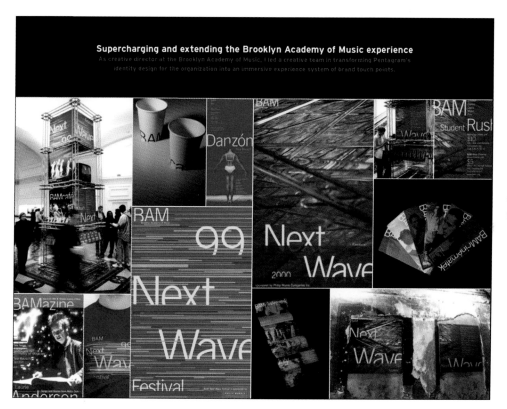

JASONRING.COM

Ring is a multitalented identity and brand design specialist. Every page of his PDF portfolio is designed with a keen eye for color and form. His collage of project images show a mastery of small as well as large-form print matter.

MULTIMEDIA DESIGNER | FOR FREELANCE OR FULL-TIME

Unlike graphic designers, who also may do multimedia design as one medium among many, a multimedia designer is most comfortable designing for the computer screen. Multimedia designers are expected to be extremely technologically adept, and their portfolios should display these skills.

Technical presentation, flair, and attention to detail are particularly critical for the design portfolio. Variety in project and approach are encouraged. Because of the emphasis on how you think, a design portfolio is a great place for process and personal project work. Craft is also highly regarded.

The designer's digital portfolio requires a concept that not only presents the actual work well but is a design project in itself. This "wrapper" is frequently interactive, although for a print-based designer, interaction might mean a simple linear slideshow instead of a complex, multilayered experience.

A multimedia designer's digital portfolio is more technically demanding, and an elegantly designed and executed "wrapper" is often a plus. Considering that you might have created sites that have been redesigned (or closed down) after you worked on them, showing prototypes or work in process is often a necessity. This portfolio is often a design object in its own right, but the portfolio should not be allowed to overwhelm the projects.

WWW.CLOUDRAKER.COM

As a company that specializes in multimedia experience design, CloudRaker has to meet high client expectations; their work and their portfolio site must be smart and on the cutting edge of technology.

PRODUCTION DEVELOPER | FOR FREELANCE OR FULL-TIME

Designers or graphic artists sometimes apply for production positions in a soft economy. If you fit this description, you may need a different balance of work in your digital portfolio than the one you use when applying for a creative position.

A production specialist is hired for one reason only—to implement—whether they are writing JavaScript, optimizing graphics, or creating Flash-based interaction. Creativity and a good eye are a bonus, not the main event. A professional developer knows this and prides herself on her speed, efficiency, and accuracy, even under pressure. This pride should be on display in a production portfolio's exquisite attention to craft and detail. Process and variety are still useful.

Motion and interaction

Designers and illustrators are adding time and motion to their repertoire of tools and media. There is a difference, however, between incorporating interactive elements into a design and concentrating on movement and imagery. Motion graphics professionals incorporate performance and storytelling into their visual skills.

ANIMATOR | FOR FREELANCE OR FULL-TIME

Animation was once identified exclusively as hand-drawn cartoon entertainment. Today, most animation is computer-based or -assisted. Computer animators make it possible to "walk through" designed virtual spaces, visualize abstract scientific principles, and merge real and imaginary elements seamlessly in film.

Technical virtuosity goes hand in hand with creativity in a time-and-motion portfolio. Variety is prized, as is a clever concept for editing clips of work together. Sound is a part of the palette and should be an integrated component in the portfolio. Process is useful in a supporting role. Personal projects are expected to make up a large percentage of an animation portfolio until the animator has been working professionally for many years.

VIDEOGRAPHER | FOR FREELANCE

In a quick and simplistic analogy, a videographer is to a photographer what an animator is to an illustrator. Instead of capturing and editing individual still frames, a videographer captures moving images. Videographers are usually freelancers who not only shoot the content but handle post-production as well. Their portfolio samples are provided in the same range of format and quality as animators' work, although there are usually fewer individual projects, and longer sample clips. Variety of subject matter and evidence of good technical skills are extremely useful.

Because both animation and video projects are extremely time-consuming, work in process or personal projects are not only acceptable in the digital reel, but expected. So are other goodies—tutorials or personal projects—that show technical mastery behind the scenes.

Portfolio sites by both video and animation professionals are often simple static sites that are used as a download space for the actual portfolio—the demo reel. No

WWW.WIPVERNOOIJ.COM

Freelance character animator Wip Vernooij's demo reel displays his talent, attention to detail, and sense of humor. It includes both professional work and personal projects.

longer a literal reel-to-reel analog film, today's reel is always digital, saved with different compressions for different purposes. The first is a highly compressed, low-bandwidth sampling appropriate for YouTube or similar sites. The second is a large, high-resolution version that can be downloaded and viewed locally or handed off on a DVD. In addition, some motion professionals offer a third version at a compromise resolution for display on a personal website.

Game Design

Game design is a collaborative category that comprises a range of specialists from established creative areas—illustrators, animators, interactive designers, information architects, programmers—who come together to create and develop a form of digital play. These specialists tend to place the word *game* prominently in front of their discipline, but they create portfolios or reels appropriate to their specialty. Illustrators and animators create game art, for example, that they display in ways entirely consistent with illustrators and animators who create for other categories. Specialists in interaction, environments, and built spaces are often game level designers. Game programmers will usually provide demo code and will work with game artists to create a DVD that contains a playable game prototype.

Most creatives in the game industry at the technical-creative end work full-time for game companies. Because no game engine has emerged as a standard, it is common for game design programmers and designers to use one or two prototypes as content for a portfolio reel to land an entry-level staff position. Once there, you'll master the company's specific engine or apply a programming language in a proprietary project.

Game artists, on the other hand, are frequently hired guns who move from project to project. Their portfolios tend to combine the game aesthetics of 2D or 3D play with the guidelines of their basic area—storyboard or character design artists have online or disc portfolios that look like illustrators' portfolios, while game animators' portfolios are always demo reels, with or without a designed wrapper.

Performance

Performing artists have joined the ranks of creative professionals presenting themselves digitally. Standards for performance digital portfolios are still evolving. Aesthetic expectations are still fairly undemanding, but seamless craft and good quality film resolution can be very important. A digital portfolio offers the opportunity for a performer to establish credibility and to provide a more professional presentation. However, as most performers do not have training in the visual arts or programming, it's usually best to hire someone to follow the professional guidelines—good quality video samples of your work, one or more high-resolution images of yourself, and a well-designed resume in PDF form.

THE GRAIN OF SALT

Don't be surprised if you come across portfolios of senior professionals that stretch the limits. These profiles can't represent the state of the profession for everyone at every point in their careers. When an individual moves upward professionally or carves a unique niche, he or she can salt the common wisdom to taste. If you are just starting out, are trying to improve your chances, or are shifting into a new area, you can't. Although you can, and should, push yourself to offer the most creative and innovative presentation and work that you can, pushing far beyond the guidelines may simply make your audience think that you don't know what those guidelines are. That's a particularly important idea to keep in mind as you move from a general understanding of your profession's expectations to the specifics of who you are in relation to your chosen audience.

PORTFOLIO HIGHLIGHT:
WILL SCOBIE | PRIMARY DIRECTIVE

WWW.REVERIECREATE.CO.UK

Generic portfolios are like clichéd characters—we know what to expect and we'd rather not waste our time. Ideally, every portfolio should be lively and unique, just as we are.

> **The website is designed to give the impression of a friendly professional illustrator. I hope this encourages people to get in contact.**
>
> **—Will Scobie**

But having a creative signature doesn't mean that a portfolio shouldn't reflect its artistic origins. Like you can tell bruschetta and sushi apart at a taste, spending a few seconds on the home page of a great portfolio should immediately telegraph whether you are sitting down to design, animation, or illustration. Spend a bit longer, and the individual personality should burst through. You'll savor every project, enjoy the presentation, and talk it up to your friends. Illustrator Will Scobie's portfolio explodes with personal style and makes you sure that you would like the person who provided the feast.

Navigation and architecture

A good structural architecture always serves as a strong skeleton for a portfolio. But nothing shows better how important the maker's personality and its creative expression can be to the portfolio's impact than a quick comparison between Luke Williams' portfolio in Chapter 1 and Scobie's here. Both portfolios use a horizontal scrolling system. But other than this fact and their shared excellence, the two creative expressions have little in common. Scobie's portfolio is as free-form as Williams' is crisply designed.

It's clear that Scobie is his site's designer. The website looks and feels exactly like one of Scobie's illustration projects, rather than a generic matte and frame, or an outside wrapper with another artist or designer's imprint. Much of his artwork, like his website, unfolds like a paper scroll. Looking at the horizontal pieces on his site imposes a linear narrative on the unfolding sequence, and encourages the viewer to linger on the individual characters and drawings to check out the details.

> **My work is formed from my imagination but it isn't necessarily saying something about me; it is about putting across an idea or concept.**
>
> **—Will Scobie**

Site navigation is compactly nested next to Scobie's name, and is very simple. The menu text brings you to individual gallery sections, each of which is either below the menu on the screen or viewable by scrolling right. Click his name and you're returned to the home page animation.

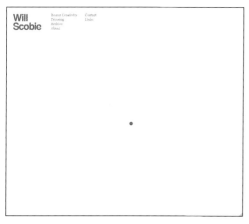

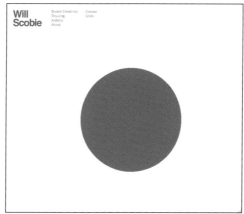

Scobie's site is built around the primary colors of yellow, red, and blue. It opens with a clean and graphically simple but mesmerizing animation. The simple circles suddenly become the frame for a complex sketch made from one continuous red line, an illustration that exemplifies his style.

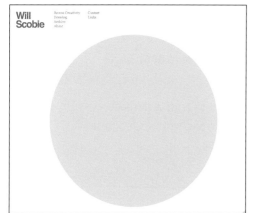

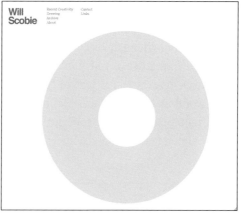

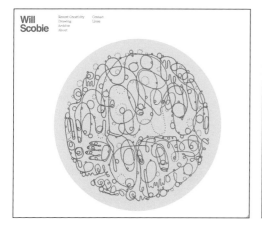

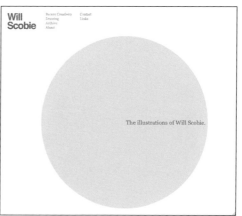

Each menu item highlights in one of the three colors. Roll over the name, and it changes to a primary color or to black.

Content

Scobie's work is loosely divided into three categories. Recent Creativity and Archive are chronological, with Recent Creativity positioned in the menu to encourage people to view it first.

Work in the Drawing section exhibits a distinctly different feel from the rest of Scobie's work. Putting this work in a separate gallery space is a very smart decision, as an illustrator's style is his most distinguishing selling point. People can explore this area, but prospective clients are channeled first to the "Recent Creativity" section, where his identifiable style predominates.

Another smart decision is what is not on the site. Many creatives struggle with how to categorize and present their material in one place. How much is too much? What will clients want to see, as opposed to other artists or friends? Visit Scobie's Links menu and you'll find a list of self-publishing sites. Although part of his strategy is just to get his work out into the world as widely as possible, he's selected each site for a purpose. Each contains a diffent type or mix of content: artist notebooks and work in progress on Flickr, thoughts and comments on specific projects in the blog.

My blog is only for certain commissions or personal projects and Behance, like my website, is designed to showcase only my best work. I always get the most feedback from Flickr, which displays raw ideas.

—Will Scobie

Except in the Recent Creativity section, where the most recent project pushes the older one to the right, the artwork is not arranged in any particular order. In this case, the lack of regimented structure is very consistent with the playful and surprising character of Scobie's work.

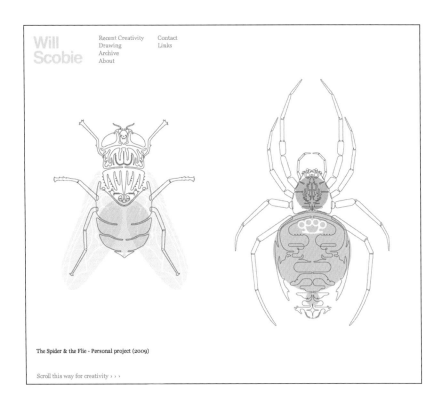

Will Scobie

Recent Creativity
Drawing
Archive
About

Contact
Links

The Spider & the Flie - Personal project (2009)

Scroll this way for creativity › › ›

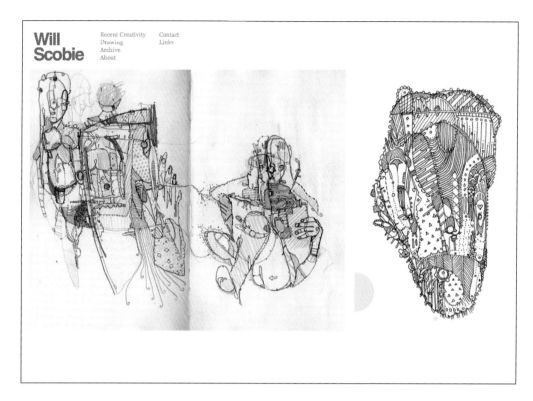

Will Scobie

Recent Creativity   Contact
Drawing   Links
Archive
About

The Drawing section is a nice counterpoint to the rest of Scobie's site. Scobie's very identifiable style is graphic and somewhat geometric. These sketches still have the flavor of his other work, but are less commercially focused.

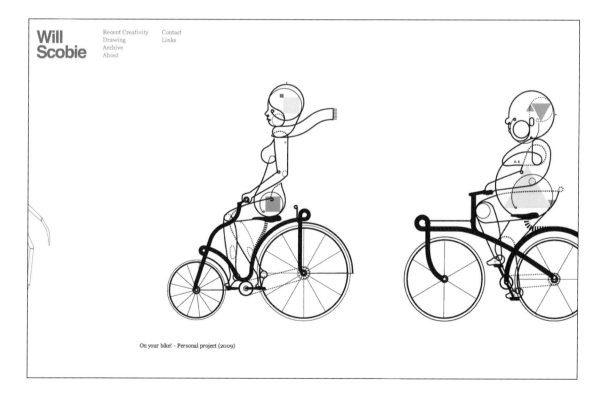

Will Scobie

Recent Creativity   Contact
Drawing   Links
Archive
About

On your bike! - Personal project (2009)

Use the scrollbar to see an unfolding stream of work. This delightful piece has distinct segments that loosely correspond to the way you would see the piece evolve onscreen.

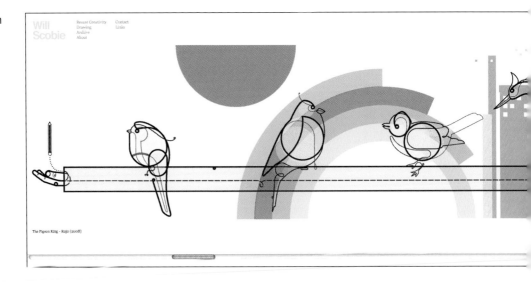

By offloading his wide variety and enormous output of work to other sites and using the portfolio website as a place for polished, completed projects only, Scobie makes explicit in the virtual world what was once standard practice in the analog one: segregating the "cream of the cream" in a portfolio, while inviting Scobie fans who want to go deeper to visit his artist's studio—in this case, Flickr and other self-publishing addresses. Everything is available somewhere, but the audience can't confuse concept and completion.

Future plans

As of this writing, Scobie's site is very new, and he has no immediate plans to change it. As Scobie says, "Before my current website I had a Flash-based site, which I felt restricted the way in which I could display work. My current site was built using HTML and CSS, which allows me to show off my work at its best."

The loose breakout by chronology makes it easy to update, and as recent work gets older, it takes its place as the first-seen work in the Archive. Because Scobie uses self-publishing sites for work of the moment, he feels no pressure to make his portfolio site bigger or update it more than once a month.

> **My website is what clients look through. In that sense it has been very successful in getting me work.**
>
> **—Will Scobie**

CHAPTER 3

Your Audience

Your portfolio is an expression of who you are. But even the unique "you" changes according to your mood and situation. Kicking back with friends sparks a different state of mind than visiting your family. It should. You're relating to people whose assumptions, goals, and values are probably galaxies apart. However, unless you're a chameleon, you don't become someone new with each group. You adapt your style to make the people you're with more comfortable with you.

Creating a portfolio that speaks effectively to prospective clients or employers might require similar adjustments. But when you are with different groups, you have the benefit of knowing their expectations already. You've had years to learn the unspoken code of conduct that each situation requires. That's probably not true of your portfolio audience. To get your share of the current opportunities, you need to be aware of what your market desires, and show that awareness explicitly with your portfolio.

With self-examination fresh in your mind, this chapter will point you in the direction of tools that will help you sharpen your marketplace savvy. We'll move from figuring out what topics you need to research, through good places to do your researching, to some practical tips on how to conduct fruitful market research. By the end of the chapter, you'll be well on your way to knowing who your target is and what they'll want to see in your portfolio.

WHY DO RESEARCH?

Part of the allure of digital portfolios is how fluid they are. Plan wisely, and you can quickly roll out a series of portfolios, each tailored to a single market, culture, or geographical area. However, you need to know a lot about each audience to speak effectively to it. Knowledge is key to chasing the right work, media, and approach.

> I tried to understand who my audience was, who my ideal clients would be. I wanted to know what they'd be looking for and how I could package the work to interest them. I found that I needed examples of work from a number of different components—like brochure, web, and signage—that surround the same brand expression. So, a client could look at the site and say, "OK. We could hire this firm to do everything for our brand and all of the commensurate applications."
>
> —Nancy Hoefig

Wouldn't it be nice if the people you'd like to work with would just tell you what they want? Actually, they do. They publicize new campaigns and give interviews about their strategic partners. They give talks at clubs and offer their opinions at student critiques. They put up websites with client lists and project samples that tell you the type of work they do and what types of firms they're pleased to do it for. Sometimes they even provide case studies that tell you all about their working process. This abundance of information tells an astute observer volumes about their philosophy, aesthetics, and company culture. You find this wealth of information through research.

Armed with solid research, you don't have to design your portfolio and hope you've made the right choices. An illustrator who has researched his targets' styles and clientele can showcase examples of appropriate work online. A designer can send an individually created PDF that shows her knowledge of a firm's client base or working process.

The word *research* makes some visual people twitch. Don't let it. You're just poking around for information, something you probably do for personal projects or just plain curiosity without giving it a second thought. The only difference here is that you'll be aware of what you're doing and have a long-range goal in mind.

WHAT SHOULD YOU RESEARCH?

Your research will be most effective if you move from the general to the specific. The further along you are in your career, the finer you might winnow the field. If you are already very focused and aware of your possible market, you might simply research individual prospects.

Depending on why you are creating a portfolio, you may pause at, stop on, or skip directly to any of four progressively more detailed research stages.

1. Do basic market research.

Savvy creative professionals always ask, "Who's your customer?" of their clients. Design and advertising are driven by market forces. Each individual market needs to be approached in a unique way. We all know—or we should—that it's hard to develop a good logo, design effective communication, or create a killer game if you haven't a clue about who you need to sell to, speak to, or impress.

We may complain about our clients' myopia, but we can be guilty of the same career crime. Although you can do every type of work for anyone, you are probably better at some types of projects than others. The end result is more satisfying and better produced, and you're proud to show it. Why not make yourself more attractive to people who can offer you such a project?

> Most people aren't able to identify anything specific about their clients. For years, I've asked, "Who's your customer?" and got "everybody" as the answer. My favorite "everybody" came from the owner of a chain of stores that sold tires and wheels for lowriders. So I said, "You're telling me that obstetricians' wives from Encino are going to drive down to get light pipes put on their Mercedes?" It turned out that "everybody" was 19- to 25- year-old males—85% African-American, 15% Latin-American...somewhat more specific than "everybody."
> —Gunnar Swanson

When you aren't consistently getting the work that you would like, you either have to look closely at yourself (as we did in Chapter 2, "Assessment and Adaptation") or your working environment. If you're not sure how to define your audience or what type of audience matches you best, the "Market assessment" sidebar provides a list to spark your thinking.

Which of these items is most important to you? Priorities matter because your ideal situation may not exist. Refer to your self-assessment in Chapter 2 to help you prioritize and narrow your focus.

You might not be sure of how some factors play out—company size, for example. A large corporation may put you to work on one mammoth project, giving you an overview of process and production. Or if you're looking for clientele, you may have prior experience with certain demographics. Should you look for a client that sells to that market? If you're not sure how some of these topics affect your job or client search, you've found a good subject to research.

For example, let's say that you want a better idea of how company size is likely to impact your project opportunities. You could move forward by selecting a small group of companies that do your type of work—half large (advertising companies or design firms listing more than one branch) and half small (firms with a single principal's name or with a creative or unusual identity are often small, personal concerns).

MARKET ASSESSMENT

Looking for a job:

- Geography: Where am I looking?
- Independent studio/agency or in-house department?
- Company size?
- If independent, what specialty? (design/concept, integrated branding, advertising/selling, and so on)
- Client or company industry category or categories?
- Type of projects? (packaging, editorial, marketing, entertainment, for example)
- Specializing in a specific media? (such as print, interactive, mass media, or entertainment)
- Specializing in specific activities or sub-cultures?

Looking for clientele:

- Other creatives, individuals, or corporate?
- If corporate client, specific industries?
- Type of work they purchase? (like identity, packaging, magazine advertising)
- Specializing in a specific media? (for example, print, interactive, mass media, entertainment, and so on)
- Type of audience each client targets?

Go to their websites and poke around to see how you respond to the type of projects on view, the type of clients (big corporate names or small local companies), and the design of the website itself. A large firm will only show work from a small client if the work represents their most creative effort—a good gauge of their creative range. A small firm may display fairly pedestrian projects if they've been done for a prestigious name—a good measure of their long-term growth aspirations.

2. Find your target audience category.

After you have created a basic definition of your portfolio's target audience, look for general data about this target. Some typical questions to answer might be:

- Is my target realistic? Are there companies that do exactly what I'm looking for, or should I be more general?
- How many companies fit my target? Can I narrow it down?
- How many companies are local? Does the geography matter to me?

In doing a general category search, you should come up with several pages of possible company targets. If you're in the triple digits, you need to be more selective. If you have only ten options, you've narrowed your options too far and too fast.

3. Select specific companies.

Now you're homing in on companies that exemplify the type of work you'd like to do.

You may have found these companies initially by exploring links from the general search or by developing a separate list from directories maintained by professional organizations. (See Appendix A, "Resources.") These companies will become the target audience against which you will "test" your portfolio concepts. You'll ask more specific questions about this group:

- What do the companies I've short-listed have in common?

- What do they have to say about their process or client relationships?

- What types of clients do they specialize in?

- What is the range of work they do?

Just like buying shoes, it's important to buy the one that fits. Some companies really push innovative work. Others are set up for larger, risk-averse clients and they know how to service them. It's a different business. One incredibly talented guy we hired got frustrated because it was difficult to sell his unique, really edgy work. He wound up the straw man—the solution that demonstrated to the client that, yes, we could push the envelope, but that never got used.

But in the long run, I don't think he had any regrets. By working in a large place, he had the discipline of a business and a branding program. When he left, he had a very impressive portfolio of large clients.

—Nancy Hoefig

The more these companies have in common, the easier it will be to create a digital portfolio that will be appropriate to the group, yet feel individually crafted when you approach each one. Understanding the visual language and work culture of the companies you admire will make it easier to winnow your existing work and develop ideas for your presentation.

If you are in possession of this information, you can use it to answer a broad range of vexing questions about your portfolio format, content, and design. Here are some examples of questions that you can find answers to through networking, periodicals, school contacts, websites, or other research sources:

- Should I put that group of photographs in my graphic design site?

- Will they appreciate my sense of humor?

- Which illustrations are likely to get me more book work?

- Will they be put off by the ad campaign work?

- How much new media work should I bring? How much print work?

4. Research the best way to present yourself.

Defining your audience and determining their basic category information should always take place before you begin your portfolio. They may be all you need. But in some situations, you want to impress an audience of few—or one. If you're well-organized (see Chapter 5, "Organizing Your Work"), you may be able to quickly compile a version of your portfolio for one special company.

Search questions to answer about a specific firm:

- Are they busy? Are they hiring?

- What is their aesthetic? Do I like it? Would I be proud to work with them?

- What's their philosophy or way of working with clients? Could I work within it?

- Does their website or other official address tell you how they like to be approached? Email? Letter? Phone?

- Who are their decision makers? What does their personal work look like?

- What are they like to work for?

You may wonder why you need to ask these questions. You're applying for a job, not marrying the company! Yes and no. If you're hired, you'll probably spend more time at the office than you do with your significant other. You need to know that those hours will be well-spent and that the projects you take on will enhance your portfolio. Also, you should consider the other side. If you are hired, but it's not a good fit, you might not stay hired for long. You could have used that time to find a more compatible situation.

For a full-throttle search on one company, word-of-mouth information from personal and local contacts is the most precious and useful source, particularly to find out if the company offers a solid work opportunity.

Designers or potential designers should know why they're presenting their work to that particular design firm, what it is that interested them, and what they're looking to do. I hired a guy, many years ago, who worked at a great design agency in Minneapolis. His was, quite frankly, the best portfolio I think I'd ever seen in my life. We hired him and in getting to know him and understand his philosophy, we started to realize that we weren't in sync. We were more about strategy and solving business problems. He was more about formal design aesthetics. It didn't work at all.

—Bill Cahan

SEARCH TOOLS

No matter the scope of your search, you'll be using tools that you probably take for granted: personal networks, periodicals, and the Internet, particularly Google.

Personal contacts

A personal network is your best resource. Do you know anyone who has the kind of job you want? If they are secure in their position, they might tell you what people at their firm say about the portfolios that get passed around. Creative professionals in related areas can be excellent contacts because they talk to the same people you want to—but about different work. They might give you a contact name in the organization who would be willing to look at your current material and give you direct feedback on it. (See Chapter 13, "Presenting Your Portfolio.") Other surprisingly good contacts are representatives of supplier companies, such as printers. They can often tell you who in your city is busy and might be ready to hire new talent.

> **You really can't underestimate the value of personal connections and networking. This has been the case since the age of the caveman in every industry.**
> **—Terrence Masson**

If there is a professional association in your field, join it. Most large national associations, like the AIGA and the IDSA (Industrial Designers Society of America) have regional chapters with contact information listed on the associations' main websites. (You'll find a list of professional associations and their websites in Appendix A.) Very active chapters will have their own websites, brimming with useful information about the local scene. Go to the meetings, and take advantage of any career events they sponsor. If you are new to your profession, volunteer your time, particularly for events and projects that will give you the opportunity to work with

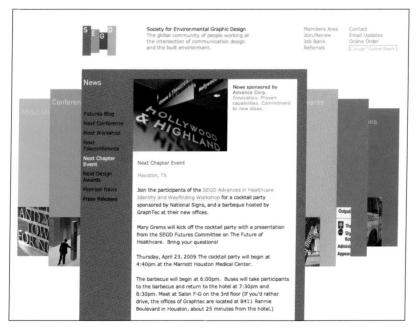

WWW.SEGD.ORG

The Society for Environmental Graphic Design is only one of many professional societies that offer networking opportunities. Each active local chapter should offer special meet-and-greet events, ranging from workshops and seminars to cocktail parties. Larger chapters may offer lectures, special events, and local job listings.

WWW.LINKEDIN.COM

This site is a professional social networking space with an infinite Rolodex. A LinkedIn profile requires minimal maintenance, but pays great dividends in building both a network of contacts and a library of recommendations.

people at different levels of experience. People are more likely to go out of their way to answer questions for someone they've met (or for the friend of a friend).

Social networking

Although it's not the same as a face-to-face encounter, a social network can often be a better way to learn about job-related opportunities than most personal encounters. It can be hard to ask an acquaintance at a cocktail party for an introduction to one of their coworkers. It's comparatively easy to put yourself out there in a site explicitly devoted to making friends and building your business network.

You probably belong to not just one, but several social networking sites already. All of them are valuable resources, because the more people you know and who know you, the better chance you have of meeting your goals. That being said, social networks with a focus are less distracting. Facebook may be a dominant network, and it's a great way to stay in touch with friends, but it has yet to prove itself as a professional destination. Although you can post artwork, other addresses may be better for a small portfolio. Facebook's superficial, short-form communications don't always lend themselves to work-related topics.

One excellent option is LinkedIn. Explicitly created for professional networking, it relies on the "six degrees of separation" concept for careers. You create a profile that can easily take the place of an online résumé, then invite people to become part of your network of connections. Once you connect with a person, you can see people in their network, and potentially add them to yours.

Aother option is to seek out professional networks that were created specifically for you and others like you. One of the very best for creatives is The Behance Network (www.behance.net). It's an all-purpose destination for anyone in the creative industries, complete with job listings, a gallery of portfolios, and its own e-zine.

Forums and directories

You can also learn a tremendous amount by visiting online forums (see Appendix A). People are there to discuss professional practice and are willing to offer advice and a reality check. One excellent source for lists of forums and discussion groups is Yahoo (groups.yahoo.com). It is intelligently organized, and topics are easy to find. General career websites like The Vault (www.vault.com) can be helpful as well if you are hoping to work for a large company with a creative services or marketing communications department. The message boards on these sites are full of people who are already working at or are former employees of the company.

Most professional organizations have statistics and surveys about your profession, from pricing structures to presentation standards, often broken down by geography or industry. While some of this material is published for general use, other parts of it might be for members only. Contact information for a selection of relevant organizations can be found in Appendix A.

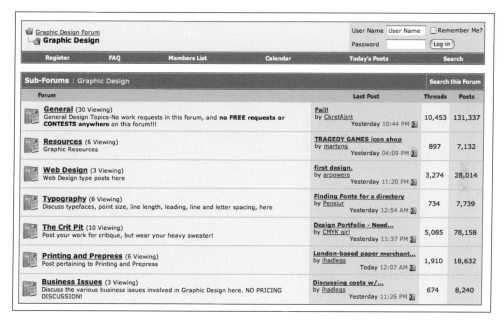

WWW.GRAPHICDESIGNFORUM.COM

The best online forums are a one-stop resource for everything from technical questions to portfolio critiques.

WWW.RISDBOSTON.ORG

RISDBoston is a very active local chapter of Rhode Island School of Design alumni that lists local firms with a special interest in RISD graduates. Firms with alumni contacts are starred, and alumni are listed with their graduation year.

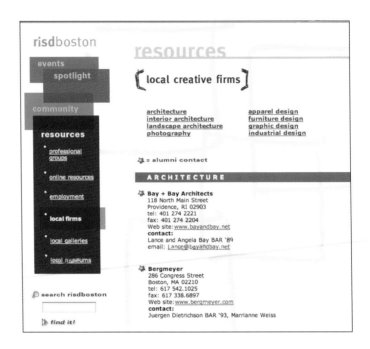

Schools, universities, and alumni associations

Did you graduate from an art school or from a university with a large department or school in your specialty? If so, you could have an invaluable resource at hand. A specialized school might offer career counseling and even placement services for alums. As a service to their students, schools often offer great career links. Even if they don't, they're usually well-connected with firms in their local area and committed to offering useful information that can be exactly what you need for your target audience search.

Some art and design schools have an intricate network of alumni associations in major cities worldwide. Local alumni clubs have lists of companies with established professionals who are willing to offer informational interviews—or even a shot at real jobs—to other alums. They can help you match your skills and interests with companies whose style and philosophy are compatible with your own. Even nongraduates can sometimes find these organizations helpful. You can use their lists of prestigious firms and contact names in a category search or to find possible targets in a geographical area that interests you.

Searching with Google

Unquestionably, the Internet is the single best tool for capturing information. There's almost nothing you can't find out about potential clients or employees—in general or in specific—by using Internet resources. And Google is the tool of choice for searching it.

Simple search

Googling a specific company, sometimes with some additional criteria, will get you their website, as well as any other sites they maintain (like a separate blog), as well as mentions of them and their principals in articles. Phrases such as *"working for (target company here)"* or *(target company)* and "resume" will get you job listings and contacts.

Remember to make bookmarks so you can return to them later and organize your search results into categories, like "job directories" and "art schools." Half of the battle in research is knowing where you put things. If you have to reconstruct your sources every time you have a problem to solve, the process will take much longer.

Googling by location

Imagine that you're a designer who has recently relocated to Montreal. You're looking for design firms that do branding and are within easy driving distance of your new home.

If you go to Google and type in "branding agency design" you may be surprised to discover that Google knows a lot more about you than you think. The list will probably be specific to your home area. Very close to the top of the list, you'll probably find a search result with a map that keys some of the companies that tag those words on their home page. The initial list is short, but if you select the "More results" option at the bottom of the listing snippet, you'll find every firm that fits your criteria in the metropolitan area.

If Google brings up results in your former home location, just click the "Change location" link to input your new city.

Google and directories

Sometimes what you need is a list of lists. If you type in your creative area and the word *directory* as a search, you'll locate a mountain of already-researched associations, job listings, and fellow travelers in your profession. An excellent resource that is indicative of what you can find this way is BusinessWeek affiliate Core 77 (www.designdirectory.com), which is a well-organized database of professionals and firms in all the major design fields. (See Appendix A for a list of some good directories to use as starting points.)

One gem hidden deep inside Google's many tools is Google Directory (directory. google.com). Select Arts, and a list of relevant categories appears. Are you an illustrator or web designer? Select the Design category and drill through the options.

GOOGLING WITH ADVANCED SEARCH

Even with Google's shortcuts and intelligence, it can offer too much information. Sometimes, you need to design a search criteria that will find information that isn't readily available. Clicking the Advanced Search option to the right of the Search button will give you the opportunity to specify words that must factor into the results as well as eliminating those that don't sound right for you. In our hypothetical search below, we've strategically slimmed down the results to only 129. That's a reasonable number to explore.

Turn to Google's advanced search function if your first easy search turns out to be too general. This search for a company that has won awards for branding in Canada turns up a million results. The advanced search applies several strategies. By putting quotes around *design agency* it requires these two words to appear together as a phrase. By adding optional words, in this case two preferred locations in Canada, these locations must be mentioned in order for a site to appear. Last, by specifying words that should not be part of the site, it eliminates the location of Vancouver (too far away) and subtracts any school websites.

Hit the books

Creative professionals frequently pore through *Graphis*, *Communication Arts*, and other magazines for inspiration. These publications are also useful for research. Look for work you admire and see if the companies or studios who've done the work fit your general audience description.

You can also use these books to create a web search, a particularly fine strategy if the companies you love don't happen to be anywhere near where you live. Go to their websites and look at the source HTML code, as shown below. There should be a descriptive list of words inside tags. These tags, and the words inside them, are called meta tags or description tags. Use these words for your local area searches, and you should find companies that describe themselves the same way and, hopefully, do the same type of work.

```
<meta name="keywords" content="branding, strategy, advertising, design,
interactive, web, brand strategy, advertising agency, ad agency, graphic
design, graphic design firm, design firm, design studio, interactive design,
interactive agency, design services, brand communications, brand consultants,
multi channel retailing, strategic design, corporate identity, logo design,
collateral, annual reports, e-commerce, packaging, package design, online
strategy, web strategy, web design, web development, web site design, website
design, marketing strategy, i-shop, web shop, online marketing, interactive
marketing, online branding, banner ads, point of sale display, point of sale
design, pos, pop, flash design, flash, direct mail">
```

Meta tags are used by web search engines to find sites that meet your criteria. Someone at the company has deliberately chosen these words to make their site come up frequently in web searches.

WHEN ARE YOU DONE?

One of the dubious delights of research is that it is never completely finished. There are always little tidbits of information that can teach you more about your target audience or change your focus. Once your portfolio is underway, it's a good idea to revisit individual websites and check for recently posted articles.

In the meantime, you should have developed a feel for the market you want to enter or the companies you want to entice. Looking at their work has helped you judge what parts of your own work might be most effective. Reading about their philosophy and comparing it to their client lists will tell you whether you should be conservative or try for a *tour de force*. If you've been researching potential clients, you'll know who they've used previously, why they continued to use them (or dumped them), and whether they might find your approach compatible.

In short, you'll know your subjects well enough to have built a little target audience construct in your head. Based on your self-assessment from Chapter 1, do your current skills and work fit that picture? If they don't, you'll need to determine the changes you need to make to bring your portfolio into the right ballpark. If they do, you can steam confidently ahead.

PORTFOLIO HIGHLIGHT:
PEOPLE DESIGN | KNOW YOUR MARKET

WWW.PEOPLEDESIGN.COM

As anyone who is old enough to remember New Coke knows, it can be a very dangerous thing to mess with an established brand. So, when partners Kevin Budelmann and Yang Kim decided to replace BBK Design, their award-winning design studio, with a refocused consultancy—People Design—they knew they were taking a radical step. After years of targeting marketing departments, they selected a new audience: corporate leaders who were looking for an innovative, integrated approach to their users' experience.

The People Design website needed to do some heavy lifting in order to reassure existing customers while convincing a new audience that they could deliver on an ambitious agenda. They decided to reorganize and redesign their existing portfolio to make it equally easy for their audience to see their work across multiple categories for single clients as well as

> **Future clients are clearly looking to see if we are an inspiring, reliable, and effective resource, and we show them that we are.**
> **—Kevin Budelmann**

To the right of the main navigation is a column of short titles, encouraging the visitor to jump directly to a topic of interest.

Because the main menu persists, it's easy to jump back after reading one of the essays.

At the bottom of the page, discreetly nestled under the logo, are a downloadable executive summary and contact options.

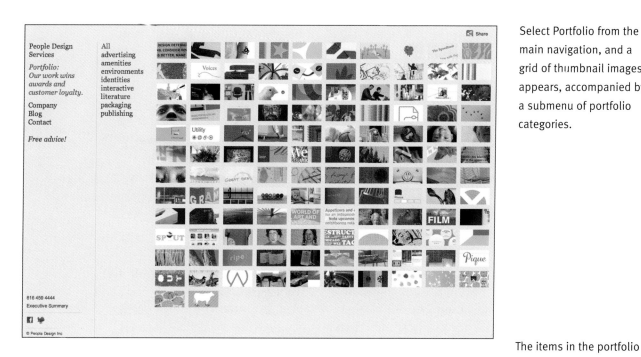

Select Portfolio from the main navigation, and a grid of thumbnail images appears, accompanied by a submenu of portfolio categories.

The items in the portfolio grid that are not part of the selected category fade and are no longer active. Clicking another category brings up a different collection of thumbnails.

Select a category from the submenu, and the topic color changes to red to remind you of what you selected. Selecting All returns all thumbnails to active mode.

Each area of the site has content that is visualized in different ways depending on the goal. We tried to keep this portfolio section very clean and simple, but provide enough information to get a sense for the work product.

—Kevin Budelmann

multiple clients within product categories. And, most importantly, to emphasize visual inspiration rather than case study analysis.

Navigation and architecture

The site structure is extremely compact. There are no Flash intros, or content prequels. Beginning with a clear statement of identity and purpose on the splash page, the main site sections appear in a standard vertical list. Each main header is a portal to its own home page, where all of the section's content displays. This strategy makes for a very shallow site that limits unnecessary mouse clicks.

The portfolio page is a surprise. Most portfolios, intentionally or by default, directly translate the organization of a physical portfolio to an interactive space. This often takes the form of a menu organized by category, client, or project list.

People Design rethinks this portfolio metaphor, in keeping with their belief that a prospective client is most interested in inspiration. The portfolio, which is accessed from one of the main menu options, is a wall of thumbnail images—snippets of interesting texture or details from the image they represent. Although it is possible to experience the portfolio by selecting a category from the portfolio menu list, this option is only one of many. You might also click any image to launch a simple slide-

Selecting an active thumbnail opens the slideshow window. If you have chosen a subset category, only the images belonging to the subset join the slideshow.
Click on the first image in the slideshow and you return to the portfolio grid.

Click on the forward arrow above the image and the sequence loads. From that point, you can either use the arrows to click back and forth through each sequential image, or click anywhere on the large image to move forward.

Interactive projects inside the portfolio play as encapsulated movies from a Vimeo feed, allowing you to see the navigation in action, or to see more than one page of the client site.

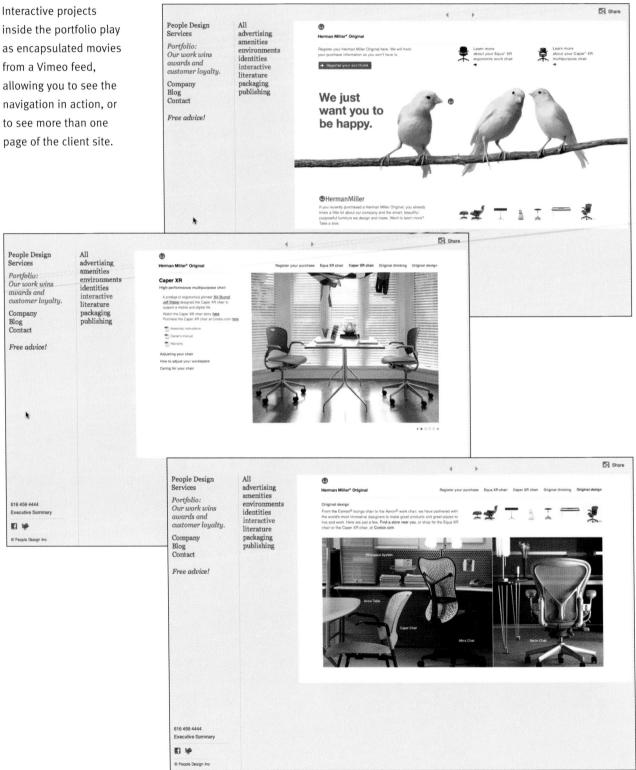

show that browses sequentially through the entire collection, or you could just randomly click on individual thumbnails.

No matter how the viewer chooses to experience the samples, it requires very little user action to tell the portfolio story, and no clicks away from either the menu or the image grid.

Content

People Design has jettisoned the case study approach to its portfolio. Instead, they have looked carefully at what a prospective client really wants to know about them. The portfolio doesn't burden the viewer with content that may not be relevant to their needs, or require a shift from visual to text processing. It provides a selection of media projects that emphasize the broad range of challenges the company has tackled successfully and gives the viewer the freedom to browse casually, or pursue a specific theme.

Instead of case studies, People Design emphasizes team, personality, and process—the common threads for all their work. Prospective clients can visit the Services section for a short presentation of People Design's working framework or visit the Company link to learn more about them as a potential design partner. Some might even decide to read the Blog, which is a prime destination for people—other designers, company fans, or aspiring employees—who want to stay on top of their thinking as design leaders. In all cases the nature of the content is clearly defined and well-categorized. The visitor can clearly engage in whatever aspect of the site most interests them without distractions or false moves.

Future plans

Portfolio sites are always in flux, and you learn from what works. People Design is constantly tweaking the back end to improve content organization and flow. As Budelmann says, "We put a lot of thought into this site, trying to marry print/analog paradigms with best practices and innovative thinking online. The structure is intentionally flexible and we intend for it to grow." By the time this case study is in print, the site features will have been expanded to personalize the experience for existing clients and to incorporate elements from social media networks (like Twitter) directly into the site.

> **We see our site as a living thing that requires care and feeding. We have already evolved the functionality since it launched.**
> **—Kevin Budelmann**

CHAPTER 4

Delivery and Format

One of a digitally based portfolio's conveniences is its flexibility. The same content can be packaged in a delightful variety of ways, depending on your needs, knowledge, and time constraints. You can begin simply with a selection of work collected in a PDF, design a slideshow presentation for a client pitch, or move to an interactive website or DVD. A well-organized digital file lets you shift elements around for multiple formats almost as easily as you might slide a brochure into and out of a binder. Even nicer, the work you collect in one fairly simple format can become the basis for a more comprehensive and sophisticated portfolio as your technical knowledge and body of work increase.

There is no "right" portfolio solution. Nonetheless, there are preferred media and delivery methods in different creative fields. And there are a few wrong choices—decisions that are inappropriate for your specific market.

Although the options for portfolio format and venue continue to expand, they boil down to one of three delivery categories: portable, email, or online.

PORTABLE MEDIA

If you want to make your digital portfolio part of your in-person presentation or need to send a high-resolution presentation to prospective clients or employers, you will need some physical medium to hold it.

CDs and DVDs

Standard-sized discs are familiar, easy to integrate into a traditional portfolio, and fairly sturdy. CDs are an inexpensive way of delivering a variety of types of relatively small files (PDFs and player files, for example). DVDs are the best choice for moving images.

> When designers or illustrators send me a CD or DVD, I often find that either I don't have the correct software installed or the disc crashes the computer. Either way, in the trash it goes. In case you're wondering, I'm not a Luddite, but I know I'm not the only designer who feels this way.
>
> —Alex Isley

People feel strongly—pro and con—about receiving a disc portfolio. The people who dislike them don't necessarily dislike discs per se, but groan because so many people do a bad job of creating them. Typical complaints range from bad organization to unreadable file formats. Unlike a website, which can be revised as you learn from your mistakes, a badly conceived or executed CD will simply be tossed—or tossed around a shop as an example of "portfolio fail"—Chapter 5, "Organizing Your Work," Chapter 9, "Structure and Concept," and Chapter 13, "Presenting Your Portfolio," address these issues, and will help you create a disc portfolio that won't frustrate an art director.

Although discs are usually welcome in 3D and moving-image disciplines, they are less attractive in 2D specializations, where there are more concise alternatives for delivering a body of work. Graphic design professionals, for example, tend to prefer receiving work via email: PDF attachments or a URL link. A disc is a commitment.

MINI CDs

Performers love mini CDs, otherwise known as business-card CDs, because they are just the right size to hold a high-resolution image, a résumé, and a small slideshow. However, they ruin optical drives, and they get stuck in slot-loaded CD trays (the skinny ones that you slide a CD into and the mechanism drags it in the rest of the way). Many people in the creative industries own some flavor of Apple Mac, and they will not thank the person whose disc trashes their computer. Avoid them, especially for portfolios and leave-behinds, no matter what type of computer you own.

Unless someone has thoughtfully provided a table of contents, you don't know how much it contains or how long it will take to look at it. And then there's the problem of where to store it if it's worth keeping.

In contrast, people with positive disc experiences swear by, not at, them. Unlike a website, where you have to consider bandwidth and window size, a disc can be viewed anywhere, anytime, even without wireless access. The disc can hold work at a much higher resolution, so typographic or rendering details become accessible. Plus, if you author a DVD (with iDVD or some other application) rather than simply drag data onto it, the result will work in a standard DVD player, not just on a computer. That consideration is particularly important if you are sending a DVD to a large com-

WWW.TOADSTORM.COM

These are enlarged details from two versions, at different resolutions, of animator Henry Foster's portfolio reel. The lower resolution (360x243) on the left is fine for a quick view, but the higher resolution (720x486) version shows the realistic modeling details of the chicken's eye and the plumage around it.

A lot of houses prefer authored DVDs because many times they'll be watched in a conference room with several department supervisors. They won't necessarily have a PC hooked up. It's easier to throw a disc in a DVD player and show it up on a screen.

—Terrence Masson

pany where your work is likely to be viewed by people who aren't technically savvy, or who don't have the latest version of your software player on the computer they're using.

In addition, discs have a physicality that can keep your work alive. Websites are great, but they aren't always top of mind. Will someone who is inundated with portfolios and reels recall your name and remember to bookmark your website? Or if they did bookmark it, will they remember why a month later? A disc full of good work, attractively packaged, can and will imprint itself on a visual person's mind. Rather than archive it in a box or file, the disc may find its way to a prominent place on a desk—ready to work its magic when the right position opens up.

One last thing: if you decide to put your portfolio on a disc for distribution, use some type of -R versus -RW disc. Not only are these formats generally cheaper, but you would rather not have someone treat your portfolio as a free storage space.

Laptop

Besides being an elegant way of transporting large volumes of work, the laptop gives you ultimate control of your presentation. You're less likely to be plagued by technical gremlins because you've tested your environment. You never have to worry about platform issues or care if the people you are presenting to can tell the difference between a DVD and a coaster. There are no surprises in type size or player speed. You can show your work in an intimate setting or hook the computer to a projection system and present it to a filled room. For all these reasons, laptops are a great way to present to a client or prospective employer.

On the downside, walking in with a laptop also requires that you be ready to use it to present under any circumstances. Your VGA adapter becomes a crucial tool if a one-on-one interview suddenly turns into a department-wide command performance. Equally important may be an alternative presentation layout if the projector has a lower resolution than you use as a standard for presentation design. Color shifts between your laptop and the projector can create awkward moments if they affect the audience's ability to see crucial details.

If you present without attaching your laptop to a projector, you'll have different challenges. You may have to dance between watching the screen and connecting with your interviewer or client. The only way around that is to have rehearsed your presentation so frequently that it's practically memorized—not a bad move in any case. You also have to take the flat panel display's limitations into consideration. If your audience is sitting at an angle from the screen they may not see the presentation well.

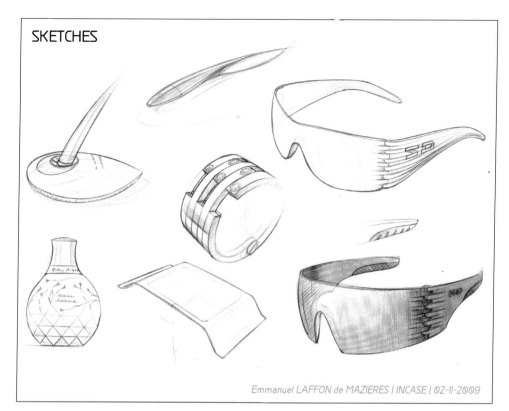

SKETCHES

Emmanuel LAFFON de MAZIERES | INCASE | 02-11-2009

On Emmanuel Laffon's website (www.emmanuel-laffon.com), he concentrates on completed, modeled projects that can speak for themselves with little context. His laptop presentation, however, contains abundant sketches: process work that allows him to discuss how he arrives at and develops his ideas.

If you plan to do regular laptop presentations, make sure that your entire computer is backed up regularly. Keep a copy of the presentation and any files it requires on a portable external drive that you carry with you in case Murphy's Law comes crashing down on your keyboard. And remember that a laptop presentation means maintaining at least one other form of portfolio as well, since you won't be dropping your MacBook Pro as a leave-behind.

EMAIL

There are two ways to use email to distribute your portfolio. The first is as an advertising conduit: providing a URL where your work can be downloaded or viewed online. The second, the email attachment, is more like a traditional direct mail sample. With it, you can target prospects individually with a fairly small outlay of time and energy. Because you don't have to design and build an interface to deliver your work, almost anyone can send a portfolio attachment.

There are very few negatives to attachments, but they are worth considering nonetheless. First, you need to keep their purpose in mind. Attachments should be little teasers. If successful, they should lead to a presentation, either in person with a physical portfolio or laptop, or as a high-resolution movie player download. They should not constitute your only foray into the portfolio world. They are also an awful

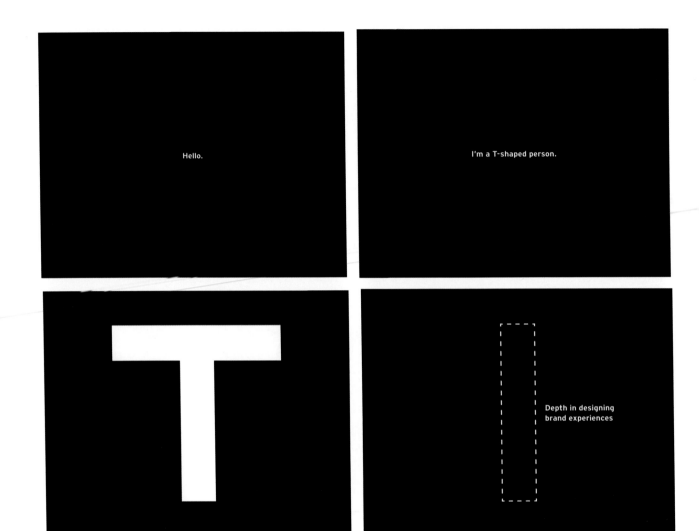

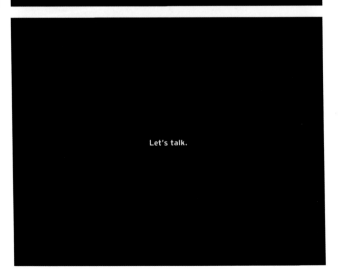

WWW.JASONRING.COM

Designer Jason Ring uses the concept of the
T-shaped person—a person with a deep principal
skill and a native curiousity about things outside it—
coined by IDEO's Tim Brown, as his lead-off and
framing device for the PDF portfolio he sends to
prospective clients. It creates the perfect teaser for
his portfolio presentation—clever, well-designed,
memorable—and smaller than 3MB, even though it's
25 pages long.

move for anyone who is applying for web-based design work and should obviously have provided a URL.

Second, standards for email attachments have risen now that most people can receive large attached files. For 2D images the expected format is a PDF file. PDFs are familiar to everyone, Adobe Reader is ubiquitous, and a PDF can be locked to prevent unauthorized appropriation of your work (see Chapter 12, "Copyright and Portfolio"). All of these good points, however, require that you own an application that generates PDF files (like Adobe applications InDesign, Illustrator, or Acrobat Professional). Designers (industrial, graphic, or architectural) and illustrators should have no problem with this. They should also be well-positioned to make their PDF a coherent design project as well (see Chapter 7, "Repurposing and Optimizing," for some PDF format guidelines).

What if you don't have strong design experience? You could still enlist a design friend or partner to set up a template file that you can update easily when you want to just add text or new images. If that's not possible, you can move images into Microsoft PowerPoint or Apple Keynote and provide a slide show player. Slideshows can be a great solution for a photographer, artist, or illustrator, as long as the size of the finished file stays within a mailable size (see Chapter 9 for more on this option).

A last possibility is an FTP (file transfer protocol) site—owned by you or, most likely, provided as a service—where you can upload your work. Dropbox (www.get dropbox.com) is one service that has an enthusiastic and growing group of users. By grouping your material thoughtfully, you can offer access to different work examples based on who you have contacted. Some FTP services provide security that allows invited guests to view, but not download or change, the content. Most, however, do not, and once you have issued an invitation, it can be shared by the invitees until you remove them or shut the access down. On the other hand, it could be a great way to share a high-resolution movie file without having to maintain a personal website or other online presence.

ONLINE

Online portfolios are like profiles on a dating service site. They enable the potentially interested client or employer to taste-test you and your work anonymously. If they like what they see, you may hear from them. If it's not their style, both you and they are spared a painful face-to-face experience.

An online portfolio is any collection of your work that people can view from inside a browser. Once you recognize that a portfolio can be defined as any venue or medium where you display your work, you may discover that you have some kind of online portfolio already. Depending on where you post and why, there are a variety of distinct sites that provide a range of levels of exposure and can make different statements about you.

Personal website

As a presentation form, a personal website is somewhere between a mailing and an in-person visit. It is unquestionably the single most valuable portfolio form you can create—even more than a physical portfolio. In fact, for many creatives, not just web designers, it is the only portfolio they maintain.

Pushed to its highest form, a personal website creates an avenue for creative expression, and a marvelous opportunity to highlight your skills, taste, and unique world view. Through linking from the other portfolio venues discussed below, it can bring contacts to you that you would be hard-pressed to reach and impress otherwise. And unlike every other online venue, your work doesn't have to compete with other posters while they are visiting it.

Personal websites are not yet a perfect medium. They are a one-way street. You can't watch how someone is responding to your work and adjust your tone, emphasis, and pacing the way you can easily do face to face. They also demand up-front design work, a host of visual and content decisions, and much more significant time in their creation and upkeep than other online options, or PDFs.

It is possible to mitigate some of the burden of creating a personal website from scratch (see "Partnering" in Chapter 1). Some people also elect to purchase and then customize an HTML or Flash portfolio template.

Self-publishing site

Self-publishing sites, from YouTube to Flickr, have pushed out most of the free, non-curated sourcebook sites that were prevalent a few years ago. Those that remain tend to be the repository of mediocre talents and part-time artists. Since most also have very limited storage space and a utilitarian interface, it's not surprising that they have been overwhelmed by the Web 2.0 self-publishing site.

The self-publishing site is a great step forward in portfolio maintenance. Although not a substitute for a personal website, it is an excellent second outlet, particularly for people whose work can be compiled into one large, well-designed package or batched by theme, subject, or style. These sites offer tremendous browse appeal, and can bring your work to the attention of people who would never find your personal portfolio site otherwise.

Most self-publishing sites are defined by their primary medium, and are organized in a way that makes them more useful to some creatives than others. For example, although Flickr posts many videos and illustrations, it mostly comes to mind as a site for sharing photographs. YouTube's obvious *raison d'etre* is moving image, which not only covers the digital videos it's known for, but also 2D and 3D animation reels, architectural walkthroughs, and portfolios full of 3D models made by industrial designers and computer artists.

WWW.FLICKR.COM/PHOTOS/
LAYLAK/
Designer Layla Keramat
keeps her extensive
collection of photographic
works on Flickr to
distinguish it from her
professional design work.

Other sites serve their own niches. Issuu (issuu.com) is a publishing outlet for everything from magazines to comic books, but it has an impressive collection of books of personal art as well as online versions of printed portfolios. Best of all, it adds the feeling of a real publication to each PDF document by using software to provide shadows and highlights to what looks like photos of a bound book. This makes it a powerful option for graphic designers as well as architectural and industrial designers who are required to own a formal printed portfolio as students. The downside of such a big site is that your work could get lost on it. Issuu, like others in its category, makes money by offering a premium publishing level that features you prominently and eliminates their advertising and logo from your work.

Creative services portfolio site

Like discounters where you can sometimes find a designer gem, free-for-all self-publishing sites can be exciting and entertaining addresses. However, they encompass enormous ranges in quality. And even with a superior search function, they offer a daunting number of results in any category. You have no control over the context of your work, and there is no curator to exercise quality control. If a search turns up twenty results and the first five are mediocre, the searcher might not bother to look at number six—aka you.

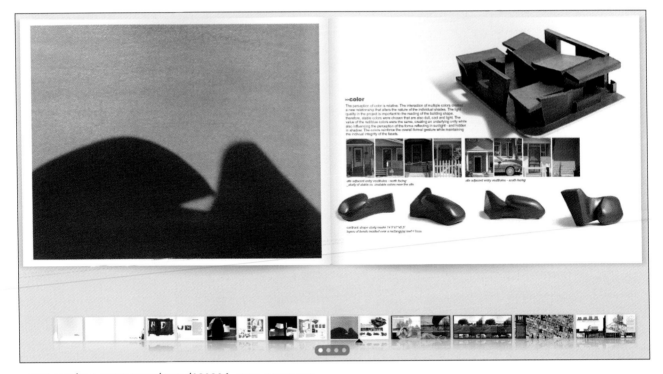

ISSUU.COM/GRACEFULSPOON/DOCS/080206_ARCH_PORTFOLIO

Issuu provides three viewing options for your work: as a flat
PDF file, as a presentation, and this version, magazine format,
which mimics the look and shadow effects of a bound book.

Paid and invitation-only sites, on the other hand, are a more upscale version of
the concept. With a barrier to entry, they're more likely to contain professionals rather than hobbyists. As with self-publishing sites, friends, members of circles, and casual viewers leave comments about the work. What's most telling is that in a professional site, those comments go beyond the "way cool" level. Most are informed, some are
critical, and the people behind them often carry the weight of reputation. A portfolio
that surfaces to the top in a professional site can easily lead to contacts and a career.

Among the well-established portfolio sites for professionals, are the AIGA mem-
bers-only portfolio site (www.aiga.org), and Communication Arts' Creative Hotlist
(www.creativehotlist.com), which offers an inexpensive six-month subscription that
allows you to post a PDF and a small online portfolio.

The relative newcomer, with an unusual combination of social network publishing and exclusive access is Behance (www.behance.net). It doesn't charge a fee, but
you can only join if you are invited by another member, or if you petition the site
editors with a detailed description of your creative work or involvement in the professional creative process. There is no way to buy yourself into a featured position.

Works that make it to the front page get there through a combination of member comments and site curators. Almost all members have personal websites as well, and a featured position in Behance almost always leads to substantially more personal website traffic.

Some sites encompass all creative professionals equally. Others draw one category more than others. For example, LiveBooks (www.livebooks.com) is becoming the professional photographer's Flickr. Although it is not free—you buy a monthly subscription—it takes all of the worry out of portfolio creation. Your site is built on a template and attractively customized by an in-house designer. Once that's done, you control updates, sequence, and content.

The pluses of this approach are that it is fast and affordable, particularly if you compare it with the price of a designer creating a site from scratch for you. A templated portfolio can be the best way to get your work online when you are unexpectedly let go from a full-time spot. The templates are attractive and take care of visual decisions like layout and fonts, as well as shielding you from having to learn a new application, like Adobe Dreamweaver.

> **There is some additional credibility when others are talking positively about you, and you're not just thumping your chest one more time.**
>
> **—Rick Braithwaite**

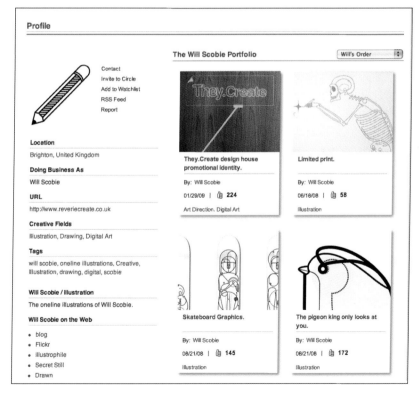

WWW.BEHANCE.NET/WILL_SCOBIE

Illustrator Will Scobie displays a selection of his recent work on Behance. His display emphasizes the wide range of projects to which his distinctive style can be applied.

Hosted gallery presentations

Many fine artists want a web presence but are intimidated by the technology or lack the resources to hire someone to create and maintain their site. For those who are established in their field, a gallery site can be a substitute for a personal site—a way of establishing a foothold in the virtual world. There are both fine art and commercial gallery sites. In both cases, the site is the product of an individual's personal vision—the curator in a fine art gallery, the artist representative in the commercial site. An artist has to come to the curator's attention, and the curator has to want to represent that artist. Assuming the chemistry is right, the artist gains an immediate increase in visibility, as well as a personal advocate.

Social networking site

There are a variety of social networking sites that provide a way for you to share short notes about your work and display images or videos. Facebook has edged out MySpace as the major website for this purpose. Companies, design studios, and working professionals are now using it as both a personal space and a marketing tool.

Any prime destination is an irresistible magnet for posting your work. Plus, a social network not only enlarges the number of people who know about you, it can provide that special sense of personality that bridges the gap between a formal portfolio and the person behind it. However, indiscriminate friending offers casual contacts access to not just your own personal quirks, but those of your irrepressible friends and family.

Key to using Facebook as a portfolio adjunct are its Privacy settings, which you can use to limit access to some elements on your page. Next you need to customize the Search section. You might want to block most people from seeing the pages you have become a fan of or from seeing your list of friends. And you must maintain these settings as you add new friends to your list.

All of this takes a lot of effort, and Facebook, like other social networking sites, is a place with a friendly, no-stress vibe. In short, if you're not committed to massaging your contacts, it may not be a worthwhile choice when there are other, more focused outlets.

Blogs

An adjunct to a personal portfolio, although not a substitute for it, is the personal or studio blog. It offers an opportunity to talk about your work in a conversational way, without weighing your formal portfolio down with opinions and insights that can seem overdone or even pretentious when visitors are concentrating on your work itself. Here is the place to talk about your creative process, and how successfully you met your client's constraints. It also provides a place to roll out experimental work, or material in a new medium.

The potential negative of the blog format is that it comes with the assumption that people not only might comment, but probably will, and perhaps at more length and with less approbation than you think you deserve. Although you don't have to publish any of these less-than-glowing comments, you'll still need to be prepared to receive them.

PORTFOLIO STRATEGIES

One format or venue is unlikely to serve all your needs. Most creatives plan on some combination of the previously mentioned media and online options. But what should you put where, and how do you end up with a coherent personal story? There are several ways to approach the multiple portfolio problem: duplicating, dispersing, dividing, doubling, and developing.

Duplicating

When you duplicate, you have a single body of work in many formats. You develop your portfolio themes, choose the best pieces to illustrate them, and create one portfolio version—the easiest to create or the one you need immediately—first. After this portfolio has been tested, presented, and, if necessary, refined, you duplicate it in other media. The plus of this approach is that it's very fast. Updates happen in tandem, and you never have to remember who saw which version of your work.

There are two minuses. First, you may be showing some work in a medium that compromises its effectiveness. More important, you have no second act. Anyone who was interested in your first portfolio will want to see more and different material elsewhere. It is particularly important that you have something extra that you can show in person.

Dividing

The divided portfolio demands more thought and preparation than simple duplication. The first stage of dividing can be relatively straightforward. Material that doesn't look right onscreen and can't be zoomed into or manipulated remains in a traditional portfolio, which you use only in personal presentations. Anything that is effective onscreen stays there. The few pieces that sparkle both digitally and traditionally remain in both versions but may be highlighted differently onscreen and off.

But once you've determined on- versus off-screen material, you may need to divide further, or differently. What if you don't need a traditional portfolio, but you have some work that doesn't feel like it belongs on your personal website? Do you have alternative concepts, or process work? These belong someplace where they can tell a story about how you think. Here's material that could be divided out and

Designers have dropped off their portfolios and the last two pages are a bunch of photos. The question is, do you think that somebody's going to hire you on the basis of your hobby? If you're serious about your other skills, then do an extra portfolio and show what kind of photography you specialize in. Don't just put it into a portfolio of design work.

—Layla Keramat

WWW.LUKELUKELUKE.COM

Designer Luke Williams' thesis project was a
photographic essay. Although he posts a sampling in
the photo section of his portfolio, he uses the division
concept to display the images in a more appropriate
venue, directing interested viewers to his Flickr site.

posted on a blog. Other times, you feel the work needs a narrator. It might work as part of a traditional portfolio, or even better as part of a laptop presentation you prepare for people who have seen and liked your website.

Dispersing

Dispersing is a variation on dividing. You create a core group of work that exists as a coherent prime portfolio. A couple of the best individual pieces, or a subset reel, can be posted on one of the self-publishing sites to build traffic.

Then you look at the pieces that you didn't include in this collection. After eliminating the ones that are really not your best efforts, you'll probably find additional pieces from a series of projects, project work, concept sketches for ideas that are still in germination, or secondary artwork (illustrations, photos, 3D art) that you are proud of but that are not your primary focus. These pieces, by themselves or joined with related pieces from the main portfolio, can be salted into other venues. Are you a designer, but consider yourself a good photographer? Maybe some of your photo work belongs on Flickr, with some commentary on how you use it to develop your design ideas. Have a good poster that you've weeded from your main site to make room for new work? It may be perfect in a blog with a discussion of your typographic decisions.

Doubling

Doubling—maintaining two completely different portfolios—is not just useful, it's required if you do more than one thing well and the two things speak to radically different audiences. Fine artists who actively solicit commercial illustration, designers who also photograph, or illustrators who design are often best served by keeping these specialized skills separate.

It is possible to create distinct areas on a single website, but think twice before you try. This tactic can work brilliantly if you are really a double- or triple-threat, or if your secondary creative outlet illuminates some aspect of your primary expertise. If the second element is only a tag-on, it weakens your overall presentation.

Developing

When you develop, you are planning on a radical break with your past, rather than an expansion or transition. A small selection of older material may combine with newly invented work—revisions of older projects or brand-new ideas—explicitly created for one new portfolio that will take the place of all existing ones.

You use the developing strategy when you are in the process of reinventing yourself, but still need to maintain a professional presence for current employment. If, for example, you want to move into a new specialty within your profession—like a photographer moving from product to editorial shots—developing may be the only way to do it. The same is true if you have been an exhibit designer but you are now studying interactive design or architecture.

The negative points of developing come down to two little words with big impact: money and time. Developing from scratch is by far the hardest strategy—short term. But it's often best to take the long view with your portfolio. Everyone has periods of feast and famine, even during good economic times. The quiet periods are ideal for developing new material, which will hopefully help to minimize downtimes in the future.

> A lot of creative energy goes into creating comps. Generally, the best ideas never get produced, or at least get "watered down" to the point that they're not as good as the original idea. So, for me, the website is a great place to showcase some of my favorite work that never got approved.
>
> —Ken Loh

PORTFOLIO HIGHLIGHT:
EMMANUEL LAFFON DE MAZIÈRES |
FORM AND FUNCTION

WWW.EMMANUEL-LAFFON.COM

Every year at graduation time, thousands of new product designers, like flocks of migrating birds, head for Core 77, Coroflot, or Behance. There they build an online portfolio nest and devour the extensive job lists. Many seldom venture away from their new home. If their portfolio is featured there, they're front and center for the prospective employers who visit these sites. But then what? The next week, a new group is featured, and they move down to the next page and join the ranks in their category.

> **I tried to make my website extremely simple to use but as enjoyable as possible.**
> **—Emmanuel Laffon de Mazières**

There's nothing necessarily wrong with sticking with this instinctive scenario, unless you count the lost opportunities. Emmanuel Laffon de Mazières, recent transplant from France to California, certainly did. Using a dividing strategy, he fields a range of portfolios in different venues, each for a different audience.

Laffon's projects work hard. A group of stills appears on Coroflot. A video on YouTube, scored to the music of Django Reinhardt, smoothly supports his 3D flyarounds, and when results are sorted by times viewed, it still appears as the first industrial design (ID) portfolio after the content featured for pay. His laptop presentation shows a full range of projects as well as process work. Most important, his prime projects are showcased in luxuriant close-ups on his personal website, to which all his other portfolio versions are linked.

Navigation

The site was designed to immediately capture the viewer's attention. The opening backgrounds, the work of a professional-photographer friend, were chosen for both beauty and visual simplicity so they would not overwhelm the portfolio itself. Once the portfolio window is engaged, your perception of them quickly changes from seeing them as content to experiencing them as color mattes around the work.

If there is one thing that should be evident in an ID portfolio, it's concern for user experience. The study of human factors and the study of product design are tightly connected, and many of the most influential thinkers in usability began as industrial designers and engineers. So it's a disappointment when ID websites are bleakly utilitarian or so dependent on Flash-based effects that a smooth experience is impossible.

> **As an ID, I could have just dropped my pictures into a portfolio website. But I did this because, through the website and interface, I could describe the way I work as an industrial designer.**
> **—Emmanuel Laffon de Mazières**

The site fills the browser window with a startlingly rich background image behind the translucent window of the actual portfolio space. The opening images remain onscreen for each visit but appear on a cycle, so each visit to the site offers a fresh visual perspective.

The navigation cues are subtle but clear. When you click on a menu link, the type highlights and its background becomes opaque. Hover on a link and it changes under your cursor in the same way but more slowly, so you will notice the process.

A blue accent is used sparingly, as the indication of another page. It appears in the link to open or close the project brief, and to move back and forth through the pages of a project.

Roll over an item in the Work or Video menus, and both the type and the rectangular space around it brighten, but fade back again as the project brief window appears.

Nothing could be further from Laffon's design. Despite its lushly cinematic first impression, it provides clear and intuitive visual cues that concisely map the portfolio space.

In particular, he uses translucency not only as a setting for his portfolio frame, but to aid in navigation and as a way to keep visual focus firmly on his work. Navigation elements react by appearing to change their amount of transparency. Project briefs never obscure the work, and are easily dismissed without any distracting motion on the page itself.

Laffon initially hoped to create an HTML-based site, because most of the sites he admired as examples of clear navigation avoided the Flash temptation. As he says, "I finally decided to go with Flash because it allows me to be more creative in terms of layout and the translucency. But there are so many things you can do in Flash that

> **I made sure that there would be some symbiosis between the background picture and the content so they would enhance each other, not compete.**
> **—Emmanuel Laffon de Mazières**

Information about the design floats above each view of the project, which continues to be visible beneath the text. The information is easily dismissed by clicking "hide details."

can distract you from your original intent. You constantly have to limit yourself because it is so easy to overdo it."

Content

Exhibit, product, industrial, and architectural designers run up against an obvious limitation with their first professional portfolio. Few of their ideas have been built. In decades past, concept designs were obvious as such. In some portfolios, they still are. Emmanuel's work is so clean, crisp, and detailed that many of his concept pieces can be easily mistaken for photos, a fact that was brought home by the many people who contacted him wanting to buy his "huit sofa"—a loveseat concept based on the figure 8. Many of these people found the project through blog articles—a natural result of having so many possible points of entry to an intriguing project.

> **Refreshing a physical portfolio is more difficult. You need to lay out a new page, and print it in large format. Honestly, I haven't shown my physical portfolio in a while. No one ever asks for it!**
> **—Emmanuel Laffon de Mazières**

As it's difficult to get the sense of a 3D object with one photo, Laffon presents his images from multiple views, and distances, at a size that makes their materials and scale apparent. Objects whose size might not be obvious are put in photographic context. In addition, Laffon's site contains his video walkthrough, which is available in three resolutions—two viewable online, one downloadable in high resolution.

Laffon's website concentrates on finished, modeled projects that can speak for themselves with little context. His laptop presentation, however, contains process work that allows him to discuss how he arrives at and develops his ideas.

Future plans

Laffon is particularly interested in consumer electronics and furniture, two areas that do not have much overlap. A few years down the road, he'll probably have to make a choice, but for now he continues to add examples of both when he updates his site. He also goes back and reworks older designs as he sees better, more workable ways to build them, while weeding out older projects to make room. However, he intends to maintain his basic portfolio design for the foreseeable future because it works so well for him. Changing the background images to refresh his content and allowing the backgrounds to interact with his projects has kept his ideas fresh.

> **My website is like a display window, so I am trying to keep on the website only the projects that reflect the best of my abilities. I remove everything that's not to my standards.**
> **—Emmanuel Laffon de Mazières**

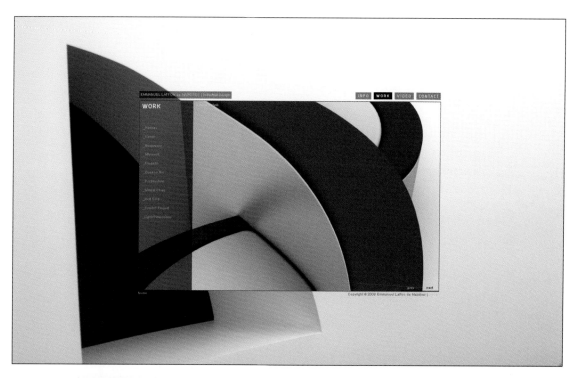

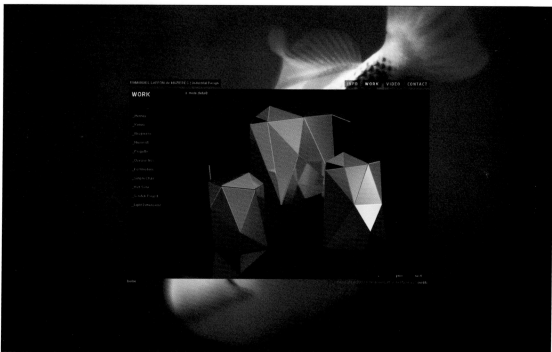

Laffon has chosen his best work, but he has also carefully selected the views that work optimally with his website design.

CHAPTER 5

Organizing Your Work

Good portfolios are not created the night before you present them. You need to look at your entire body of work to evaluate its condition and current relevance. And that's hard to do when it's scattered on multiple discs, file folders, and flat files.

Let's face it: organizing isn't sexy. Creatives aren't supposed to be organized...it's part of our mystique. But wouldn't you rather be a little less exotic and a little more rested? When developing a portfolio, being organizationally challenged will set you up for extra work every time you need to redo or revise. If revising is a chore, you'll wait until the eleventh hour to do it. Unpaid work on a personal deadline is just about the worst creative nightmare. Inevitably, you'll cut corners, make mistakes, and miss important details.

It's better to approach your working process with the idea of making your work "portfolio ready." Take the time to organize as you go—it's only hard at the beginning. Once you get used to the process, organizing your work becomes second nature.

COLLECTING MATERIAL

Unlike people in other lines of work, everything you do results in a unique creative product. Don't trust your employer or client to archive your work. Everything you do should remain in your possession in some form: original, sample, slide, print, or disc. For some professions, ideas and work leading up to the finished piece also should be retained. This might seem obvious, but it bears emphasis. To keep your work secured and up to date:

Keep process materials

Ask yourself at the beginning of every new project if this piece might be a keeper. If so, hold onto your process work. From quick pencil sketches to detailed storyboards, the first stages of creativity are seldom found on disc. Your concepts can be a powerful tool to help you illustrate your creative process in your portfolio.

Keep editable backups of computer files

If your artwork is digital, keep the original, editable files, not just player versions or PDFs. You may want to change frame rate or scale them later. If your final product is a printed piece, don't assume that's all you need, especially if the work is product packaging or oversized flat art. As you'll see in later chapters, the original art is sometimes more useful in a portfolio than a photograph of the piece would be.

Students: retrieve your graded work

Between summer break, co-op stints, and faculty requests to borrow student work for their own needs, student work often falls into limbo. (Limbo is also known as the trash.) Instructors often don't have a permanent affiliation with the schools where they teach, and work left with them can easily be misplaced. In addition, most art and design departments discard unclaimed student work. Does it sound as if you shouldn't trust your school and faculty to get your work back to you? Exactly. Be responsible for your own career and get your work before the school year ends.

Request samples when working for hire

If you're freelancing, don't neglect to ask your employer about sample copies before you start your work. Even if you are not retaining copyright (see Chapter 12, "Copyright and Portfolio"), in most situations you'll be allowed to use a sample in your portfolio or reel. If you can't, you'll know the limitations before you imagine the project as your portfolio's centerpiece.

Get plenty of samples

You can never be too rich or have too many samples. Speak to the printer directly if you can. If the client is handling the printing, request your samples from them in advance. Print runs are not an exact science and most jobs result in more finished impressions than the quote specified.

Photograph artwork

Most artwork is one of a kind. Even computer art is often output large in a variety of individual forms or on special materials. As soon as the piece is dry, shoot it yourself, even if you plan to hire a professional later. If the worst happens and your artwork is stolen, damaged, fades, or ends up sold to someone who disappears, you still have a portfolio record. See Chapter 6, "Transferring Physical Media to Digital," for the best ways to get your work into the computer.

STORING ORIGINAL ART

Mounted boards bend, glues lift and yellow, and badly framed prints bubble with moisture. You learn these lessons in school or from miserable experience. Yet people who are craft-conscious in traditional media can be remarkably careless with digital output or samples. Could you afford to reprint a poster? Store the work you're saving with care no matter whether it's made of atoms or bytes.

Storing traditional materials

Always store your two-dimensional work flat, between acid-free paper, out of direct light, and in a cool place. If you must roll the work, store it in a closable tube with as large a diameter as you can find. If you have a portfolio case full of work, store it on a shelf without any bulky items or additional folders inserted, and never place anything on top of it. Keep it away from damp places, and never leave your portfolio case in the trunk of your car on a hot day. If you need to take it on an airplane, carry it on. Baggage handling can be hard on your case and the things in it.

If you are storing process work, set aside a sketchbook or file folder for these non-digital project materials. Keep these folder materials off your working surface. Coffee rings and grease smears do not improve marker sketches.

Storing digital output

Some work is only output digitally, not offset printed or chemically developed. The quality may look great initially, but some inks, toners, dyes, and even the papers you print them on are unstable. If you are unsure of your digital printer's (or its inks') archival quality, see the sidebar, "Is your digital output stable?," that follows.

Other problems can arise with stored digital output, even when the ink and paper archive well. Some inks chemically react with portfolio books' plastic sleeves. Copier and laser prints can stick to the inside of vinyl, ruining both the sample and the portfolio page. And almost all output—even the very best—will eventually fade, especially if left in full daylight. If your only original version of the piece is a digital print, store it just like traditional art.

ORGANIZING SAMPLES AND ARTWORK

Keeping your work in prime portfolio condition is an imperative first step, but it isn't enough. You need a storage or documentation system as well so you can find a piece later, either to use in a traditional book or to shoot or scan for a digital portfolio. Being organized is particularly important if you create unique works of art. If you ever have to put in an insurance claim because of theft or damage, you'll need to show physical proof of the work's existence before you can recoup any losses.

The simplest and easiest way to handle small-format printed pieces is to use a good, old-fashioned file drawer with Pendaflex folders. Most people file work either alphabetically by client or consecutively by date. Some people create folders based on the type of work (like branding or identity) or client industry (like biotech or fashion). You can use any quirky system, just apply it consistently.

Store original, non-printed art, or printed pieces too big for a file folder in flat files, shelves, or artist racks. But wherever you put it, keep a record of it (see

IS YOUR DIGITAL OUTPUT STABLE?

To check for fading, run a CMYK bar test (a full page of output with each of the four printing primary colors running vertically) on the paper you're using for output. Cut the output in thirds so each portion has all four ink colors. Pin one up on a sunlit wall. Put one in a flat box with a lid, and put the box someplace dark. Leave the third one out of direct light, but uncovered. A month later, run the CMYK test again.

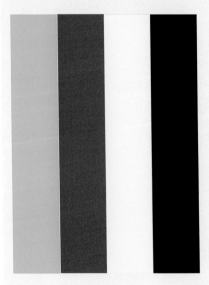

Now pull out all three pieces and look at them, using the newly printed copy as a guide. In many cases, there will be color degradation in the print that was hung in unprotected bright light. (That happens to traditional photographic prints, too.) Has there also been a shift in the other two pieces? If you see color problems in the third piece, you should use a different printer for your portfolio work. If you see any change in the copy you left in the dark, the inks are chemically degrading. Not only is the printer wrong for your portfolio, you shouldn't use it for anything other than quick proofing.

archiving strategies in the next section) as well. Use a camera to shoot the piece for identification, add text (including where you've stored it if you're absent-minded!), and print the page.

Document now: the further you are from creating the artwork, the more you won't remember. It's most efficient to do this all at once—scanning batched photos, or hiring someone to shoot your work—but it's better to do this work in smaller clumps than to be caught empty-handed.

ORGANIZING DIGITAL FILES

Keeping traditional materials in good order is painless compared with organizing computer files. They are hard to recognize, harder to find than a buried piece of paper on a messy desk, and all too easy to delete. Even if you start naming and filing every project starting today, reorganizing all your previous projects is exquisite torture. Fortunately, there are useful strategies that can at least deaden the pain. Most of them work best if you combine them with an archive made with database or catalog software.

To organize your files, you'll have to master six disciplines:

- Group
- Name
- Show
- Weed
- Catalog
- Back up

Group

The first step is to keep your working files in order. Everyone is occasionally guilty of hurriedly saving a file on the desktop. But if your desktop becomes the home for all your files and folders, you'll waste valuable time hunting for work when you need it, and even more time trying to clean up between projects. Here are some grouping guidelines:

- **Use folders.** Create a separate folder for each client or project series. Each time you start a new project, create a new folder inside the client's folder. Put new files in the appropriate folders when you save them the first time.

> I would hope that my project hard drive could be easily navigable by a stranger, typically starting broad (like "Columbia"), then being divisible by course, followed by category ("diagram," "3D models," "renderings," etc.), then lastly organized by date.
>
> —John Locke

- **Link folders.** Make aliases of your folders so you can jump directly to them. Put one set of aliases on the desktop, but don't stop there. Make multiple aliases of each folder, and put them inside your other live job folders. You'll be able to reach any folder almost immediately, and you'll be less tempted to put files in the current directory or on the desktop to "save time."

Name

Once you've found the folder, you still have to find the right files inside it. One of the best timesavers is to develop a file naming method. Here are some guidelines:

- **Name uniquely.** Avoid generic folder and file names. Be concise but descriptive. Filling a hard drive with multiple versions named "image1," "newproject," or "brochure" can be almost as useless as deleting them.

If you create an alternate version of a file, describe what's different in the name. These file names document variations in typeface and color.

OralHistgridV2.psd   OralHistgridV2-altRed.psd   OralHistgridV2-Small.psd

MAKING A FOLDER ICON

Mac OS X makes it easy to create custom icons for folders. Anything that you can copy into the OS X clipboard can be used as a folder icon, including text. The process is simplicity itself. Once you've copied your desired image or text (Command+C), open the file in an application and then select all or part of it. Highlight the folder you want to change, and press Command+I to Get Info. Click the folder icon in the Get Info box to highlight it, then paste (Command+V).

Replace generic icons with unique ones, and you can quickly zero in on what you need. In the top row of icons, the first is PostScript text from Adobe Illustrator and the second came from a Word document. In the next row, the left icon is a JPG and the right is a Photoshop file.

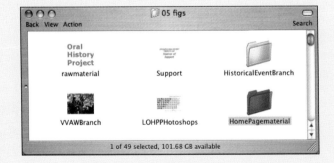

- **Name descriptively.** If you are designing a homepage image for a new website, HomeHeader_Greenway—what the image is, and the client it's for—might be a good naming convention. Calling alternative files "JimBroV1" and "JimBroV2" may seem to make sense, but if you do many versions, will you remember what was different about each one? Add a little description and you will. Avoid numbers in file names unless they refer to a series (like pages or book folios). Numbers work best as "save as" devices for chronological stages of one working session.

- **Name briefly.** Really long names truncate (get cut off) in directory displays and make poor icon labels. If you must use a long file name, start it with the most unique information, moving toward the least unique. For example, if you are archiving artwork for specific pages of a book, try "Fig57ARev-P210-Ch5-DDP.psd" rather than "DDP-Ch5-P214-Fig67ARev.psd." You'll be able to scan for the most unique portion of the name more easily.

You can use a similar strategy in Windows. File icons themselves must be ICO files, and you'll need third-party software to create them from BMP artwork. The artwork will have to be square and created to the right size. But Windows XP and Vista let you add a picture to the generic folder icon instead of completely replacing the icon with another picture.

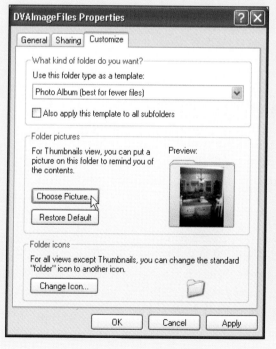

To make a folder more visual in Windows XP, right-click the generic folder icon you want to personalize, then click Properties. Click the Customize tab and then click Choose Picture from the Folder pictures section. Browse to the image and select it.

Long file names are easier to read in list view but are still not always clear. Some operating systems truncate in the middle like this one, others at the end. Since the bottom three names start with the most important information, it's easy to identify them anywhere.

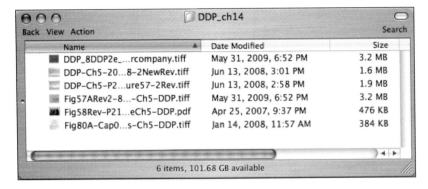

- **Name inclusively.** You might need to show your digital portfolio on different platforms. When possible, use naming conventions that are legal on all operating systems. For example, avoid colons, semi-colons, and slashes.

If you haven't been good about file naming, you aren't condemned to disorganization. See the following sidebar, "Bulk renaming," for strategies for name cleanup.

Show

Since you're a visual person, identify files by using a visual method—icons.

- **Use catalog thumbnails.** You can't depend on the little image icons on your files. It's too easy to confuse images that look the same but have radically different resolutions or sizes. Cataloging software (more on this under the "Back up" section) creates bigger thumbnails, and can identify the difference between files by their file size. If your work is cataloged, it's really easy to pull up a file in the middle of a presentation, even if you hadn't originally planned on including it.

- **Customize folder icons.** You can replace a generic folder icon with a custom one, although older operating system versions (such as pre-XP Windows) limit you to specific file icon types and work best with square images. Windows XP and beyond and the Mac OS X give you wide latitude on the file format you use for the icon and will display rectangular images without distortion. See the previous sidebar, "Making a folder icon," for the basic how-tos on each platform.

Weed

Sometimes the best way to stay organized is to throw things out.

- **Simplify.** When you're certain your project is finished and billed, review your project folder and hard drive. Put any process ideas in a "process" folder and then throw out errors while the project is fresh in your mind.

• **Update.** When last-minute changes happen while a job is on press, it's tempting to say, "Whatever," and be glad the job is done. Don't give in to temptation. Unless the correction won't affect some future version of the piece, make the edit in the original file. Guaranteed: you won't remember the change if you need to output the file again.

Catalog

If you are a prolific imagemaker, archive your images in a program designed for photographers. Apple Aperture or Adobe Lightroom both have excellent tools for archiving, tagging, and organizing.

If the file formats you're using are more of a non-photo mix, try catalog software. Windows Expression Media is available in both Windows and Mac versions. I use it because it recognizes and manages not just image files, but also all Adobe Creative Suite extensions and other program-specific formats. It's the software I used for the examples in this chapter.

All good catalog software offers a slideshow feature, and some export the slideshow to a player. If you're in a desperate hurry or are not in a field where portfolio technology and sophistication are crucial, your archive can become a portfolio in minutes. All you need is the catalog software and a drive containing your selected images.

You can drag whole folders into the catalog or bring in individual files. As long as the original images remain where the cataloging software can find them, they can display at full size onscreen. If you change your mind and don't want to show something, you can just delete it from the catalog. (It won't delete from the drive.)

After you've arranged your material in order, it's easy to set the slide show options for how long each image remains on screen or whether there are transitions between images. You can even choose a typeface and font size for any captions.

Back up

All of these techniques make it easier to retrieve your files for portfolio building. But the job is even easier if everything is in one place. As you finish a project, copy the final version to a dedicated disc or removable hard drive, either by hand or by using your operating system's tools, like the Mac's Time Machine. If you have to create your portfolio fast, everything you need will be there—ready for output, presentation, or web conversion.

BULK RENAMING

There are strategies on both Windows and Mac computers to rename groups of files.

Windows XP/Vista lets you rename groups of files alphabetically or by date. Select all the files, sort by name or date, press F2, then type the text you want them all to share. Windows will rename and number them from top to bottom in the window, maintaining the file extensions. To do more sophisticated renaming in Windows, you'll need a software program for batch conversions. Several programs can do this for you, Microsoft Expression Media among them. You can browse a file download site such as www.shareware.com for others.

 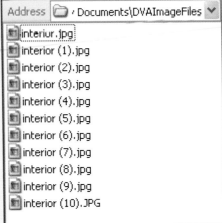

Macs come with the Automator app. It uses actions like those in Photoshop to help you automate tedious tasks. Although you can write your own, the actions you need for failsafe file renaming come with the program. Open Automator, making sure that Applications is highlighted so you'll see all the Finder-related actions. They're alphabetical, so drag these actions to the workflow window in this order:

1. Get Specified Finder Items
Click the + symbol in the lower left of the window, navigate to the folder that holds the files you want to rename, then click Open.

2. Copy Finder Items
Select a folder from the dropdown list to put a copy of these files into it temporarily. Doing this saves a copy of the files in the original naming state in case something goes wrong. Once you've renamed, you can't undo!

3. Get Specified Finder Items

Click the + symbol, navigate to the folder that holds the files you want to rename and open it. Select all (or just the ones you want to rename) and click Open.

4. Rename Finder Items

Select the change you want to make from the dropdown list. In this example, I've searched for the file name I want to replace, then typed the text I want to replace it with.

Click the Run button at the top right of the main Automator window above the Actions section, and you're done.

When you drag an action from the alphabetical list to the window, it becomes part of a series of small dialog boxes in the action section. The numbers in the upper left of each action indicate the step order.

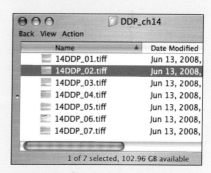

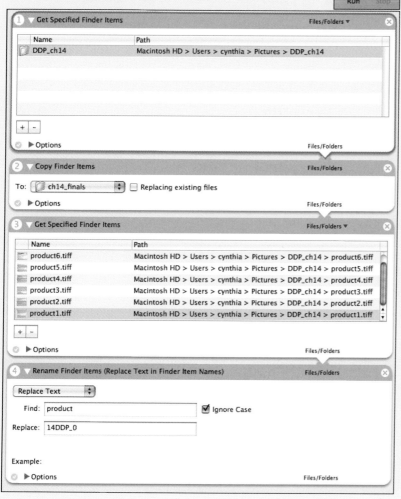

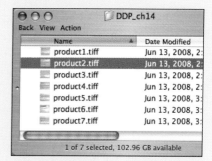

Automator's actions will rename all the files in the folder you select in the order they appear in the folder.

PORTFOLIO HIGHLIGHT:
JOHN LOCKE | LEFT BRAIN, RIGHT BRAIN

GRACEFULSPOON.COM | ISSUU.COM/GRACEFULSPOON | LIONINOIL.NET

When we can't find a sketch on our desks or a file on the computer, we use the excuse that our analytical left brain is underdeveloped. Yet we can cook a tasty three-course meal, micromanage a party, or arrange our clothes in color groups. Lack of organization in our work is a bad habit, not a missing gene. Talented creatives who recognize the virtues of organization generate precious free time that others waste. Instead of struggling to finish just one thing, they prolifically explore new ideas and ultimately excel in their chosen field. Architect John Locke is one of these happy souls. He proves that both sides of the brain can coexist in perfect harmony.

> **I spent four years working in an office. When you have 16 people opening files from the same location, you quickly realize that a logical filing system is key to avoiding a lot of wasted time.**
>
> **—John Locke**

Locke's creativity is not debatable. He has two beautifully produced PDF portfolios on Issuu (issuu.com/gracefulspoon), one created for admission to graduate school, the other as a final statement of his work as a graduate student at Columbia University. These generate extensive feedback, particularly from college applicants who ask for advice or help. He shares a blog of non-architectural projects with his creative partner, photographer and designer Jackie Caradonio (lioninoil.net). His personal portfolio website (gracefulspoon.com) is the most comprehensive record of his work, and links to everything else.

> **I believe in the Internet as a means to share information, and hope that my site is not only a record of my work, but also part of the global network of research and mutual assistance.**
>
> **—John Locke**

Navigation and architecture

Most people reach Gracefulspoon.com from Locke's elegantly designed Issuu publications. Based on these books, you expect a certain style of navigation: perhaps a Flash splash page introducing categories of work, that in turn lead to projects. Instead, everything in the site loads into one infinitely expanding, vertically scrolling page. As you explore, it dawns on you that you are looking at something rare: a portfolio that is both open-ended and extremely well-organized.

There are echoes of a print newspaper both in the site's initial layout and its sense of immediacy. Above the fold are the main topics, masthead and wayfinding info. A Twitter feed styled as a bold headline speaks directly to the viewer. Images, each a link to one of Locke's featured works, fill the bottom half of the window.

Select any category or project, and links to all of Locke's other portfolios, self-publishing sites, and social networks appear in the top bar.

Sited compactly at the top of the page is a text nav bar of work categories, alongside a bio and a list of contact options.

A 4x4 rectangular grid contains large thumbnails linked to each featured project.

Click a grid image, and a link to Locke's design studio replaces the grid, loading the selected project.

Each thumbnail has a label with the project title, type of project, and date.

In the design blog window on gracefulspoon.com, research, process work, and the evolution of Locke's design concept for a project (in this case, Global Panopticon) are presented in chronological stages.

By scrolling down through the vertical presentation, viewers can follow the way Locke approaches a project. The goal is to make his design thinking transparent.

Anyone who wants a closer look at each graphic can click on it, and it will launch in its own window.

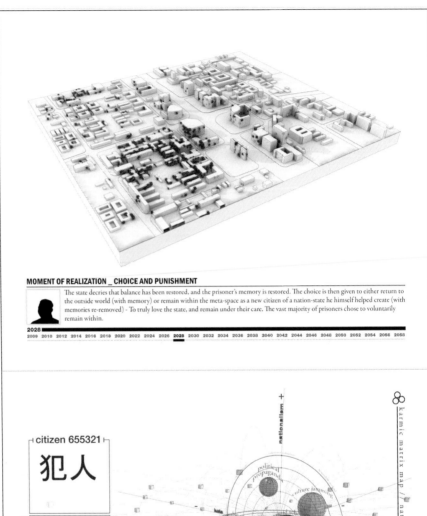

MOMENT OF REALIZATION _ CHOICE AND PUNISHMENT

The state decries that balance has been restored, and the prisoner's memory is restored. The choice is then given to either return to the outside world (with memory) or remain within the meta-space as a new citizen of a nation-state he himself helped create (with memories re-removed) - To truly love the state, and remain under their care. The vast majority of prisoners chose to voluntarily remain within.

2028
2000 2010 2012 2014 2016 2018 2020 2022 2024 2026 **2028** 2030 2032 2034 2036 2038 2040 2042 2044 2046 2048 2050 2052 2054 2056 2058

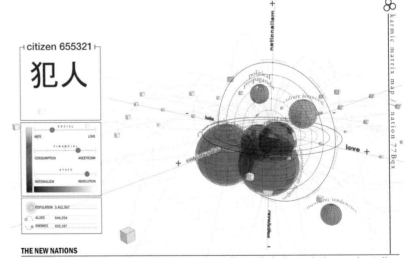

THE NEW NATIONS

In a virtually connected world, national identity is no longer determined by physical borders. Groups in a limitless space are determined by their individual, common relationships based on past deeds, or misdeeds. This leads to a new values-based economy modelled on beneficial trade relationships. What types of person would make you a better person? A new social network is created that precisely maps all possible relationships. Loss of contiguous spaces creates new possibilities for fragmented, franchise model of atiguous space.

2028
2000 2010 2012 2014 2016 2018 2020 2022 2024 2026 **2028** 2030 2032 2034 2036 2038 2040 2042 2044 2046 2048 2050 2052 2054 2056 2058

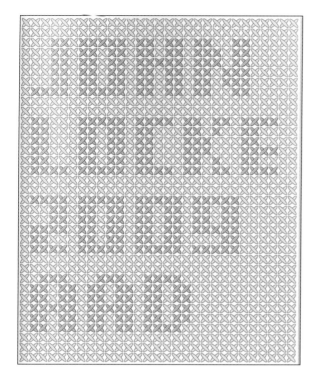

Political Fever

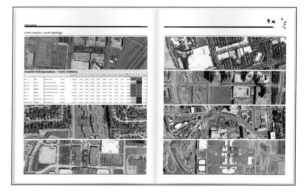

The project becomes a version of American Flag 2.0, something that doesn't only wave from above in the wind, but rather demands work, a back and forth engagement between

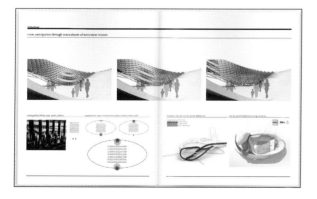

Locke presents his content differently depending on his audience and purpose. Here, the material from the gracefulspoon site is reorganized into a formal portfolio book. Although static and carefully composed, each of the project sections in the book version could be easily reconfigured to create subset portfolios of his work.

On the site, I use the keywords to help with searches and to allow visitors to quickly find all posts with the same keyword.
—John Locke

The newspaper analogy, however, is not adequate to the navigation. There are two obvious navigation methods—the topic menu and the project image grid. But every project is in a database that can be accessed by descriptive tags located above its header. Want to see Locke's studio work at Columbia University's Graduate School of Architecture, Planning and Preservation (GSAPP)? Select the Studio tag at the top of a project and the window will reload with only the relevant material. No matter how many high-resolution images there are in a project, the reload is extremely fast, so skipping around is encouraged.

Lion in Oil's design and photography often appear as featured projects on Locke's Gracefulspoon site, making it more than just a record of school projects.

Content

Gracefulspoon contains not just finished project images: it is the repository of Locke's creative history. All work Locke creates is digitized and organized as it's completed. As he says, "Any process work—including physical models—I'll extensively photograph, then discard. I scanned my pre-2005 work, which included hand-drawn plans and sketches, at a high resolution, then archived it digitally for easy dissemination and sharing."

As an architectural designer who has lately spent a significant amount of time on graduate projects, his content is dominated by his concept work. Each project begins with a final image and a project description. His renderings, which combine his photography with physical and computer models, are interspersed with research material and side comments, all in the form of a linear presentation.

However, the flexible way Locke has organized and divided all of his creative work allows him to highlight his photography and design interests without changing his primary identity. His photography actually lives at Flickr, and his non-architectural design is at lioninoil. Each can be experienced separately, or loaded into the grid space without the viewer having to leave his main site.

Future plans

Locke's PDF portfolios are static, complete works. They'll probably be joined by at least one new PDF book now that his student days are over. With all his content accessible, he can create smaller, targeted portfolios for various markets and opportunities: architectural firms, academic positions, or freelance jobs in a variety of other realms.

Gracefulspoon's content will undoubtedly change on a regular basis. As Locke says, "I see the 'design blog' section as being a constantly updating, thorough record of my work; while the 'featured work' section is more selective, static, and includes 16 projects that are the most highly indicative of how I want to present myself. This selection of 'featured work' is also partly generated by what is most popular on the site." This volatile and responsive tool will likely continue to be the access point for all of Locke's interests, and the real-time repository of future work.

> I think there are many new fields where architects can take a more active role. I hope that's what is conveyed in my portfolio: the sense of possibility in fields as diverse as programming, photography, interactive art installations, science fiction, theory, politics, and research.
>
> —John Locke

CHAPTER 6

Transferring Physical Media to Digital

If all or most of your work was created (or printed) in traditional media, getting it into digital form will be a major project. Like any other task that is light on creativity and heavy on production, it can take an effort of will to begin. It's also tempting to underestimate how important it is to digitize well. Failing at this crucial stage can make the rest of your effort a waste of time.

In the end, your portfolio is all about your work. Digitizing that work successfully is the first step to a quality portfolio. Fortunately, you probably already have the technology you need to do it right. Your skills and some patience will take you the rest of the way.

This chapter will outline the best methods for capturing different types of material for a digital portfolio, how best to move your work into a digital file, and the most frequently needed software remedies for materials that aren't portfolio-ready.

DIGITAL CRAFT DEFINED

Craft is just as important in making digital files as it is when doing everything by hand—in some ways, more so. People are far less forgiving of bad digital craft because it is so much easier to fix a digital image than it is to repair a dinged or folded corner on a sample. You owe it to yourself to keep the focus on your ideas and creativity, not your production.

Not having the original at hand, people judge images in digital portfolios by two criteria. The first is image quality—sharpness, cleanness, size, and load speed. The second is image appropriateness—whether what you've chosen to show actually helps them judge your work.

> **We try to think about how the world interacts with our work. In showing a spread in a magazine, I would never show the flat "digital file." The paper properties and the slicing and distortion caused by the binding all affect the viewer's experience. These realities should not be cast aside simply because the work is being viewed on the web.**
>
> **—David Heasty**

Unlike your physical portfolio, the appropriateness of your digital work doesn't depend just on its style or subject. Some of your portfolio material might transfer poorly to the digital medium. Be prepared to evaluate your work twice: before you digitize it and when you see the results of your work. No matter how much you want a digital portfolio, trying to doctor a terminally ill file will just make you frustrated.

On the other hand, don't do a detail-for-detail comparison, or you'll never use any non-digital work in your digital portfolio! You can't ever totally replicate the experience of a real printed piece. Evaluate the work based on how you feel about presenting this material to someone who may never see the original.

If there is an overriding theme, it's GIGO: Garbage In=Garbage Out. Keep each stage of your digitizing process as precise as possible. Start with the cleanest original material, and remember that bad quality can be introduced inadvertently at every stage of digitizing and cleanup.

And don't be afraid—or embarrassed—to look for help when you need it. It is better that your portfolio process be a learning process as well than to present a flawed finished product.

GETTING HELP

If you want to learn how to use the software for digitizing your specific artwork type, I encourage you to buy the appropriate book in Peachpit Press's *Visual QuickStart Guide* series and to look for local workshops for training on digitizing analog tapes and photographic film. Scanning has to be done right, but it's drudgery, and it competes with paying work. If you have an enormous backlog of work to digitize, some money to devote to the enterprise, or feel that you can handle some parts of the process but not others, there are viable alternatives.

PHOTOGRAPH OR SCAN?

Should you use a flatbed or film scanner? Or should you photograph your work? The best way to bring your work to the computer will differ based on its exact type.

Garden variety flatbed scanners are great for flat, low-contrast images. That makes them extremely useful for printed art and illustrations but less effective for images with a broad value range. If you scan to hold shadows, you'll lose the highlights, and vice versa.

If you have strong highlights and shadows and compara- tively few midtones, you may lose detail at both ends, as happened in this image. The bright foam is too bleached out (center of the image) and there is no detail in the rock shadow in the lower- right corner.

Although you can scan prints on a flatbed, if you are a professional photographer you should try to go direct from film. You should also look for a slide scanner. Flatbeds market- ed as photo scanners have better dynamic ranges than standard ones, but even with trans- parency attachments most can't complete with a good film scanner. Use them only if you print on special paper or make post-developing changes to the print.

What about not-quite-flat art, like books? Your ideal solution is a large-sized flatbed scan- ner for page spreads (an option at some service bureaus and schools). But if you can't find one, taking photographs using a copy stand (see "Shooting 3D and oversized work") and some non-reflective glass is usually better than trying to graft two scanned pieces together in Adobe Photoshop.

Hiring students

If you live in or near a college or art school, inexpensive help might be close at hand. Most art and design students are well-versed in software technologies, particularly scanners and Adobe Photoshop. Many schools have clearing houses or bulletin boards (or placement offices for part-time help, co-ops, interns, and so on) where you can post your needs. In some cases, you might find that hiring a creative student can help you produce a better portfolio, not just get your artwork on a flatbed.

Service bureaus

If you have negatives or slides, look for a place that advertises photo scanning. Ask them about their process and how they ensure quality for images that may need special handling to maintain color or dynamic range. Avoid service bureaus that specialize in document scanning. They make their money by putting standard-sized materials through scanners in batches.

DVD services

Most places that make video copies and transfer home movies also have facilities to convert an analog tape to DVD-R. They're likely to charge by the hour, so you'll get the most cost-effective result if you have them transfer your original analog demo reel first (never one of the copies!), rather than whole project tapes.

> **We've set up a basic photo studio in the office, and sometimes we'll shoot pieces on white background, knock it out, and put the shadows back in.**
>
> **—Michael Borofsky**

Ask other film and video people in your area to recommend a video service, or a member of the community who owns the software and equipment you'll need. If you can't get a recommendation, at least try to talk directly with the person at the service bureau who will do the conversion, so they'll know what you need the film for and why its quality is important.

SHOOTING 3D AND OVERSIZED WORK

Digital art is flat; 3D art isn't. There's no perfect way of getting around this, but it shouldn't prevent you from showing your 3D work to good effect. Even traditional portfolios require photography to transfer dimensional art into flat containers.

In fact, short of being in the physical presence of the work, a digital portfolio can be a great way to show a 3D piece. With a little skill, you can create the illusion of three dimensions in Photoshop. Even without image editing, you can show multiple views of the same art or even just a standard product shot in glorious full-screen.

Most of what you will need to get acceptable results on a budget are time and patience. You'll also need access to some of the standard tools of a photographer's trade: a camera, a copy stand and/or tripod, and some professional lighting. If you don't own all of these things, you can rent them, rent studio space, or barter.

Choosing your camera

Your camera should not be a small consumer model, because these do not have good depth of field. It must have optical (not just digital) zoom, capture images at 4 megapixels or better, and have a mounting hole in its base for a tripod. It should have white balance features and an adjustable flash.

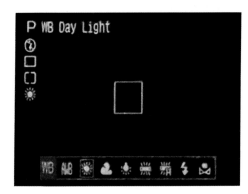

A standard white balance screen allows you to shift how your camera "sees" colors in different ambient light settings, from full outdoor daylight to fluorescent or incandescent indoor lighting.

Ideally, use a camera that has a raw file format option, not just JPEG. Raw files contain all the visual information the camera captured, whereas JPEG files are processed in the camera, where they are sharpened and stripped of "redundant" information, which might not be redundant to you. (See the "Cleaning up digitized art" section below for some basic hints on image editing.)

One last thing—you'll enjoy shooting more if your digital camera has a display screen that pivots like those in the Nikon COOLPIX series, particularly if you'll be using a copy stand (See "Setting the stage" below for more on copy stands.) That way, you won't have to crane your neck to see the display no matter how you've had to mount your camera.

Lighting

Lighting is very important because it will determine the range of colors you shoot. The way the lights are positioned is also critical. If you don't have a copy stand or a room with professional lights, try to locate a bright, day-lit room, and make sure that any lights in it are turned off. If your artwork is framed under glass or reflective plastic, take the frame apart. There's almost no good way to light a framed piece to avoid hot spots and reflections. Place your flat art so that no shadows are cast on it. (For 3D art, shadows behind or below are fine.) In general, avoid using a flash. It will create hot spots and inappropriate shadows.

Another alternative if you don't have professional lighting available is to wait for a dry but overcast day. The light will be nicely diffuse.

Adjusting your camera

Correcting white balance ensures color fidelity—a must for any serious designer or artist. Setting the perfect white balance for a shot is a basic skill for a professional photographer, but if that doesn't describe you it's still possible to end up with a good color match.

In every uncontrolled lighting situation, color shifts with lighting. Our eyes adjust, but cameras do not. Fluorescents (found in offices everywhere) tint everything blue-green. Incandescent light (sometimes called tungsten) moves colors toward the yellow. Even scanners can be a problem as some shift colors toward magenta.

WWW.PEOPLEDESIGN.COM

Although some people shoot everything against a white background for stylistic consistency, sometimes individual projects beg for different color backgrounds to show them off to best effect.

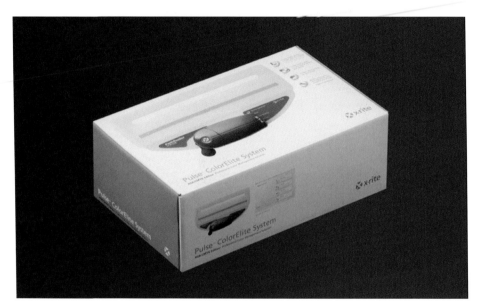

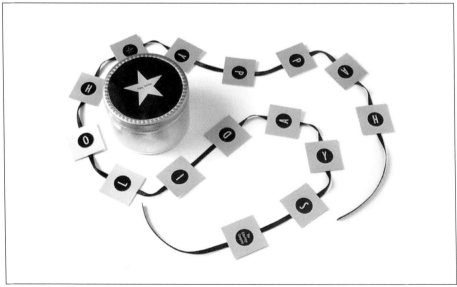

Fortunately, all decent cameras have a white balance setting, although you will have to depart from the automatic settings to find it. The white balance menu offers several presets for a variety of standard lighting situations. When in doubt about the type of lighting you are shooting in, you should take sample shots of one object in each of the presets, and compare the picture in your camera display with reality. Use the preset that most closely resembles your work's color range.

Setting the stage

For books, mid-sized prints, or pieces with accordion folds or die-cuts, your best bet is usually a copy stand. A copy stand is a flat board with a camera attached above it and lights at an angle (usually 45 degrees) on two sides. The bulbs should be the same type and brightness to eliminate shadows. Ones with double copy lights on each side and a large bed are best, but you can get a small stand, lights and all, for under $150. If you can't buy a copy stand, ask your friends and your professional network; libraries and art departments at schools and universities often have them.

If you can't get access to a copy stand or your artwork is flat but too big to fit on the stand's base (like an oversized architectural sketch or an etching), mount your artwork on posterboard with a large enough margin to create a uniform background for the art. Pin the mounted art on a wall in a large room. Attach your camera to a tripod and shoot away.

> A very important thing to remember is that almost anybody interviewing someone is thinking, "Is this person going to make me look like a chump? Cost me money, reputation?" So you're looking for reassurance in a portfolio. You're looking for a portfolio that says, "I do everything perfectly."
> —Gunnar Swanson

If your artwork is three-dimensional, you'll need a large, flat table as well as a wall. Photographers often shoot against smooth, pure white matte backgrounds (referred to as "seamless") to emphasize the object's dimensions and cast clean shadows. Seamless is also your preferred background if you plan on making the background transparent in your portfolio design. Ideally, you should use a professional fabric, but if you can't, a stretched white sheet can be a good stand-in. On the other hand, not all objects will show to best effect with a white background. If you don't feel comfortable masking the art in Photoshop and adding in appropriate background colors on the computer, consider having a black background available as well. The material should be non-reflective paper or fabric.

Worst-case scenario, find a clean, level floor. Again, put your artwork on a non-reflective background. Raise your tripod as high as you can, point the camera down, and shoot. Tripods that allow you to rotate the head mount so the camera points straight down will allow you to shoot flat art without angling or distortion. Try to avoid the temptation of a wide-angle lens.

The bigger your artwork, the harder it will be to shoot. Oversized printed material can be pinned and shot from a distance to capture it, but this strategy has two disadvantages. First, you can't see details. Second, all sense of scale disappears. Murals, sculptures, and environmental design projects become indistinguishable from brochures. The ideal is to shoot the artwork in pieces, and then reassemble them into one image. To minimize distortion, shoot standing at the center of the work and use a tripod. Try not to set up too close to the work, or you will need too many "tiles" to avoid distortion.

Many digital cameras have a panorama function that makes it relatively easy to shoot your images in visual tiles of overlapping segments. Leave plenty of overlap—at least a third of each image should overlap the one before—so the software can figure out where to position each puzzle piece. However, you should use Photoshop to merge these and adjust for distortions, rather than using the stitching software that probably comes with the camera and that is optimized for landscapes, not flat artwork.

DIGITIZING FLAT ART

I encourage you to use a good-quality scanner for your digital portfolio, even though the cheapest scanner on the market scans at an optical resolution better than you'll probably need for onscreen display.

Why? Color, features, and time. A good scanner will faithfully read and reproduce more colors than a cheap one. It will have software with features that can save you lots of Photoshop work. In addition, on a cheap scanner, you'll wait for an image preview and even longer for the scan itself. The time difference isn't significant for one or two scans, but you'll come to dread it for a larger batch.

Be sure to scan line art in grayscale mode, not in bitmap. Otherwise, your result will be pixelated, as this image is.

Then, adjust the Brightness/ Contrast slider in Photoshop until you get the line thickness that most closely resembles your original art. Use the Sharpen Edges filter to reinforce the changes you made in your line weight and make the line edges feel crisper. When you're done, scale down the image to your preferred size.

Line art

Line art—pen and ink illustrations, marker or pencil sketches, and etchings—looks like it would be easy work to reproduce. In fact, it's the hardest. Because it only contains two elements (black and white), the lines break up into bitmaps. Diagonals develop stair-stepping, and crosshatching can look like jagged arrangements of dots.

Scan line art at a much higher resolution than the screen quality you ultimately need (1200 ppi is good). It's also a plus to have an original that is much larger than the final image needs to be. Scaling down line art always makes it look better.

Flatbed scanning hints

There are several things you can do to improve the quality of your scans, some of which are very low-tech:

- **Clean the scanner.** Every speck will reproduce. Don't depend on scanner software that offers to clean up dust and scratches as you scan. It does a terrific job on the obvious places but can sometimes mistake a critical detail for a speck and eliminate it.

- **Square up your art.** It's easy to square up a small photo on a flatbed. It's much harder to do that with a book, or an artwork that you'll need to scan

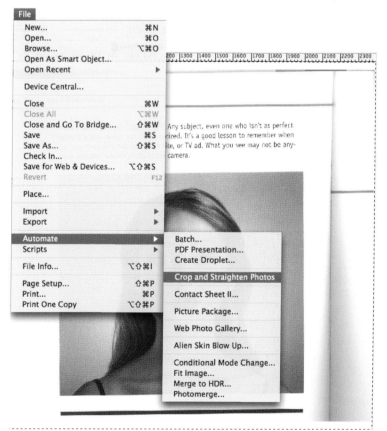

To square up scanned art, select all, then choose File > Automate > Crop and Straighten Photos while holding down the Option (Mac OS) or Alt (Windows) key.

If Photoshop divides your scan into separate elements, step backward. Select Image > Canvas Size, make sure the canvas extension color is white, and that the artwork is anchored in the center of the grid. Increase the canvas size, then try Crop and Straighten again.

RESOLUTION DO'S AND DON'TS

It would be nice to be able to scan everything at 72 ppi and not have to do a thing to the files, but you'll end up with much better results if you scan them in with more resolution and detail than you'll end up using. The trick is to know how much more you need, and when you're just wasting time and disk space.

If you expect to edit a photographic image, not just scale it, try scanning at 150 ppi. If you scan at too high a resolution, then downsample—resample the image at a lower resolution. Your image may soften so much that you will find the result unacceptable.

Your best rule of thumb is to scan so your pixel dimensions are roughly double what they'll end up on screen. If you want each image to end up about 400 pixels wide, scan at whatever resolution gives you approximately 800 pixels to work with. That may mean scanning in a business card at 300 ppi but a tabloid image at only 72 ppi.

Line art can get very jagged when scanned. You'll need to scan at high resolution and then clean up the art before you scale it down.

Scanning printed work with great type design or sharp, flat art can drive you crazy because you're moving lovely vector art to rasters. Always scan such artwork to at least double the resolution you'll need to show onscreen and then scale it to 50%. This will help to clean up the edges.

After you've chosen a resolution and made your scan, don't ever scale the work up. If you've miscalculated and scanned too small, rescan at the correct percentage.

If you have several pieces of the same type to scan, test first. Scan one, making whatever changes you think are necessary to bring it successfully to the size at which you'll show it in your portfolio. If you discover that you've scanned too high or too low, you have time to adjust before scanning the rest of the batch.

in pieces and stitch together. Fortunately, there's a quick and easy fix for that. Scan the art, and open it in Photoshop. Then use Crop and Straighten Photos to square your art up automatically.

- **Scan tiled work twice.** If you're scanning art in two pieces, you may find that one side of the artwork is slightly brighter or darker than the other if the artwork doesn't lie completely flat. To guard against this, scan the work twice, the second time with the halves rotated 180 degrees. Try merging the left side of the first pass with the right side of the second, or vice versa.

DIGITIZING SLIDES AND NEGATIVES

When you use a film scanner, you don't have to worry about screen moiré or lost dynamic range. Yet even with a slide scanner, your image quality can vary. Most of the unpleasant changes can be avoided by keeping some simple concepts in mind.

- **Clean your slides.** Spray your slides with canned air before you scan them. Dust can affect film just as easily as it can a printed piece.

- **Use film negatives.** If you have the choice between scanning a film negative and scanning a slide, use the negative. They're both films, but the slide is actually second generation art, just like a photo print. The negative contains more faithful color and a better quality image than the slide does.

- **Scan right side up.** If you scan with your slide or film wrong side up, you could end up with your image looking as if it was shot in a mirror. To avoid this, scan with the emulsion side of the film facing away from you (or down, depending on how your slide scanner is set up). To recognize which side is which, look carefully at the film. The emulsion side will look slightly textured, and often has the film logo printed on the holder. The other side will be much shinier and smoother.

- **Don't overscan.** Ordinarily, you need to scan a slide in at a very high resolution (2700 ppi isn't unusual) to use slide art for printing. (Slides are so very small—they need to go up about 900% to fill a letter-sized sheet.) But when you're heading for a screen resolution of 72 dpi, there isn't much point in creating a mammoth file. 400 ppi should easily give you a large enough image for the web.

Hopefully, you are only digitizing your very best work for your portfolio. But photographers with decades of analog work may find their "very best" list runs to the high double-digits and beyond. If that is the case, you will need a deeper understanding of color management and workflow to keep you sane and guarantee that you finish the process. I recommend *Scanning Negatives and Slides: Digitizing Your Photographic Archives* by Sascha Steinhoff as a good introductory book on the subject.

DIGITIZING VHS TAPES

One of the most frustrating realizations to a film and video person is that there is no digital video equivalent of the flatbed scanner. The process is time-consuming and often disappointing.

If you have already edited digital video using professional software like Adobe Premiere or Apple Final Cut Studio, or if you have easy access to a digitizing studio, it may be worth your while to do your own digitizing. (Handling your own process is always preferable because you have more control over the final product.) But if you're a digital neophyte and you need a portfolio soon, your energies would be better spent learning the ins and outs of digital video and the above-mentioned software, while you pay to have your tapes digitized for you. Then all the clips you work with will be digital when you create your DVD.

Video digitizing hints

Some of the same issues in scanning flat art arise in bringing analog video to the computer. Alas, because of the added complexity of dealing with sound, larger files, and better frame rates, they can be easy to miss until it's too late. Like scanning errors, the only way to remedy them is to redigitize.

- **Start with a good tape.** If your material has been processed twice—once when you edited pieces onto a demo tape and again when you made copies of the demo tape—you won't get a good quality digital result.

- **Transfer to DVD.** Moving from interlaced video at 30 frames per second (fps) to non-interlaced digital display can result in dropped frames and sound and video that don't always sync. Always make a DVD copy of your video, no matter how you intend to use it later. You'll need that quality. Unlike flat image files, you can't clean up your video by simply showing it in a smaller window.

- **Use the right tool.** Although you can use either consumer software such as iMovie or professional software like Premiere or Final Cut Pro to digitize tape, there is a crucial difference between them. Professional tools can edit uncompressed video; consumer tools can't. A consumer tool will compress your video every time you edit and save it. Compression throws out visual information to save space. (See Chapter 7 for more about compression.) That's not a serious issue if you have shot digital video. But with analog, the quality will suffer, sometimes tragically.

CLEANING UP DIGITIZED ART

Even when you scan and photograph under optimal conditions, the result can be disappointing. The problem may be in the artwork itself. Pieces that have been damaged will be captured warts and all. Or perhaps the art is so large or complicated that you've scanned it in pieces and need to put the pieces together. When you can't start over or substitute other work, it's time to pull out your software tools.

As anyone who edits digital files daily can tell you, a compendium of all the editing techniques you could use to perfect your files already fills hundreds—perhaps thousands—of computer books. To stay focused on portfolios, this chapter highlights only the most frequently needed remedies. For more details or problems that this chapter doesn't cover, I suggest almost any book by Katrin Eismann, but particularly *Adobe Photoshop Restoration & Retouching*.

WORKING PROCESS

Post-scanning issues occur with all types of digitally captured art, both still and motion. In fact, video-editing software packages, particularly the simplest encoders like Windows Movie Maker and Apple QuickTime Pro, have many of the same filters and tools to affect multiple frames as you can find in image-editing software like Photoshop. The best adjustments are found in professional programs, like Apple Final Cut Pro. If you understand the concepts behind issues like tone, color, resolution, and sharpness, you can apply them equally well in any digital file.

It's critical to do your work on the right types of files, and in the right order. Follow this sequence:

1. Change your file type.
2. Adjust brightness, contrast, and color.
3. Clean up and retouch your art.
4. Save a copy of the image.
5. Adjust document size and resolution, if needed.
6. Sharpen, if needed.
7. Optimize and save in a compressed format. (This is covered in Chapter 7.)

The video-editing process steps are the same, although the size of files usually makes it necessary to edit first before applying cleanup filters and effects.

CHOOSING A FILE TYPE

File types (formats) serve different purposes. You should select the format that best suits your purpose at each stage of your working process.

If you are using a digital camera, you will either have no choice (JPEG is the default) or you will be able to shoot and save in raw. Raw files can be opened in Photoshop, but must be translated into an editable format before you can work with them in the application or use them in a portfolio. When you create a digital file with a scanner, you usually have a choice of what file format to save the file in.

When you create a file in an application, or move it into an application for editing, you are working in a native file format—one "owned" by that application. Although some native files open in other programs, most of the time a native format is specific to the application that creates it.

When it's time to archive a file, move it into another application, or open it in a different OS, you should save a copy of it in a universal format—one that many applications can read and edit. For photographic or continuous tone files, that format is usually TIFF. For illustration and print publications, it's usually EPS. For onscreen moving image, AVI and MOV are the formats of choice. Good universal formats allow you to save and return to editing without quality loss.

For onscreen work that will be transmitted over the Internet or played back on a computer, your files must be compressed. Compression formats minimize file size in different ways. Two common image compression formats are PNG and JPEG. For publishing layouts, PDF is the standard. Sound and moving-image files can be compressed with many formats, such as the familiar MP3 and MP4 files. Currently, the most common video compression formats are MPEG, DV, and WAV, but there are dozens of others, some of which may well become standards over time.

Never edit a JPEG...

...or an MPEG file, for that matter. These files are efficiently compressed. They can look as good as the original files, but they have lost information in the compression process. In fact, they continue to lose more information every time you open one, make an edit (no matter how small), and resave it. That's why some online artwork ends up so awful.

Compressed files should be the culmination of your editing process, not the working format. If you must edit a compressed file, resave it first into a non-compressed universal format. When you are finished, save a copy of the edited universal file in the compressed file format.

CONSIDER YOUR AUDIENCE

In many ways, the platform you use is irrelevant to designing and developing your portfolio. One of the times it becomes a factor is when you are setting values for your images. Mac machines are brighter than Windows. So, artwork created on a Mac will often look a little dark and muddy to a Windows person, and work created on a PC will look garish and harsh to a Mac user.

If you aren't certain that the people who count use the platform you do, look at your artwork in the other platform's color space before you adjust Levels. If you own Photoshop, you have a control panel called Adobe Gamma. (On Macs and PCs, you also have system-specific methods of setting gamma. Check your online help.) Use it to set your Mac to a gamma of 2.2 to see how a Windows user will see your work. Set it to 1.8 if you are a Windows user wanting to know what a Mac user will see.

EDITABLE ISSUES

When problems with photos or scans arise or you've made a design decision about your portfolio after your photo shoot, you may need to correct your material. The following issues are the most likely to cause you grief.

Tonal Problems

Even when you use white balance and are careful when you scan, images can suffer from bad contrast or color shifts. As long as there is readable image information in an image's shadows, highlights, and color channels, it's possible to bring that information out, improving and preserving the artwork's details.

Briefly, an image's *tonal value* is its range from darkest to lightest areas. Many images that seem to have multiple problems really just need a tonal value adjustment.

Tonal problems respond best to a software program that generates histograms. Linear sliders for brightness and contrast, like those in consumer programs, will not do the trick. Professional editing programs (still and video) offer histograms and level tools, as well as brightness and contrast sliders. Some programs also offer other tools, like Photoshop's Curves or Adobe After Effects' Levels and Channels. You're free to experiment with any of these options to find the ones that feel most intuitive to you.

WHAT IS A HISTOGRAM?

A histogram is a chart of thin vertical lines that shows the distribution of brightness in an image, from 0 (black) to 255 (white). The taller the line, the more pixels the image has at that level of brightness. Darkest pixels are on the left, and brightest on the right.

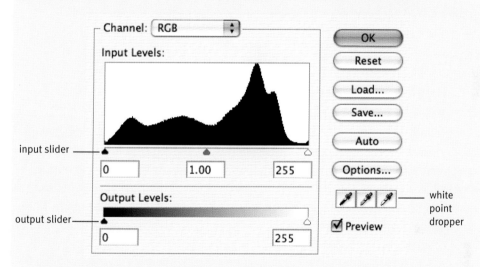

The input sliders regulate the distribution of brightness. The output sliders regulate how much contrast the image has. There are three small eyedropper boxes on the lower right. The one on the far right sets the white point, which is the brightest place on your image— pure white. The one on the far left sets the black point, the place of deepest shadow. Used together by clicking the whitest and darkest image areas, they treat an image's value range like a rubber band, stretching it out in both directions to use the entire value range.

IMAGE-EDITING TERMS: A CHEAT SHEET

Artifacts: Random image distortions, often introduced by too much compression, or by saving a file in the wrong format.

Channel: The portion of an image containing a single color's tonal information. For example, an RGB file has channels for each primary color: red, green, and blue.

Curves: A feature to fix color range problems. It allows you to change the number of red, green, and blue pixels in an image, and their relative brightness.

Levels: A feature to fix value problems. It generates an interactive histogram so you can adjust the number of pixels at each brightness level.

Mask: An electronic frisket, or defined area, that protects portions of an image from change, or determines by its level of opacity how much change will be applied. Masks can be created from selections, and saved for future use as a channel.

White balance: An in-camera lighting calibration that determines pure white in the current lighting and balances the internal camera settings for the shot accordingly. If white is correctly displayed, all other colors in the spectrum should also display correctly.

Brightness and contrast

Most image-editing software has an automatic levels function that can do a decent job on an image. For a portfolio, however, decent is not always good enough. The automatic function tends to increase contrast at the expense of maintaining detail—not a good feature for a photographer's portfolio, or for a designer whose work includes textures and subtle ink variations. Most of the time you should use the manual levels function, which gives you much more control. Curves allow even finer adjustments in color and tone, but they also require more experience and understanding of color management than levels do.

Moiré

Color printing depends on fine-screened overlays of dots to mimic continuous-tone color. Unfortunately, the dots are created with screens that do not have a one-to-one correspondence to pixels. When screens and pixels collide, you get wavy, distracting patterns. Most scanners come with software that includes a "Descreen" setting, which usually does a very good job on the problem. But sometimes moiré persists, or the scanner you're using is too old to have software that includes Descreen.

If you scan and discover that the file has moiré, the first thing to do is to rescan it. You can often eliminate or decrease moiré simply by finding a sweet spot—

an angle where most of the screen dots don't create pixel patterns. Then a few simple tweaks in Photoshop can make your printed pieces sing again.

Place your artwork slightly off-kilter on the scanner, at about a 6- to 8-degree angle, then scan at least double the final screen ppi. Avoid a number that's evenly divisible by your final resolution, or the moiré could return when you scale your art down. For example, 150 ppi works nicely for an image that will be seen at 72 ppi.

Backgrounds

If you've followed the guidelines on photographing your artwork from earlier in this chapter, you may not have to worry about backgrounds at all. A well-shot object can be cropped and shown in its own background.

An image background can need editing when you finalize the design of your site interface. Some people arrange several scanned objects together, adding a drop shadow to each object. Or they've shot a bright object against black for contrast, and

A

B

C

If the image still shows moiré after you rescan it and use the Descreen option (**A**), look at each color channel. You may discover that one is in much worse shape than the others, like this blue channel (**B**). Select this channel, and use the Gaussian Blur filter with a very small radius setting to eliminate most of its patterns. The improvement can be enormous (**C**).

then realize that they want to show the art against a different color web page. If this strikes a chord for you, you'll need to separate the background from your image.

Because you've shot your work sensibly, it's on a white or black background. That means it should be easy to select—probably much easier than trying to select the object in the picture. In Photoshop, once you've selected most of the object background with the Magic Wand, you can use the Polygonal Lasso tool for those places where the differences between the background and the object are too delicate for the Magic Wand to see, and to clean up areas where the Magic Wand hasn't given you a clean line.

RESIZING

The default for a digital photograph is only 72 dpi, but it has an enormous document size. Document size and resolution are two sides of a mathematical equation that describes how much information is in your file. To avoid throwing away valuable information, always uncheck the "Resample Image" check box in the Image Size dialog box before you change your document size or resolution on a newly imported photo.

To be safe, before you crop or resize any file, save the file you've been editing and crop a copy. You may discover that you need more resolution after it's too late to get it back without redoing all of your adjustments and edits.

RESAMPLING IMAGE FILES

Eventually, you'll downsize your files to fit your portfolio design. When you downsize, you are asking the software to resample the file. The program will throw away information, downsampling to reach the smaller size. Downsampling is like doubling your resolution while shrinking the onscreen size. It makes some art look much better, although somewhat softer. Never upsize your scan. That's called interpolation, and results in the computer creating pixels by mathematical guesswork and adding them to your file—very bad for a portfolio piece.

It's better to resample only once, since files can require a little sharpening if they come down more than 30 percent. Each time you sharpen, you coarsen your image, potentially introducing artifacts. Resize and sharpen more than once, and your artwork deteriorates. If you have Photoshop or another application that offers a Save for Web and Devices function, use it to handle your resizing at the same time that you optimize (see Chapter 7). It will offer a better result than resizing by hand.

SHARPENING

Only sharpen images that really need it, and then use the least amount of sharpening to get your result. Avoid the standard Sharpen filter: It's a blunt instrument for a surgical task.

The correct image sharpening tool is the "Unsharp Mask" filter, one of the Sharpen menu's alternatives. It only affects areas where abrupt color or value changes indicate visual edges. The filter's strange name describes how it works. It takes a blurred copy of the image and uses it as a pixel mask, then compares each pixel with its blurred version. Pixels that aren't at the edges are untouched, or masked out. The filter then does some complicated math to determine how much to change the edge pixels.

If you have images that develop outlines when you use Unsharp Mask, try working on each image channel separately, sharpening the noisiest channel (usually blue) the least, and the cleanest channel (usually green) the most. But be careful. Sharpening one channel much more than the others can lead to color shifts.

Make sharpening the last thing you do before you save a file in a compressed format. As with other edits, never sharpen a file that is already compressed. Return to a universal file format and make your changes there, then resave the file for the web.

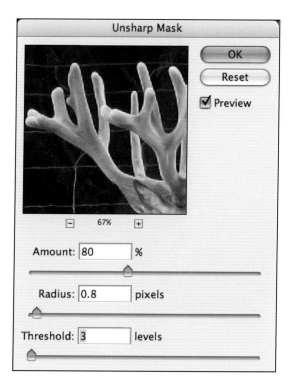

Unsharp Mask's Radius and Amount should increase with your resolution. At 72 ppi, Radius should be between .3 and 1.0 pixels, with .5 to .8 usually giving optimal results without oversharpening. For Amount, I start at a default of 75% and move up to 175%, watching for harsh lines that warn me that I've gone too far. Threshold should decrease as resolution increases. A Threshold of 3 to 5 is appropriate at screen resolution.

PORTFOLIO HIGHLIGHT:
TRIBORO DESIGN | APPLAUSE IN TRANSLATION

WWW.TRIBORODESIGN.COM

Of all the creatives who need an online portfolio, graphic designers are held to the highest standards overall. They were the first design professionals to migrate their work to the web, so there is a decade-long string of trailblazers both to emulate and surpass. Those who are primarily print-based are faced with the toughest challenges. Many of the decisions that separate journeyman print designers from those who are truly gifted are very hard to convey in the flat, rectangular frame of a browser. Yet without an impressive online portfolio, a graphic designer might never get the chance to present his or her physical portfolio in person to a prospective client. This conundrum makes the online portfolio of New York City's Triboro Design particularly notable.

> **We aimed to create an interactive experience that mimics, as closely as possible, the physical experience of viewing our printed work. This is of the utmost importance.**
>
> **—David Heasty**

Triboro Design is designer David Heasty and his wife and collaborator Stefanie Weigler. Although a relatively young design firm, they have carved a distinctive place in the competitive world of identity and publication design through their attention to the very physical details that disappear in most online portfolios. Yet their site illustrates how it is possible to transcend the limits of the medium while staying true to the things that they do best.

The Triboro splash page is a compelling introduction to the portfolio experience.

Select a category and a third column lists the relevant clients in this group, automatically displaying the first client's work in the list with a client brief on the right. You can move backward and forward through the work with the simple arrows.

Click the portfolio link and a column of project categories appears to the right of the main list. Categories highlight in black as you roll over them in the menu. The breadcrumbs that orient you within the site architecture are also indicated by black type within the columns.

about	identities	roth gallery
portfolio	printed matter	moma
news	magazines	bigshot magazine
contact	albums	william rast
	illustrations	central europe art
	books	sodium sodium
	book covers	mahou cup
	products	triboro promos
	typefaces	misc. invites

Navigation and architecture

Their novel approach is immediately obvious. Load their URL and a bold field of horizontal stripes fills the window. Click their name, and a pop-up window appears, framed perfectly by the stripes. If you close the rear window, the clean, pure design of the second window persists. However, the dimension and layering it provides is the perfect foil for the portfolio itself, and precisely the kind of design thinking that makes good print production.

As in many design portfolios, the menus are no-nonsense sans serif columns. Theirs nestle at the top of the page, building from left to right as the categories become more granular. The menus are always available but never obtrusive. The first two columns persist as you explore the portfolio, with the client list and briefs changing as necessary. Separating the copy and internal navigation of the projects prevents the text from becoming a wall of gray, and clarifies the difference between the general navigation and the project group.

Content

So far, the portfolio indicates clarity and good taste, but so do many other portfolios online. It is in how they approach their project content that Triboro stands apart. With the exception of graphic representations of logos and type designs, all of their work has been photographed and presented to emphasize its physicality. They shoot books at an angle, displaying cover and binding the way a book would actually be observed and experienced on a table. They celebrate the reflective shine of light on glossy paper and indicate thickness and scale by the expert placement of lighting to cast shadows.

> **When possible, we avoid using images in a standard rectangular format. We didn't like the restricted feeling of these rectangles, which flatten the site.**
> **—David Heasty**

It's easy to see how Triboro approaches book design when you can experience an entire range of layouts, cleverly sequenced to emphasize spot color and visual balance.

But of course, there are other designers whose work is shot expertly. The difference is that Triboro not only shows each work as a complete object, they zoom tight into the details that define what makes each piece special. In some cases that means a shot from inches away to capture the texture of a woven label. In others, it's a series that shows how an identity is used in different ways. In still others, varnish glistens on an extreme closeup.

They manage this strategy with a consistent visual vocabulary. As Heasty says, "If the viewer sees an image in a circle, they instinctively know they are viewing a detail. If the object is floating free in the whitespace of the page, then they can be sure they are seeing the piece in its entirety. By floating the pieces in a

Showing details is also key. Our physical pieces' aim is to inform and communicate, but secondarily we are out to seduce.
—David Heasty

Triboro makes every effort to present their printed work from the angle and distance that the work would really be seen in. This decision makes every product shot on their site pop with excitement and provides an almost 3D experience.

white background the space around the work becomes energized and there is an illusion of dimension. It's as if you are in the same room with the work."

Future plans

The website was coded by collaborator David Correll, but the partners update their site themselves. They change the portfolio section frequently as they complete new projects, with the latest project appearing as the first image in the portfolio section. The portfolio is not a historical record of their work, but a curated combination of their newest and best efforts. As David says, "A good portfolio is never finished. It grows and changes as the designer grows and changes."

Most designers will show a category of logos or identities as graphic artwork. However, the crucial test of an identity is how well it translates in a variety of settings and materials. That's particularly critical for fashion design. This combination of objects and closeups answers the test masterfully.

Triboro uses different strategies to show off each piece in a series to best effect. A flier is displayed on the site as it would be seen by a recipient of the physical original: with creases after folding. The People's Liberation logo, seen as flat art on the previous page, is expressed in a variety of materials and purposes in the porthole details.

CHAPTER 7

Repurposing and Optimizing

Many of us who work on the computer view our finished, printed art as the final step in a long creative process. When we gather our work for a portfolio, it's natural for us to think of that physical artifact as the work we should show. After scanning, shooting, and agonizing over lost details, it can suddenly dawn on us that sometimes the best art is the original file version.

Returning to your original file is sometimes your only option. When you freelance, or leave a company while a project is still in production, you may never receive a copy of the final, printed work. Then there are the times when you create something you're particularly proud of, only to see the final, produced work and groan. The printer erred, or the client decided to make last-minute changes against your better judgment. Website designs, particularly those where you provide templates, are especially dangerous. After they're out of your hands, anyone with technical competence and no taste can "improve" your best decisions.

You're much more removed from the print work in a digital portfolio. Many of the subtle production choices that can make or break a great piece are simply lost in a 72-dpi image. Paper weight, finish, size, scale, varnish, binding— all those cues are lost in the digital world. The only things you have left are shape, color, and imagery. I've seen pieces online that don't even begin to resemble or represent the real thing.

—Michael Borosky

You can return to your original file, but you can hardly ever use it exactly as it is. Working files are too big, and in the wrong file format. This chapter provides some suggestions for repurposing and optimizing your existing artwork for your portfolio.

FILE ADAPTATION STRATEGIES

Designers, as well as many artists and illustrators, do more than create onscreen. They choose colors and types of ink, select paper, and specify die-cuts. Sometimes those choices are the ones that make a project great. Unfortunately, finesse can be hard to capture in a scan or photograph. Even with a large-sized image, some details are a challenge to visualize onscreen. You can accept the limited representation, and bring samples of special work to interviews. But doing that with too many pieces negates the point of a digital portfolio. And if the pieces are part of your best work, not showing them online hurts your marketability.

Repurposing is particularly attractive for oversized work, like a poster, that has no special paper stock, but it can work in lots of other situations. What follows are a few suggestions to illustrate possible solutions. If your knowledge of Adobe's CS applications is not quite comprehensive enough to imagine how to accomplish these ideas, Appendix A has suggestions of resources that can help you.

- If you have an original file and a paper sample, scan in the latter and use it as a texture with the original file.

- If the paper sample you chose is transparent or translucent, you can mock up the finished piece and use a transparent layer to let a background slightly show through. Experiment with blend modes to avoid having the work lose saturation with the transparency.

- Using animation, you can show a piece at various stages of opacity if it was printed both front and back, or create the effect of turning pages to show a transparent overlay.

- Shooting an oversized book can leave shadows in the gutter, obscuring details. You can take a two-page spread into Photoshop, and use a dis-

The things that I bring to my print work are often hard to photograph. If I've done a piece that has metallic inks, it might have this mysterious glow in person, but when it's printed in an annual or turned into a JPEG on a website, the shimmer is gone, and the ink just looks lifeless.

—Gunnar Swanson

placement map to give the "book" a curve and a slight, non-destructive shadow in the center.

- A metallic ink often just looks like a flat color when scanned. Use a camera instead, and light the piece at an angle to bring out the highlights.

- Embossing is impossible to capture in a scan. It's easier in a photograph, particularly if the embossed piece can be lit to emphasize shadow details. If that doesn't work, bring the original file into Photoshop, select the embossed element, and then sharpen its edges. Run a light brush over the insides where the sharpening effect is too obvious.

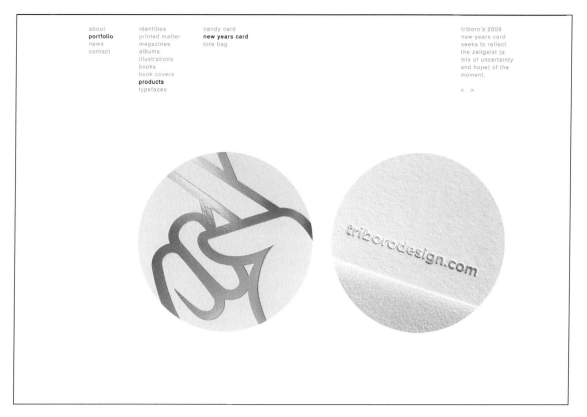

WWW.TRIBORO.COM

Triboro employed a professional photographer to capture important details about their print projects. Here, the camera was focused very close to their self-promotion piece, where ink selection and embossing are both key. The result is featured on their website to emphasize these defining design decisions.

REPURPOSING WITH PDFs

One of the best ways to repurpose published work is to create a PDF. It can be a good way of presenting a file that was originally created in a page layout or illustration program, or to bring together multiple image files in a coherent single file.

PDFs are pretty easy to make, but they deserve just as much attention as larger, more complete presentations. They can often be the key to winning an interview. Many applications allow you to save your files directly as PDFs. However, a full version of Acrobat will allow you to create an integrated portfolio, not just a loose affiliation of files.

Automated PDF creation

Adobe Acrobat Professional 9 has a feature called Portfolio, which makes it very easy to combine different types and sizes of files, including some moving image formats, into one document. If you are not a design professional but your audience requests a PDF, this feature is a wonderful way to give them what they need. You can customize a welcome page and a header with a typeface and color scheme of your choice, and select one of four ways for your individual files to be displayed: as a grid of rectangles, as a "desktop" with a background JPG and documents represented as icons, as a 3D revolving flipbox of rectangles, and as a sliding horizontal row of icons.

For a design professional, you can use this feature to bundle a cover letter with your designed PDF portfolio, and add a SWF or other moving image file if you design both still and motion content. That way, everything in your email package will stay together.

The Portfolio function is a good start. However, it emphatically does not take the place of a professional's portfolio file, as its customizing features are too limited. It is the equivalent of using a social-networking site as your only portfolio website. A designer, or anyone who needs their portfolio package to be a memorable representation of their skills and tastes, will still need to design their PDF themselves using a layout program, with a redesigned résumé as part of the package.

PDF creation hints

You owe it to the people who'll receive your files to create your PDFs correctly, and in a format they'll find easy to view. That can be a critical difference. Many people quickly print a PDF they've received and take it with them in paper form for review. They won't want to fuss with settings, or multiple files.

Here are tips for creating good PDFs:

- **Create a cover page.** Make sure your cover page contains your contact info, then place your name and the page number as a header or footer on each subsequent page. If your work is printed, the pages will still be identifiably yours, and will remain together.

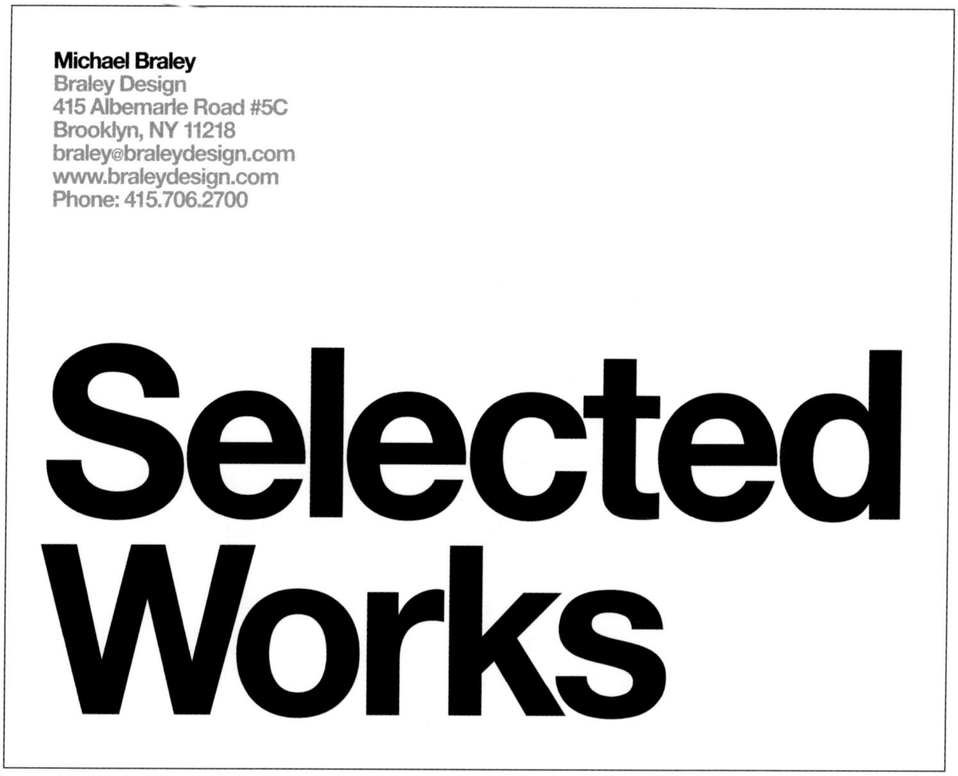

Michael Braley
Braley Design
415 Albemarle Road #5C
Brooklyn, NY 11218
braley@braleydesign.com
www.braleydesign.com
Phone: 415.706.2700

Selected Works

WWW.BRALEYDESIGN.COM
A well-designed cover page sets the tone for the presentation. Design one that will print equally well in color or on a standard laser printer, as Michael Braley's does.

- **Avoid scrolling.** Create letter-sized pages, so viewers can view and print them out easily. Set up your PDF in landscape format to fit better onscreen.

- **Shoot original files.** Always return to your original file for onscreen shots of web-based material for your PDF. For example, when possible, screen shots of Flash-based websites should be shot from the FLA file, not from a browser window, to preserve higher resolution for typographic decisions.

- **Use TIF files.** If you're creating screen shots, shoot them as TIF, not JPEG, files. You are certain to end up needing to scale them as you lay out your pages, and scaled JPEGs quickly lose quality.

- **Watch your file sizes.** Even in these days of cable modems and DSL, no PDF should exceed about 3 MB. Recipients who have fast connections still might have limited storage space on a mail server.

- **Label your artwork.** Just as you would on a website or disc, you should include captions with your artwork that identify it.

A PDF is more flexible. It's like showing boards, because you can put pieces on different pages and they can be various sizes.

—Yang Kim

WWW.BRALEYDESIGN.COM
As Rita Armstrong points out about designer Michael Braley's smart PDF portfolio, listing the number of pages in the heading for a project is a great idea. It lets the viewer know that this page is just a small taste of what the project was about.

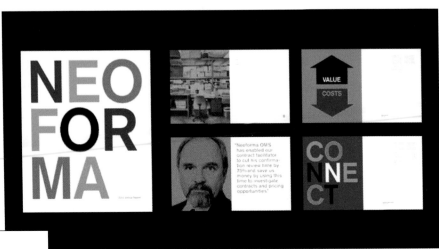

Neoforma
Annual Report
36 pages

- **Name your PDF sensibly.** Don't call it "mywork" or "myportfolio." Use your full name in the file label. If you must send more than one PDF, name the files similarly, so they'll appear together when sorted.

- **No headshots.** Unless you're a performing artist, don't ever put a picture of yourself in your PDF. You're not entering a beauty contest, nor are you a member of a corporate sales force. Creative directors and placement agencies target you as clueless as soon as they see the photo.

OPTIMIZING IMAGE FILES

All your files will eventually need to be optimized—altered to fit the requirements of transmission. Websites, emailed images, and image files dropped into PDFs will need the most shrinking. CDs and DVDs have less stringent requirements, but optimized files will take less time to load.

A well-optimized file looks good onscreen, but takes up very little file space. The smaller the file space, the faster the file. With the exception of your creativity, nothing will have more bearing on how your portfolio is perceived than how much time the viewer must invest to see it.

Optimizing basics

Optimizing is a delicate balance of four elements: color, image quality, image dimensions, and file size. The ratio among these elements shifts as technology improves. Browser and platform differences still compromise color (see the sidebar "ICC color profiles and JPEG files" later in the chapter), but good image quality is readily attainable. So is a large onscreen image size. Unless you have an unusual cli-

The number-one killer on a website is speed. Corporate clients will run out of patience. They have high-speed connections, and they're not used to waiting.

—Yang Kim

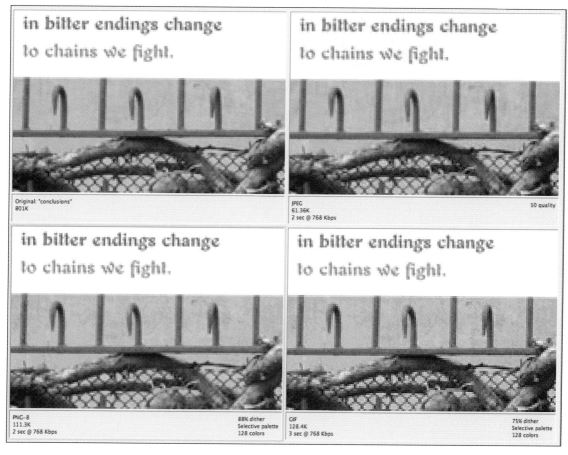

A graphic image with a mixture of flat areas and smooth blends (upper left) should be tested as GIF, PNG, and JPEG. Here, the JPEG (upper right) is too soft, the GIF (lower right) has too many artifacts, and the PNG (lower left) does the best job of holding onto the crispness of the type while not losing the image quality.

What makes us pass on a portfolio? Not enough attention paid to details both in the portfolio itself and in the work. Even in the simplest of portfolio designs, every detail has to be addressed and perfected.

—Thane Calder

ent base, you can optimize for 16 million colors on *at least* a 17-inch monitor with a 1024x768 resolution.

In most urban markets, the minimum standard is a DSL or cable modem connection, often with a download speed of 6 Mbps. But that doesn't give you the license to throw anything you'd like into a portfolio. Image sizes are cumulative on a page, and even as options have increased, viewer expectations have too. No one will wait 20 seconds to watch a portfolio page render. And during really high-traffic times, even a cable modem connection can slow to a walk. Every 10 kb saved in optimizing will still be appreciated.

You'll optimize before you begin actual portfolio production, but you'd be wise to already have sketched out a layout grid for a typical page before you optimize. Although you can downsize art in HTML or Flash, the closer you are to optimizing your work at 100% of its onscreen size, the happier you'll be with the results.

THE OPTIMIZING PROCESS

There are some specialized optimizing tools, like DeBabelizer Pro, but the easiest and most common method is to bring files into Adobe Fireworks or Photoshop CS4 or later, which incorporates Fireworks' optimizing windows and range of variables. In Photoshop CS3 or later, these features are found under "File > Save for Web and Devices"—in Fireworks, they are under "File > Image Preview."

In either software, you can choose between optimizing the file as a JPEG, a PNG, or a GIF. The standard rule of thumb has been that photographic images are optimized as JPEGs, and graphic images as GIFs. Most browsers now support PNGs, which addresses many of the GIF/JPEG tradeoffs. However, the PNG format has many variations and makes larger files than GIF. For size and compatibility purposes, GIF and JPEG still often prove to be the safest routes.

Applications for optimizing provide presets as jumping off points. Many people who don't know much about optimization select one of these presets and apply it globally to their images. That's better than not optimizing at all, but it usually leads to files that load too slowly, or are significantly smaller onscreen than they need to be.

ABOUT SLICING

Slicing is a way to break up large images and interfaces into small, bite-sized elements that load more quickly than a single image would. Many applications, including Photoshop, offer a slicing feature that helps you to slice an image before you optimize it. But slicing is often an unpleasant distraction. Unless you have a good visual place to break the file (like in the center of a two-page spread), it's better to use optimizing techniques to have the file load progressively, or simply keep your file sizes down.

SKINNY GIF

Why should you optimize your file visually, instead of just saving it for the web? Every second of wait time counts. On the left is part of a large file that will take 3 seconds to download on a fast cable or DSL connection. On the right, the steps for optimizing visually.

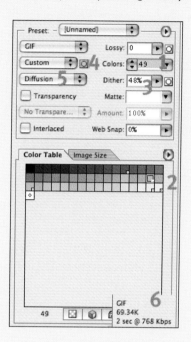

1 Minimize the number of colors. Starting with a 64-color preset, I dropped colors from the palette one by one until I reached the minimum acceptable number for the image.

2 Several colors dropped too soon. I stepped backwards, selected the most important colors to preserve, and locked them. Locked colors can't be dropped as colors decrease.

3 This image has a lot of flat color and type. Through experimentation, I've found that I need much less dither at this size. In fact, the type is crisper without it.

4 It was important to hold some details in the book cover when decreasing the number of colors. I created a mask of that rectangle and saved it. Then I enabled the mask by selecting the mask button next to the palette type and protected this small detail from being posterized. This strategy is called "weighted optimization" and it works for both GIFs and JPEGs.

5 There are different methods of selecting colors for a palette. I used Diffusion here because it gave the best color fidelity and smallest file size.

6 As a result, the final optimized image will take a full second less to load. That doesn't seem like much, but when your entire page goal is five seconds, one second is 20% of that time.

Both Fireworks and Photoshop use a 56K dialup modem as the default speed estimator in their optimizing window, giving you a "worst case scenario." To get a sense of download time for Cable/DSL, hold down the Ctrl key in the speed/size estimation box and select one of the other options from the list that appears.

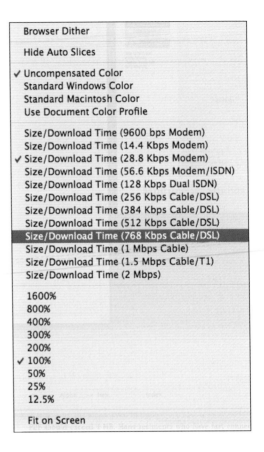

Optimizing hints

Let's examine the best ways to approach optimizing different types of files. To begin, set a goal for each page's download. For a standard, non-animated portfolio, a good goal is five seconds, based on DSL or cable access. If your images are detailed photographs, double this goal and use progressive JPEGs to let your audience know that more detail is on the way. Assume that your portfolio image will represent the bulk of that time, since it's the focus of your site.

You can process files in bulk, using a standardized optimization setting and the software's automation menu. I only recommend this shortcut for PNGs, which have very limited options and are therefore more conducive to automation. Otherwise, automation is only appropriate for steps such as bulk preprocessing the height and/or width of your image to meet the standards of your portfolio template. Fireworks offers a "Batch Process" function for these needs, while Photoshop offers more advanced scripting options. However, the time spent developing a proper batch process may be better spent working through each image; optimizing still requires a commitment to examine every image—individually.

ICC COLOR PROFILES AND JPEG FILES

A *color profile* holds information about the color space of an image or a device. If every device you use is calibrated and has a color profile, the computer can translate color between the devices so you will always see the same colors no matter where your file is.

Photoshop allows you to embed an ICC color profile in an image. And if the browser your viewer is using is color-managed, i.e. one that reads these profiles, what you show on screen will be what you expected.

Unfortunately, some browsers (like Microsoft Internet Explorer and most other Windows browsers) don't read these profiles. They show all artwork with their default profile, which is sRGB. To gain an accurate assessment of what colors will look like in a browser, prepare your files in sRGB, and check them in a browser window before you create your portfolio.

These are exactly the same JPEG file, with the same ICC profile, captured on the same monitor and operating system.

The top image is color corrected. The bottom image is how it appears in a non-corrected browser.

GIFs

It's not a problem to get acceptable-looking GIF files. The difficulty is to shave little bits of file size from them without making any dismal changes in the appearance of the finished file. The sidebar "Skinny GIF" shows the finicky yet valuable optimizing process for a GIF.

JPEGs

There are fewer elements to consider when creating JPEGs. The most important thing to remember is the difference between the general categories—Low, Medium, High, and Maximum—and the quality gradations within each category. You continue to have a high quality at any setting between 60 and 79, but the file size you generate can be radically different at these settings.

One extremely useful setting when optimizing a JPEG is the Progressive setting. Choose this, and your JPEG will begin to load immediately at low quality, improving as it goes until it's completed. Viewers will be much more patient with an extra second of total load time if they are already able to see artwork in process.

PNGs

For PNG, be sure to export using the special optimizing windows discussed above. Don't just bring the file into an application and save it as a PNG from the File menu. Some programs, like Fireworks, save out a more complicated version of PNG that web browsers can't interpret correctly. This format includes scalable vector graphics (SVG) information that makes the file size significantly larger—information that is just "thrown away" by the web browser. The PNG export options "flatten" the file and put all vector information into bitmap format before optimizing.

OPTIMIZING VIDEO

Unlike regular still images, which have well-established guidelines and types of file formats, there is no standard video format, which is a tremendous headache for portfolio creators and viewers alike. The lack of standards makes it even more important that you take the time to optimize your video files correctly, as a misstep could mean that your target audience will not be able to view your work.

After editing a video file in a non-linear editing program, you encode it: save it in a different, compressed format. Your major decision is to figure out what format or formats you should use to create your new file. From there, you select settings that determine the final quality and file size of your clip.

Each format is optimized to be viewed from within its own player (see the next section, "Encoders and players"). Some players allow you to view other formats, but the quality is often compromised. Unless you are quite certain of your target audience's platform and technology, you'll have to output in more than one format.

VIDEO OPTIMIZATION TERMINOLOGY

Aspect ratio is the proportion of the horizontal to the vertical dimensions of an image. The computer/standard TV ratio is 4:3. Film/HDTV (the new standard, and the ratio of Apple Cinema Displays) runs at 16:9.

Codecs are algorithms that are built into software. They are converters that **co**mpress and **dec**ompress digital data, particularly video files. There are dozens of video codecs, including DV, MPEG-4, and Cinepak. Some are better for your purposes than others.

Fast Start is pseudo-streaming. When you play QuickTime and Windows Media Player files from a regular web server, the file downloads to the viewer's computer at the best speed for its connection and begins to play while the download is still taking place.

Hint Tracks tell a streaming server how to prepare video clip data for successful streaming. Without a hint track, the video will not stream. Hint tracks aren't needed for downloading or pseudo-streaming.

Streaming is the process of sending data to a computer in real time. The viewer doesn't have to wait for the clip to download before they can see it.

ENCODERS AND PLAYERS

To see encoded video, the viewer needs a player in your format. The "best" player format for you is one that is already installed on your viewer's computer. Because you can't always predict what that will be, you'll need to create files for more than one player. The players mentioned below are the most popular ones.

If you are creating movies for both Mac and PC users, save your edited files in at least two formats—AVI (for Windows users) and MOV (for Mac users). Even though both movie types can be played on both platforms, very few Mac users have Windows Media Player. Conversely, although a reasonable number of Windows users have QuickTime, all have WMP.

- **QuickTime.** QuickTime is Apple's cross-platform video software. It imports many other file formats, including AVI, and outputs to a variety of codecs. Windows users of IE5.5 and later need to download a special ActiveX file to be able to see QuickTime content. Note that not all AVI files play correctly on a Mac, while more and more Windows users have QuickTime support because of the popularity of iTunes, which requires it.

- **Windows Media Player.** Windows Media Player is installed on all Windows computers, making it the single-most popular player. The player is cross-platform, but Mac users must downloaded it. The Mac version does not support all formats, such as "secure" versions of Windows media.

- **RealPlayer.** RealNetworks is a provider of a format for streaming video. Because large corporations use RealPlayer to deliver music and video content, RealPlayer has good coverage on Windows and Mac computers alike. Products such as Adobe After Effects have built-in support for RealMedia export, but this is not as common as AVI or QuickTime export. Although limited support for the SMIL format is built into QuickTime, most RealMedia files can only be read by RealPlayer.

There are three additional ways of encoding and/or playing audio and video on the web or on a disc. Each of them relies on one of the main technologies listed previously, but requires an additional player or software on the user's computer:

- **Flash and Flash Video.** Flash allows you to import video from other sources and add an interactive layer to it. You can output files as SWFs, or as a QuickTime or Windows Media file. Adobe CS3 and higher as well as many third party encoders also create files in Flash's FLV video format. Adobe estimates that 97% of web browsers have Flash Player 8 or higher installed, so this is a well-supported video standard.

- **DivX.** DivX is a popular codec with 3D animators and DV enthusiasts. It offers high-quality, large window sizes, and fast performance. It uses the Windows Media Player in Windows, and QuickTime on the Mac side. If you use DivX, you will want to include instructions for your viewers on how to install the codec; however, chances are that you will still lose some viewers if this is the only option you provide.

- **Vimeo, YouTube, and similar sites.** Video sharing sites are increasingly popular because of their "one step" approach: upload the video and receive a link back to the web-optimized version. Although these sites are working to match the quality of the other formats mentioned (including offering HD encoding options), you still have to deal with a site watermark and possible advertising on your videos—not the best impression for your portfolio.

You can't offer too many formats, but you absolutely can offer too few. Yes, you can include a player on a CD or ask a viewer to download one, but most people find that extra step extremely irritating—if they are willing to do it at all.

ENCODING SETTINGS

After you've determined what format or formats best meet your needs, your next step is to select the settings that will determine the final quality and file size of your clip. Rule number one is that the more you compress, the smaller your file is and the faster it will download and play, but the worse it will look. You can maintain more quality by keeping your window playback size small.

Rule number two is that no setting is perfect for every clip. You'll want different settings for two clips in a web-based portfolio if one is a full-motion video and another is a 2D typographic animation. Also, every person's eye and tolerance is a little different, so what looks great to you on your computer screen may be less sharp or too fast for someone someplace else. The best course of action is to find willing guinea pigs to test your result before you finalize it.

Window size

Everyone wants to show their work as large as possible, but unless your web portfolio will reside on a streaming server, you'll have to compromise. Although standards are always improving, it's safest to display motion video in a small window,

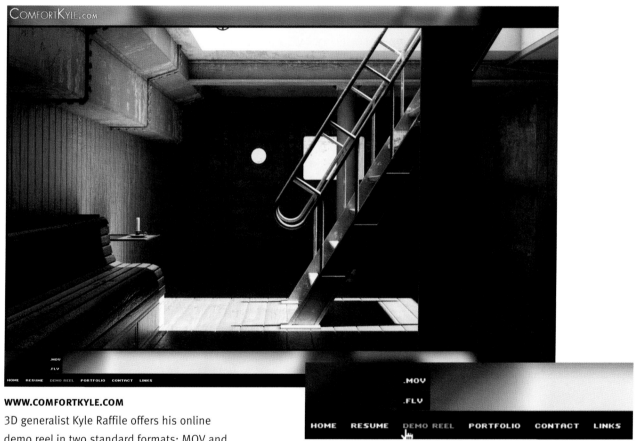

WWW.COMFORTKYLE.COM
3D generalist Kyle Raffile offers his online demo reel in two standard formats: MOV and FLV, to make sure the maximum number of people can view it.

usually 320x240. If you really want to upsize to take advantage of better technology, create two window sizes and allow your viewers to choose. Or make a high-resolution file that can be downloaded for viewing.

Work on CD can be somewhat larger, with 720x480 for standard or widescreen DV and 1280x720 for HD being good starting points. DVD is usually designed for a full TV screen, although you can use it to show smaller clips.

Compression type

There are too many compression types to choose from, and it can be bewildering to see the list of codecs in a typical export menu. In fact, most of them are completely useless for your portfolio. Some are for videoconferencing, for example, and others are actually almost obsolete. Even more frustrating is the list of audio codecs. Unless you have high-quality music as part of your video, you won't want to compress audio at all. Compressed audio sounds really bad, and you don't even get the benefit of smaller file sizes.

After you eliminate all the unnecessary complications, you're left with one codec that solves most problems: Sorenson. The Sorenson codecs are used for Flash Video and QuickTime, and also work with various Windows formats. If you are unsure about Windows support and you don't want to use Flash Video, Cinepak is the safest choice for creating AVI files for Window and MOV files for Macintosh.

Frame rate

A higher frame rate per second gives a smoother look to your clip, but adds size to the file. Over the web, you should probably stick with 12–15 frames per second (fps)—a good formula for a starting point is to divide your original video's frame rate by two. Moving up to 15–20 fps on a CD should be fine. DVD compression assumes a full 29.97 fps.

Key frame rate

Encoders can determine how much a movie changes from a reference frame (called a *key frame*). To make movies smaller, they only send information about the things that change in the frames that follow. The more key frames, the smoother the movie will appear, but the larger it will be. Too few key frames, and the movie will be small but jerky. I recommend 5–7 key frames for a CD. Web settings should be tested, depending on how much actual movement takes place in the clip. A setting of 15 ensures an update every second if your movie is playing at 15 frames per second. The Sorenson encoding tools (both Squeeze and the Flash Video Encoder) provide named defaults that give you a sense of the intended purpose of each setting.

File naming

It is very important to name your files with the correct extensions. Be careful not to delete these extensions by mistake, or they will not be recognized properly by their players. QuickTime uses .MOV, Windows Media uses .AVI and .WMV, and RealPlayer uses .RM, .RA, and .SMIL.

AFTER THE ARTWORK

Repurposing and optimizing are the tasks that will seem the most time-consuming and thankless in your portfolio process. Like most production work, this stage can feel like an obstacle in the way of the fun, creative part of portfolio development. But when you're finished, you'll be able to reuse most of your work again and again as your portfolio requires.

maya | after effects
modeling, rigging, lighting, shading, compositing

WWW.HERCFERN.COM

Optimizing a detailed animation file with composited backgrounds and foreground characters always pays off in the end, as viewers are delighted by the results.

PORTFOLIO HIGHLIGHT:
THOM BENNETT | OPTIMAL DETAIL

WWW.TBGD.CO.UK

The best technology is invisible. If you do everything right—select, repurpose, optimize—nothing will pull attention away from your work. But invisibility only goes so far. The more astute the viewer, the more they will appreciate how the things they don't see make possible the elegant things that they do. That connection is obvious in British designer Thom Bennett's portfolio.

I always take my time and make sure that the images show off the work to the very best quality they can.

—Thom Bennett

Bennett's 2006 site, which is still linked from his current one, excited the attention of the digiterati who comb the ether for exceptional websites. For some people, such attention would result in an extended run of the "don't fix it if it ain't broke" variety. But Bennett, although justifiably proud of the work and pleased with the attention, is a perfectionist. He executed a complete revision in visual design, image preparation, and programming development.

Bennett's presentation may be technologically adept, but it does not draw attention to itself. In fact, his design choices are conservative—in the best sense of the word. They consider the needs of the visitor the way a good host does with a house guest. His typography plays against the prevailing look and feel, comfortably scaled and extremely legible.

Bennett starts with a short animated build of the site from background to navigation to his center statement, which boldly states the purpose of the site. The design supports the statement with subtle colors and cool gray background. The look is a nice break from design-default white matte, while still providing a clean, understated look.

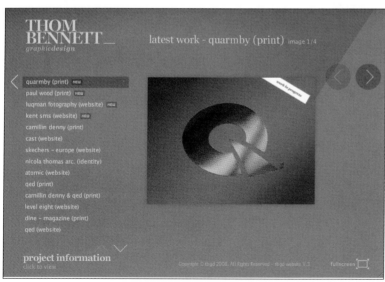

These two images are the result of resizing the window of Bennett's site. His header and nav bar always remain in the same place on the page. Everything else floats in the window relative to the size and position of the project image.

Navigation and architecture

Technology can affect navigation choices, usually by presenting limitations to creativity. One can see Bennett's command of his medium in the apparent ease with which he provides navigational feedback and options that most developers would avoid, or never even think of attempting.

In one of its most elegant uses of technology, Bennett's site readily adapts itself to the viewer's screen size. Most Flash websites are designed at an optimum aspect ratio and size. If you enlarge the browser window, you simply get a lot more of the designer's background. If you shrink the window down, eventually you have to scroll to see the entire page. Bennett's site scales; if you have a cinema screen, you can see his artwork at its largest size. But if you're on a 13-inch laptop, the navigation tools adjust to the browser window, maintaining their relationship to the image window and always remaining accessible.

latest work - atomic (website) image 1/3

The menu and header provide a wealth of orientation information. The header reminds you of the main section you're in, the project name and type, and how many images represent the project.

The main menu has two large arrows that point back to the main heads and down to indicate that there are more projects below the ones you can see listed. Unvisited projects are in light type, visited ones are in dark. The selected project has blue type in a dark box. Hover over another project and it highlights with a mid-value box.

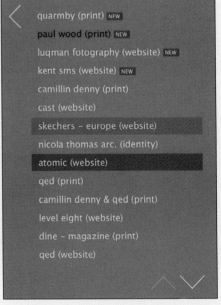

The menus are full of visual feedback and clever thinking. No visitor will feel the frustration that arises when you realize that you've just unintentionally loaded a project you've seen before. Simple color changes in type and background act as breadcrumbs to help the viewer stay oriented to where they are and what they have already viewed. The menus themselves are clearly organized, with navigation that makes it easy to change levels or topics with one click.

As you might expect, all of Bennett's project images appear with blinding speed. But even so, he provides feedback for each project group as it loads with a "percent complete" readout. The images stay in the computer's cache for as long as you remain on the site, so if you do decide to review a project, there is no load time at all.

This was one of the main goals when developing my website: to try and produce a high-impact portfolio that would fill a user's screen as much as possible.

—Thom Bennett

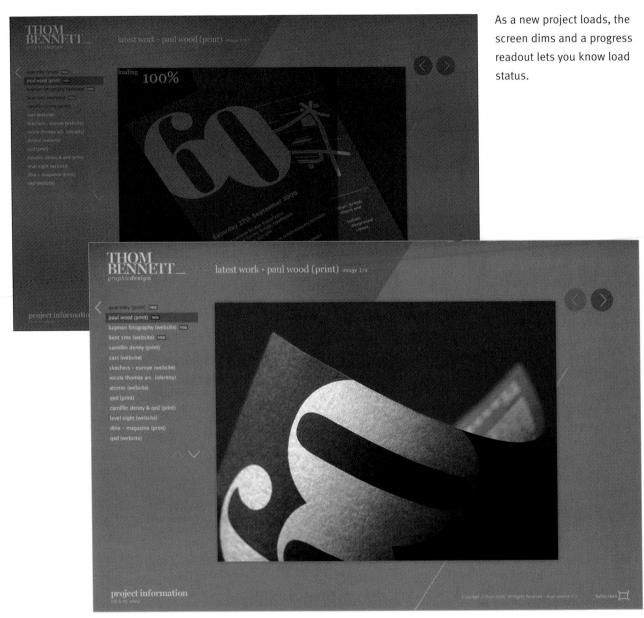

As a new project loads, the screen dims and a progress readout lets you know load status.

Select project information for a print project, and Bennett identifies ink and paper decisions.

Print projects are photographed in innovative positions or lighting to emphasize the difference between them and web work, and to show the textural details that Bennett's optimizing process maintains.

It's a juggling act trying to get the balance right between the image looking sharp and crisp and it not being too large in file size. But it's worth the effort, as this is what decides the speed it will load on a user's system.

—Thom Bennett

Content

Bennett is a self-employed web and graphic designer, and his portfolio site is by far his main presentation form. Most potential clients base their decision to use his services on the site without a face-to-face portfolio presentation. Given its importance, he's given a lot of thought to what brings a prospective client to his site, and what they expect to find there. As a web designer, he needs to show a range of site design projects in addition to his own site's obvious object lesson. As a print designer, he needs to show his non-screen work in a way that indicates his sensitivity to traditional issues. And that means shots of finished print work, to avoid confusing one type of medium with the other.

Bennett never forgets that ultimately it's all about the work. Every project image is of stunning quality and shows a different aspect of the whole, framed and cropped individually to show off the defining design elements. He shoots only high-resolution photos, and he spends the extra time in optimization to maintain the exact color levels he needs. Each image is compressed to exactly the optimum file size: big enough to hold even delicate details, but small enough to load as fast as possible. He describes the key to his process: "I will set up a document to the actual pixel size of the final image I want for my portfolio. From here I will copy and paste my hi-res project photos and images into the document. The advantage of working like this is that it allows you to play around with the images position and size so you can crop into it where you feel it looks the best."

Future plans

Bennett created this redesign to make his site easier to update and to provide more visual impact with each image. One of Flash's drawbacks is that it creates sites that can take constant effort to stay current, in contrast to a standard HTML site that can often be updated with minimal fuss. Like Jonnie Hallman in Chapter 1, Bennett has separated the wrapper from the content—he updates using XML and linked images. As a result, this site will likely remain present for the foreseeable future, hopefully to gain its own share of approbation from potential clients and other design professionals.

I hope my website shows users that the graphic and website design work I create is both considered and intelligent.

—Thom Bennett

CHAPTER 8

Creating Written Content

"Someone showing their art should at least pretend they're competent," I heard a student sneer while surfing a site. That was harsh, but it's easy to criticize when you know the difference between good and bad work. Writing is no different. Even if you're dyslexic or just hate writing, you can't afford to be embarrassed publicly.

The easiest way to avoid the issue is to design a portfolio with no written content—just your contact information. This strategy can work for some disciplines (animation comes to mind) but it is deadly for most design areas. Too much of what makes a good designer is in the decisions. To appreciate the decisions that went into your finished pieces, viewers need some context.

Fortunately, most of what you need for competent writing can be learned, and what's left can be handled by a combination of software and patience.

This chapter will help you figure out how much text your portfolio requires, prevent you from making the worst writing errors, and help you keep your portfolio's visual and verbal elements in sync.

AVOIDING WRITING ERRORS

You choose your samples carefully and attempt to craft a seamless presentation. What you write is equally important.

As someone who sees lots of student résumés and portfolio packages, I've been treated to many remarkable writing errors. They don't make a potential employer feel confident, although they can brighten up a tense day at the sender's expense. My personal favorites...the student who claimed proficiency in "Adope Photoshot" and the person who misspelled his own name. Then there was the poor applicant whose résumé design had a large initial letter at the beginning of each major heading. The problem was that these initial letters were for the words Louis, Objective, Schooling, Experience and References. Oops.

Want to look bad in print? Here are a few ways to do it.

Sad spelling and grammar

In the age of spell checkers, there is no excuse for misspelled words. They tell people that you are sloppy. Spell check even if you think you are good at spelling. Everyone has some words that they consistently spell incorrectly, and everyone makes typographical errors.

The paragraph below is an excerpt from a real online résumé. The résumé itself was very nicely designed but had a remarkable number of errors—indicated in bold—for one short paragraph.

> Work with the design team developing new brands, as well as **(verb missing)** strategies for moving **extisting** brands online; present design mockups and **iteration** to clients; and **manageeing** the production of final media assets. **Resposible** for text production and layout, as well as digital photography.

If you don't spell well, chances are your grammar isn't perfect either. This paragraph also had a grammatical problem. The word "managing" should have been "manage" to match the verb tenses for "work" and "present." Grammatical errors are trickier to catch than spelling errors but can lead to real embarrassment. Not only did these errors make it hard to appreciate the writer's design, they raised a horrible question: Why was this person in charge of text production?

Unless the program you are using contains a spell-checker *and* a grammar checker—or you are both an accomplished typist and good writer—write everything in a program that has these helpful tools. Then cut and paste the text into whatever development program you're using.

Microsoft Word can be irritating, but it does a pretty good job of preventing the worst grammatical goofs. In it, you can select Tools > Spelling and Grammar at any point and check your document for errors. If you don't mind interruptions as you work, set Word to prompt you. To do this, go to File > Preferences (Windows) or Word > Preferences (Mac OS X). In the dialog box, you can choose to have Word highlight spelling and grammar errors as you type, so you can fix problems as they arise.

Fractured headlines

One little-known fact about spell checkers is that they don't check words in all capital letters unless you tell them to. You are less likely to notice mistakes in all-cap words because they are usually headlines or captions. While you're setting preferences for checking bad grammar, ask Word to spell-check uppercase words as well. It is usually worth the added hassle of false positives.

After you've unchecked the default "Ignore words in UPPERCASE," Word will stop on every acronym it doesn't know. To avoid this problem, create a custom dictionary. In the Word Spelling and Grammar preferences dialog box, click Dictionaries. In the next dialog, you can add a personal dictionary. (I like to put mine in the Office folder where Word's default dictionary lives.) The first time Word stops you on an acronym such as AIGA, add it to your custom dictionary. Not only will Word stop bothering you, but it will alert you when you mistype the acronym in the future.

Sloppy typing

Having a program with a spell-checking tool is only half the battle. You must also remember to use it. It's human nature when you're pressed for time to type something in without checking it, because it's only of few words long. That's how mistakes happen in navigation bars and headlines.

Verbal diarrhea

Strange but true—people who hate to write almost always write too much once they start. Just as minimalist design is the art of deleting until you get it right, the trick to good writing is good cutting.

Too many "and"s

Don't use the word "and" unless it's in a series of things. "Books, periodicals, *and* annual reports" is fine. "This project was created to serve the needs of the client who wanted to focus their brand *and* they planned to use it for future online projects," is incorrect. It's actually two sentences glued together. Run-on sentences, besides being bad writing, are hard to read and understand onscreen.

Capital objects

In general, you should only capitalize words that begin a sentence, are proper names, or are acronyms (such as UI for user interface). Excessive capitalization puts emphasis where emphasis doesn't belong. Be particularly alert for this problem if English is your second language. In German, for example, capitals are used much more liberally than they are in English.

PORTFOLIOS IN SECOND LANGUAGES

Creativity is international. It's possible that you are now working in a different country from where you started. If so, you might not be as solid a writer in your adopted language as in your native one. To a point, potential employers or clients will accept imperfections in your writing if they know that you are working in your second language, particularly if you present yourself well in person.

That doesn't give you carte blanche to butcher your adopted language in print. In fact, if you are looking for a job where you are likely to be working with text, not just image, it is extremely important that you convey your ability to maneuver in your second language. If you don't, people could wonder if you will misunderstand instructions or make expensive or embarrassing errors under deadline pressure.

You should not only follow the guidelines in this chapter for proofing your work—you should take them one step further. If at all possible, have a native speaker read your text before you post it.

WHAT TO WRITE AND WHY

Now that you've had a quick refresher on how to avoid the most frequent writing mistakes, it's time to put your knowledge into action. People often look to your portfolio package to find out about your career or education, what you contributed to a project, and how you solve visual problems. Particularly if they will be bringing you into a close-knit team, they need a sense of who you are. The right text in the right place can help them put you and your work into personal context.

Some types of text are more important in your portfolio than others, so if you don't write well, you can concentrate on these critical elements. In order of necessity, you will write to:

- Identify your work.
- Introduce yourself.
- Explain your ideas and process.
- Speak directly to your audience.

IDENTIFYING YOUR WORK

Even a minimalist portfolio includes a way to identify each project. Your labels or captions should include the client and a short title. If there is any question about the role you might have played in the project (art direction, illustrations, or programming, for example) either the title or another line of the caption should specify your

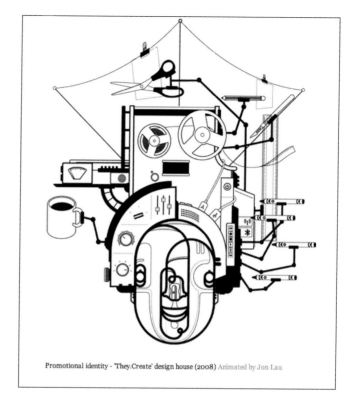

Promotional identity - 'They.Create' design house (2008) Animated by Jon Lau

share of the creative result. The title can be descriptive ("graphics and art direction for") or a formal work title ("Beyorn identity package").

Distinguish between these captions and any descriptions you provide of the work. Captions are not the place to explain your design ideas and process.

Check your facts...don't depend on your memory for titles, names, and spelling. Don't use abbreviations for the client name unless it is so well known (like IBM) that everyone will recognize it.

INTRODUCING YOURSELF

Your portfolio presentation must include basic personal information to identify you and orient the casual visitor. You provide that with some text about yourself—a résumé, a bio, an introductory statement, or a cover letter.

The résumé

The classic professional writing requirement is the résumé. There are scads of books and workshops on creating effective résumés. Beyond the most basic guidelines, they don't apply well to creatives. With the exception of academic vitae, the résumé is secondary to your portfolio. It could get you in the door at a large company's human resources (HR) department, but it will never get you a job.

It can, in fact, have the opposite effect. In many large organizations, someone in HR is often making a first pass among a large volume of candidates. A sloppy résumé will give that person an excuse to toss you into the circular file without anyone ever seeing your portfolio. Later, it can be the tipping point when a company is having a tough time choosing among a short list of candidates.

The best advice anyone can give you about writing a résumé is: Keep it clean, visually and verbally. Then make sure that it contains no errors. Use a spell checker every time you edit it. Get other people to read it—the more eyes, the better.

Clean also means spare. Few résumés need to be longer than one page, even if your career spans decades. Older experience tends to become less relevant as time passes and can be cut or radically condensed. Education is an example. It's important when you've just graduated, but after you've had even one job in the real world, your academic history or honors usually belong at the bottom of the page. By the time you're heading for your second job, details like your grade point average should disappear.

Another "delete me" is the Objective that management gurus tell you to put at the top of your résumé. The only time it might be useful is if you've had an unusual career. When you've done a variety of work that you need to tie together or you're making a radical change (from exhibit designer to interactive designer, for example), an objective can help you explain the transition: "My objective is to leverage my experience with wayfinding in physical space to designing for the virtual environment."

Brevity is a creative blessing. Text-heavy résumés written by and for creatives simply don't get read. No paragraph should be longer than four sentences, and no sentence should run longer than four lines, assuming about 30 picas a line and 10-point type. Shorter is even better. Stick to your responsibilities, range of work, and most significant accomplishments. Or simply take a sentence to explain what you did and then list the clients you did it for. You can always elaborate in person.

A résumé is best written and designed to be printed and read offline. That means it should not include anything that will slow the download and tempt someone to break the connection. No placed art of any kind. And use your name as the file title, not "résumé." How will anyone remember whom your PDF belongs to otherwise?

The bio

People don't need your full story on a portfolio site. A good compromise is a note that describes your experience and expertise. An online bio, like most web text, should be as short as you can make it while still hitting what you feel are your most important points. If you are looking for clients instead of employment, your bio should emphasize your capabilities or the type of work you do.

A text introduction on your splash page is not a résumé replacement, nor should it be deeply personal. It's a centering device to give a reader a way to look at

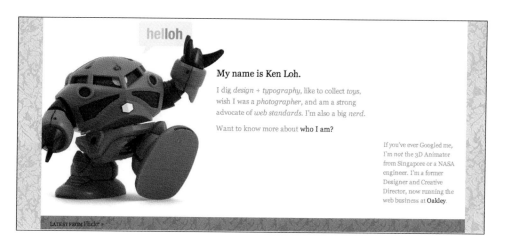

JOHNLOCKE

Featured Work	About	Contact
Design Blog	Hello. I'm currently completing the last semester of a Masters of Architecture program at Columbia University's GSAPP. Prior to that, I spent four years working with Randall Stout Architects in Los Angeles after graduating from the School of Architecture at the University of Texas in Austin. I also tackle freelance graphic and photography work with my partner in crime, the multi-talented Jackie Caradonio at Lion in Oil.	john.h.locke{at}gmail.com
Photography		310.735.3333
Graphic Design		CV (pdf)
Lion in Oil		Portfolio 2002-2007 (issuu)

GRACEFULSPOON.COM | KENLOH.COM

How you approach your bio depends on your career path and your portfolio site's purpose. Young architect John Locke offers a front-and-center solution to his biographical note. Nestled between his navigation and contact information, he provides immediate context. Ken Loh, on the other hand, has moved into management and uses his site to stay engaged and creative. He can afford to treat his bio more playfully.

your work. Although you can include light personal information in this text, unless you can tell your story succinctly it is probably better to let your work speak for itself first. If you really can't put yourself in context in three lines or less, it might be better to let the viewer select an "about" link should they decide that they want to get to know you.

Cover letters

When you send a portfolio or samples, you'll need a cover letter to accompany them. You'll also need to respond if someone sees your website or contacts you from some other connection. The fact that this response or accompanying note might be "just email" doesn't make it any less subject to issues like grammar and spelling.

Whether it will be tangible or virtual, you should compose as much of your cover or response text as possible in advance—a particularly important step if you are not comfortable with any writing beyond messaging and tweets. A cover letter should include a standard salutation, a short reference to who you are, why you are sending your material, and a reference to any intermediary who might have arranged for the connection. Don't forget to end with a thank you (in advance) for their interest in your work.

EXPLAINING YOUR CREATIVE THINKING

Your portfolio doesn't have to include a written commentary on your projects. Many artists and designers prefer to wait until they present their portfolio, particularly if they are more articulate in personal interviews. But some form of explanation can be a valuable asset in your portfolio.

WWW.CLOUDRAKER.COM
CloudRaker provides a concise and well-written description of their brief for client Buffalo David Bitton.

Buffalo David Bitton

The challenge?

With the launch of its 2007 Spring-Summer collection, Buffalo David Bitton set out to mark a new era in the jean fashion industry. Adopting a daring new London look steeped in punk chic, the company replaced the traditional red of the Buffalo David Bitton logo with black, white and silver. They turned to CloudRaker for the online campaign.

Creatives in different disciplines take a variety of approaches to commenting on work, and the areas do not adhere to the same standards. No fine artist has ever had their work rejected because of fuzzy thinking or typographic errors in his or her statement.

Design professionals, however, are at the opposite end of the spectrum. Although an eye-candy presentation can be sufficient for a potential client, when the audience is another design professional, it's another story. To fully appreciate the design, it helps to know something about the project and its challenges.

Providing a project description can also be useful in the growing discipline of game design, particularly in the area of serious games, which usually have a goal beyond sheer entertainment. Understanding the project's purpose, the project's medium (online, iPhone, Xbox, etc.), and, if relevant, clients' expectations, can be critical in determining the success of the observed gameplay.

Artist statement

One of the few exceptions to the "less is more" dictum for portfolios is for the portfolio fielded by a fine artist. Fine artists' statements generally speak about a recent body of work and its inspirations. It is a big plus to have a statement that is both personal and well written, but content is far more important than form.

> Copy is one of the many tools that can be effectively used to engage the viewer/consumer. We utilize it whenever possible to create the link between our client's message and their customer's needs.
>
> —Rick Braithwaite

Although you should still avoid obvious bloviation, there is some purpose to explaining your personal mission or artistic philosophy or to discussing the inspiration for a series of images you have created. If you have a long career or an impressive history of one-person shows, or you are creating your online portfolio or disc because you are applying for an academic position, it's actually a necessity to provide some type of statement. Most important is to make sure that your statement is clear, grammatical, and well proofread. If you have any doubts about your writing ability, enlist a friend you trust or find a partner to barter with to make sure you present yourself as articulate and clear.

Process comments

In disciplines where work evolves in stages, such as most areas of design, it can be enormously useful not only to show examples of your process, but to annotate your sketches with comments. What led you to your final color choices? What inspired the form for your product design? Here, as in most other writing, avoid duplicating in words information that a viewer can get by looking at the sketches themselves. Process comments can usually be treated like captions—short, direct phrases are good.

Design brief

Because design work is done in response to a set of requirements and constraints—usually called a design brief—it can be very useful to take the extended captioning one step further by including the brief, so the viewer can better understand the route you traveled. Design briefs can be minimal—a capsule overview of the client and their project—or they can be more complete explanations of the project and its criteria. Just remember that in a portfolio, "brief" is the operative term.

Case study

If you decide to share a full analysis of the design problem and its solution, you are writing a case study. Case studies should not be undertaken lightly, because they require good writing and analytical skills. Because they are usually at least a full page of text, you should give the viewer the choice to opt in. Put the case study in its own window or frame, or separate it out entirely from your main portfolio by making it a downloadable PDF.

Overview | Character Gallery | Screenshots

CLICK HERE TO PLAY THE DEMO OF GECKOMAN!

The Story: In "Geckoman!", a lab accident has shrunk Harold Biggums to the nanoscale and flung him to the ceiling of his new environment. His lab partner Nikki is trying to help him develop a device to reverse the shrinking effects, but in order to do so, she needs Harold to collect missing nanoparticles.

The problem, Harold soon discovers, is that he isn't alone on the ceiling. An alien race, the Nanoids, have been stealing Harold and Nikki's technology one nanoparticle at a time. Now it's Harold's job to stop them, using his newfound nanoscale powers!

Harold, now known as Geckoman, must steal back parts from the Nanoids, while preventing himself from gaining too much mass and falling off the ceiling. As he journeys through this strange new world, his lab partner, Nikki, helps him to better understand "real world" nanoscale forces.

The Science: Van der Waals forces involve the alignment of electrons in very small particles: the distribution of electrons within the object causes a slight positive charge to form.

Funded in part by National Science Foundation grant #EEC - 0425826

WWW.METAVERSALSTUDIOS.COM

Game designer Jay Laird and his team at Metaversal provide a thumbnail description of each game on the web page for its category, but link to a comprehensive case study, complete with plot, educational context, and detailed game play description.

Blog

For a person with a Renaissance mix of professional interests or an acknowledged gift for writing, the blog has become a value-added way to talk about ideas and process. However, because it comes with a different set of expectations from most portfolio text, it should be considered carefully before it becomes part of your portfolio mix.

There are two types of blogs, the personal and the professional. Under no circumstances should a blog of the first type ever find its way into your portfolio site. If you have one, keep it at a separate address whose title page does not make it so easy to Google that it will come up before your portfolio in a search. Or make it a part of your Facebook page that you only share with close friends or relatives.

As for a blog of the second type, think twice. Do people sit at your feet and hang on your every word? Do you turn down the opportunity to judge at award ceremonies because you're just too busy giving TED talks? I'm betting on "not yet."

If I'm right, you can still blog about your design philosophy and social observations, but separate the blog from your main portfolio in some way. It's very possible that people will read your writings and find them entertaining and intriguing. However, others may disagree with what you say or how you say it. Your work itself should be the primary medium where you demonstrate how you think and what you believe about your profession.

> Humor is one of the ways that we make people like us. In its simplest form, you smile at somebody; in its more complex form, you say something that makes a person laugh and enjoy the contact between two individuals. I think in a portfolio, it works exactly the same way. What you're trying to do in a portfolio is make a friend on the other side of the table, and humor is a wonderful way to do it.
> —Stan Richards

WRITING TO YOUR AUDIENCE

In Chapter 1, "Assessment and Adaptation," I emphasize how important it is to know who will be viewing your portfolio and what they'll be looking for. That guiding principle applies to writing your portfolio text. Whether you are writing to CEOs, small design studios, or to a highly focused niche audience, adapt your vocabulary and style as needed. Generational slang, pop culture references, and other elements that might make the text hard for your target audience to understand should be stripped away.

One of the easiest ways to check your tone is to hand your writing to someone who is similar to your audience. For example, if you're young, enlist a mentor or older relative. If you can't find the right reader, go in the other direction and read what your target audience writes. You don't have to imitate it, but you should be sensitive to the differences in tone and language. In particular, pay attention to how loose or formal the writing seems, and try to strike a similar level of formality in your own text.

Obviously, the more like your target audience you are, the easier it can be to write appropriate text, and the more of your true personality you can expose. But even if you are quite different from your audience, it can be an enormous plus to be able to project a little of yourself into your writing. Light humor (see the "Humor" sidebar), a friendly tone, or a brief anecdote about a project can all help to get the reader on your side.

HUMOR

Nothing is more valuable—or trickier—than adding humor to your portfolio. Humor can be a great leveler. When someone makes us laugh, we instinctively warm to them and often to their work.

Unless you are as good verbally as you are visually, the best way to add humor to a portfolio is to show it. A project that includes humor can be valuable in a portfolio filled with serious, restrained work. Don't grab just any funny project, though. Avoid any humor that relies on putting down others. You never know the sex, religion, age, or ethnicity of a potential employer or client. And gross-out humor is just as likely to alienate as amus

WWW.WIPVERNOOIJ.COM
Animation is often humorous, but you may not get the joke in the snippets that make up a reel. Vernooij displays his light side immediately in his interface. Click on the plate to reject the egg his "restaurant" offers, and the waiter brings you a new one.

WWW.CLOUDRAKER.COM

Montreal-based digital branding agency Cloudraker is unafraid to entertain as well as enlighten. The visitor who, through inattention or patience, stays on their site without interacting with it will be treated to the Sherpa guide's displays of impatience and occasional indiscreet scratching in tender places.

If you don't have any projects that allow you to show your clever side, you can add some playful elements to your interface. Your portfolio presentation is a perfect opportunity to let people peek behind the curtain and see what you can do without client constraints.

Most importantly, consider your audience. If you are primarily targeting small studios and other creatives, you can probably be a little looser than if you are attempting to speak to the corporate market. Until you are established and can afford to break the mold, humor in the business world is best left to personal encounters, not incorporated into your personal sales tool.

PORTFOLIO HIGHLIGHT:
SANDSTROM PARTNERS | GET YOUR WORDS' WORTH

WWW.SANDSTROMDESIGN.COM

One of today's portfolio rules is that prospective clients visit your website to see really big, shiny pictures of your work. Rules like that exist because they are mostly true. Oregon's Sandstrom Partners is a brand development company that for years has used its portfolio to reinforce its reputation for great copywriting and a killer sense of humor. A glossy gallery was never their main focus. How could they rise—or lower themselves—to this eye-candy challenge without defaulting to a site that looks and sounds just like everyone else's?

> We hope that prospective clients might realize that effective communication can be unpredictable, engaging, and bold.
>
> —Rick Braithwaite

The answer, it seems, is to have it both ways. Sandstrom's site is a beautiful and tasty piece of work, starting with its lush landing page. The words "our company" and "your company" trade places on a richly colored full screen. The background colors loop through a rainbow of shades that have been carefully selected to match saturation and to segue beautifully. It makes a commanding display of smart design in the service of great concepts.

A window-shopping prospective client can move on to verify Sandstrom's successful track record and see if it's the approach they need. Existing clients and fans will still find their dose of the amusing and unpredictable. Sandstrom's portfolio, like the company itself, is insidiously unique.

Navigation and architecture

Select the "your company" option, and you're presented with conversational navigation choices, not categories. If you are looking for options like "packaging" or "advertising," you won't find them here. Or you will, but not by expected names. Each choice presents a potential client scenario—some straightforward, like "needs an identity," and others, like "wants to talk to grown ups," tap shrewdly into emotional wants and needs. Sandstrom is leading you to their case studies through narrative.

Once you've made a selection, the navigation disappears. It's replaced by a frequently tongue-in-cheek description of a client's situation and Sandstrom's response, complete with a clear description of the results of their work—and sometimes a punch line. After you've read the introductory text, your only navigation option is "see the work," flashing onscreen. Yes, you could use the Back button, but who could resist the invitation? If you do resist, you can select the last menu option, "just needs some arty types to do whatever you tell them."

> Anytime that you do things differently, you can expect polarizing feedback. Some clients love it while others would prefer a site that is more conventional. You can't have it both ways, so we default to thought leadership.
>
> —Rick Braithwaite

Click on a headline and its drop-down menu appears in a rectangle that shifts color in sync with the main background. As you roll over the choices, they highlight in hues that interact to give the impression that they are also changing color—although in fact they are consistent throughout.

Sandstrom's navigation copy, like their site design, is sharp, clever and unexpected. Reading the options, you don't know exactly where they'll lead you, but the light humor of the approach encourages you to stay longer to find out. Even better, the savvy potential client gets the message that this firm can deliver visual and verbal excellence in equal measure.

FULL SAIL BREWING

Full Sail Brewing had an amazing product, a loyal following and (some would say) the best location of any brewery on the planet: Hood River, Oregon—the windsurfing and kite boarding capital of the world, just minutes from Mount Hood. The problem was that younger beer drinkers were gravitating toward imports. So we did the unthinkable: we told the truth about Full Sail. We decided to position them as an authentic, independent, employee-owned brewery located in the board sport epicenter of the universe. All of the new identity, packaging and brand elements reflected this authenticity. Result: better distribution and increased sales that messed with brewery production. (We should warn you that this is a problem we like to create.)

see the work

Well-crafted, client-centric case studies provide a window into Sandstrom's creative process. There is exactly the right amount of copy to make their point, while staying well within a visitor's attention threshold.

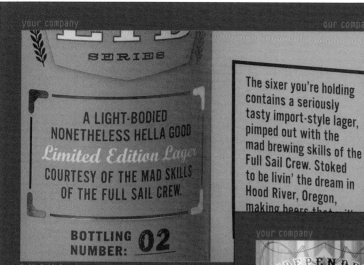

Shots of astutely chosen product artifacts emphasize Sandstrom's stated areas of expertise: sensitivity to color and color interactions, and a gleefully playful attitude toward product packaging. The copy communicates a distinct personality for Full Sail Brewing.

The Color of the Month page, like the Moment of Zen on *The Daily Show*, is a holdover from the beginnings of Sandstrom's web presence. It's another way that Sandstrom brings their copywriting and design strengths together.

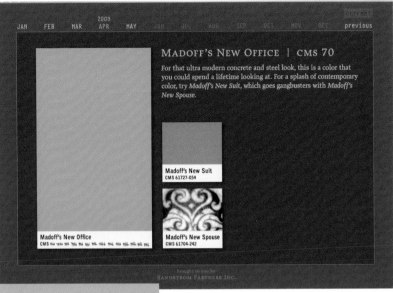

Sandstrom's interactive phone, probably the last place a prospective client will visit on the site, will leave an indelible and positive impression on a client who appreciates the company's style and approach to their work.

Have you explored their website and developed an irresistible impulse to join the Sandstrom cult? If so, research demands that you click the phone's "2" button, and discover what the firm looks for in a member of their creative team.

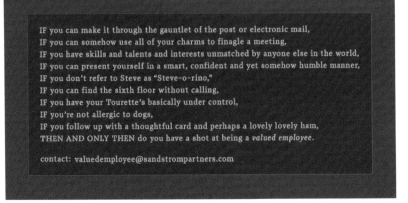

Our work has always been more about ideas than style, except when the style is the idea, or the idea is the style, or the style is the ideal style. Huh? What I really meant to say is that conceptual design, whether it includes copy or not, is far more interesting to us, and far more effective in the marketplace.

—Rick Braithwaite

Never has a company been so clear about the type of client they're *not* targeting. Their window closes, and the unsuspecting heathens find themselves at a "make your own logo" software site.

If you select the "our company" menu, you're presented with three options: a contact link, a client list that offers another entrance to the case studies, and "has a knack for color," which opens a new window: Color of the Month, one of the site's most popular features.

Content

Sandstrom serves up many portfolio images, accessed through the case studies. Collectively, they provide a complete feel for each project. The photos are beautifully shot and composed, and they are displayed at such high resolution that you can recognize typefaces and read package text without difficulty. There are also many close-ups of copy—in brand books, on the backs of wine bottles, in magazines—that highlight how all this company cleverness gets put to work for the clientele. Although not all of their client projects display their comedic gifts, they are unafraid to use humor—the disarming, slightly wacky, laugh-with-you style—when it is appropriate for their client's message.

And if you're already a client or have some extra time on your hands, there's the equivalent of a software Easter egg. Select the contact menu, and a very slickly programmed interactive phone offers a staff list. A tickertape display urges you to press buttons for contact and information, but in fact most of the buttons on the phone have text or sound messages attached. Press 3 for their internship program, and delightfully smarmy text ensures that anyone who applies gets a taste of the company culture. And finally, hover over the blue button. The people who bring you Color of the Month still have a marked card up their sleeves.

Future plans

As with previous versions of their site, Sandstrom keeps updating their content while keeping an eye on its continued relevance. They've had to redesign infrequently, as each iteration has been far enough ahead of its competition to give them some breathing space. Although Rich Braithwaite, who set the tone as president of Sandstrom, has handed the reigns to Jack Peterson, they are both satisfied with the current version. As they say, "There's a sense of discovery, from the navigational user interface through the writing. It's a unique experience."

From a business perspective, the new site has been great. The right people have visited the site and, seeing enough to gauge whether we would be appropriate for their project, have scheduled meetings.

—Rick Braithwaite

CHAPTER 9

Structure and Concept

You've brought all your work onto the computer and transferred it to an appropriate file format. You've written sparkling text. You know who you want to impress, and why. Now, finally, you want to get your work into a portfolio. Should you start creating a nav bar and laying out a page?

Not so fast. In order for your interface to be appropriate and effective—and not distract badly from your wonderful work—it needs a foundation. The foundation is the skeleton that your artwork relies on to stand up to scrutiny.

A portfolio foundation requires three things: an appropriate technology, a structure, and a consistent visual concept for your interface. You need to consider all three before you make a single decision about graphics or page content. All of these elements affect one another, and should be influenced in turn by your work.

The chapter begins by exploring the types of portfolio you can design, and how much technical knowledge each one requires. It connects concept and technology, and introduces the metaphor as a development tool. By the end of this chapter, you should understand the choices that will define your portfolio, and be ready to create a site map and start brainstorming your interface design.

CHOOSING A DELIVERY TECHNOLOGY

Technology has a big effect on design, particularly at the beginning, when you are looking at how much time your project will take and figuring out how to optimize your work. (See Chapter 7, "Repurposing and Optimizing.") It will certainly act as a constraint on your design decisions, perhaps making it difficult to implement some of them. So you'll need to understand the limitations before you allow your creativity to go wild. The following overview moves from least- to most-technically demanding.

> **Being able to bookmark pages is always super-important, especially if you're giving a recommendation to somebody. If it's a Flash site, there's no way to bookmark things and say, "I really thought this person was good because of this particular project."**
>
> **—Layla Keramat**

Everyone seems to approach digital portfolios thinking that theirs must be an interactive masterpiece. Unquestionably, a web developer must display both creative and technical knowledge, and many other design professionals are finding it advantageous to indicate their comfort with interactive technologies as well. But for people whose *métier* is more traditional, or whose portfolio will primarily be a DVD demo reel, too much technology and interaction can be the wrong move. In all cases, what's most important is to show your work in a favorable light. And indeed, no matter what technology level you're comfortable with, simple interactions are often best.

Instant portfolios

Instant portfolios are the "just add water" solution...with water, in this case, being images. They require no design decisions, just the ability to upload optimized pictures to a site. In most cases, the site provides step-by-step instructions on how to do this, and sometimes even offers a small desktop application to help you prepare and upload your files. Most social networking and group portfolio sites make it easy for you to turn your space into a gallery.

An instant portfolio can be a life-saving stopgap while you either find a partner or get comfortable with web design and production. And there is no reason to take it down once you do have a personal site, so the time you spend in the process of making an instant portfolio is never lost. In Chapter 4, "Delivery and Format," I go over the options and their pluses and minuses in detail.

Portfolio helpers

Your only design decision in an instant portfolio is curatorial. With a portfolio helper, you do have some control over the look of your site. The simplest portfolio helpers start with a selection of templates. These usually offer a limited choice in layout, but allow you to customize colors and fonts. Some go one step further and allow users who are comfortable with HTML coding to incorporate custom code and Cascading Style Sheets (CSS). If you take advantage of these options, you can quickly create a site that displays your aesthetics. Two good examples of these options are iWeb, a free application on the Mac, and Google's Blogger.

In both of these cases, the resulting portfolio website is housed as part of the service's URL. If you don't want viewers to have to drill down through a group site to get to your work, it's easy to use simple HTML code to insert this portfolio onto an otherwise blank web page at your preferred address.

Instead of using web tools for a disc portfolio, you can use software that creates slideshows. Web layout programs make it relatively easy to combine linear navigation with a simple uploaded player file. A video editor will also create a non-inter-

Blogger is not specifically a portfolio program, but its format and flexible tools allow you to pick a template off the shelf, or explore customization options that can make it a great way to provide a quick portfolio—and even get some useful feedback on your work.

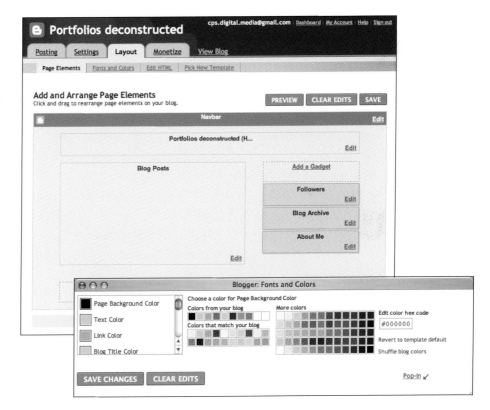

APPLICATION SOFTWARE

What software will you need to create a portfolio of your own, not just one on a group or social networking site?

At the very least, you'll need a portfolio helper like Apple's iWeb to create a simple static site. For more creative control, you'll want a web publishing program like Adobe Dreamweaver. To design an interactive, self-contained portfolio, you'll need Adobe Flash, or you'll have to be clever with coding in JavaScript, CSS, and HTML.

If you're making a CD or DVD portfolio, invest in software that creates *hybrid discs*—discs that are readable in both Mac OS X and in Windows. For a DVD, you'll need DVD-creation software to make your interactive DVD menu and link your work to it. On the Mac, that means iDVD (free with OS X) or DVD Studio Pro, which is part of Apple's Final Cut Studio suite. The premium versions of Windows Vista include Windows DVD Maker, Microsoft's version of iDVD. Prior to Vista, or for more options, seek out a third-party program. Roxio DVDit (www.roxio.com) has many good features, and is fairly simple to learn and use.

If your portfolio is a straightforward slideshow you have hundreds of options, but you should only use applications that create a self-contained file—one that doesn't require your viewer to own any software or to use a specific operating system. That's crucial if you will be sending out the slideshow on disc, or making it downloadable from your site. Anything that creates files readable by one (or both!) of the standard video players—QuickTime and Windows Media Player—will work fine. If you own Acrobat Pro, you can create an interactive file that can be viewed in Adobe Reader.

Presentation programs create slideshows, but they need the application to run. So if you want to put your slideshow on a disc or on your website, you'll need to convert the slideshow to a player. If you use PowerPoint, an inexpensive shareware program will do the trick. There is even one, Wondershare PPT2Flash Standard (www.sameshow.com), that will turn your slideshow into a Flash SWF file. If your program is Apple's Keynote, versions 8 and below will directly output to Flash. Unfortunately, this option was removed for Keynote 9, so you'll probably need a third-party solution as well.

active slideshow. You will only need to sequence the work, determine how long each image stays on the page, and (if the software supports it) select any transition effects.

If your forte is design but you know nothing about preparing work for the web, your ideal portfolio helper may be an InDesign or Illustrator file, exported or saved as a PDF. Print designers sometimes own a web address that's one page deep and functions solely as a staging space for a downloadable résumé, mailto address, and PDF.

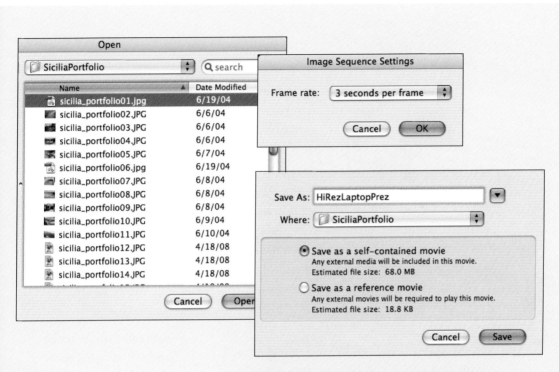

To make a simple slideshow using QuickTime Pro, name all your files sequentially (see the Bulk Renaming sidebar in Chapter 5, "Organizing Your Work."). Go to File > Open Image Sequence, select the first file, and set your frame rate. When you save the file, be sure to choose "Save as a self-contained movie."

Static page site

A *static website* is one that doesn't contain any interactive coding. That doesn't mean there's no navigation. A static page can have text links between pages, as well as links from thumbnails to larger, higher-quality images.

Static pages are one step up from a site created with a portfolio helper, because they give you more freedom to design, and you can scale them up as you learn more about web design and development. In fact, static pages that use CSS stylesheets can often be very visually sophisticated. The inspiring CSS Zen Garden

WWW.CSSZENGARDEN.COM
Each of these designs uses the same text and basic HTML code. The widely various interfaces are the product of using CSS to specify fonts, div blocks, and other web page elements.

(www.csszengarden.com) can give you a taste of what you can aspire to without heavy JavaScript or any Flash.

Simple motion or interaction

With a program like Dreamweaver, moving from a static page to one with simple interface interaction—rollovers, drop-down menus and the like—is a relatively small step. Good web layout programs write the JavaScript that runs basic interactivity for you. As a result, you can either design site navigation from scratch, or add interaction to a static website.

Complex movement and interaction

It is a big step to go from a simple layout to one that takes advantage of HTML's power. If you want a website that includes animated elements, plays video inside the page, uses unusual or customized navigation, or simply protects your code and images from being downloaded, you'll either have to master JavaScript, or use Adobe Flash. Mastering Flash is not trivial. It has recipes for frequently used interactive elements, but you'll still need to learn a little ActionScript (Flash's internal programming language). But if you're willing to put the work in, there is almost no limit to the things you can do once you've mastered Flash.

DEVELOPING FOR WEB OR PORTABLE

If you create your portfolio to work within a standard browser, you can maintain the same design and navigation for both a website and a portable portfolio version. Don't just copy one to the other, though. It doesn't make much sense to send a CD if you can send an email that points to your URL. Instead, take advantage of the many pluses of a disc portfolio (see Chapter 4) by adjusting your presentation to provide full-screen renditions of your video and animation, increase the size and quality of your still images, and provide extra material for personal presentations.

If you are dealing primarily—or exclusively—with video or animation, you'll probably have to separate the web and disc portfolios. Although your design concepts for the two should be related, the contents for each will be optimized differently, and may even run at a different aspect ratio.

THINKING ABOUT STRUCTURE

You will face technology decisions every day as you design and produce your portfolio. But once you gather your materials and whatever software you'll need, your focus should shift. If you are creating anything beyond an instant portfolio, you'll need to find the ideal way to sequence and group your work, and then the very best way to "wrap" it. As you'll see in Chapter 10, "Designing a Portfolio Interface," you should always start with grouping and arranging, because the way you create your categories can and should influence your design concept, which will in turn affect the look and feel of your site.

> We look for work that begins with an idea, is developed deeply and with a deft touch, and is presented simply and with honesty.
>
> —Rick Braithwaite

SELECTING A METAPHOR

A metaphor can be a useful way of thinking about your portfolio structure. A metaphors can be a powerful tool to help you visualize your digital portfolio—a hazy, virtual collection of megabytes—as a concrete form. It provides a framework for an appropriate organization and interface. A metaphor implies that your portfolio is organized in a certain way, and is like something we know in the real world. Once your site is up, it also helps to provide the visitor with a familiar frame of reference for your navigation and mapping decisions.

Designed by Janine Fron and Jack Ludden, Ellen Sandor's virtual photography site uses a gallery metaphor. Each major category of work (in this case, virtual architecture) has its own "room." The individual images are previewed from thumbnails running along the bottom, and can be selected for closer view. As with a museum or gallery in the real world, a short label identifies the work and its provenance.

(art)^n

contact
features
new work

The Jewel of the Mile II: The Wrigley Building Along the Chicago Riverwalk, 2008
credits

ellen sandor
Virtual Photography PHSColograms : Portfolio : Virtual Architecture :

Terminology for portfolio metaphors is neither standardized nor precise. At best, it's an attempt to focus the concept process. Even so, most portfolios do adhere to at least one of the following basic metaphorical concepts:

- Gallery
- Spec sheet/brochure
- Outreach
- Diary
- Narrative
- Experience

But it would be a mistake to believe that these are the only ways to think about structure. Nor is this list a suggestion that you exactly mimic a real-world format in an electronic one. Even if you could, you shouldn't. Doing so would not only artificially limit you to real-world constraints, it breeds a tendency to make your site boring and literal.

Gallery

The museum or gallery is a formal space where you come to see work. When you use this metaphor, you say, "This is my work. Draw your own conclusions."

Gallery sites can be as simple as one intimate room, or they may inhabit a number of differentiated spaces. Some explicitly mimic a museum space, with frames and captions, but there is no need to maintain any or all of these literal forms. Gallery sites are often linear, or linear within sections. In a gallery portfolio, the interface itself is very understated, to emphasize each image. Although it's possible to make a gallery site very rich and complex, it's not a requirement. A gallery portfolio is one that can be implemented with very little technical knowledge.

Spec sheet/brochure

Spec sheets and brochures provide business information. The brochure does so in generalities; the spec sheet provides functional details. In portfolio terms, this is a capabilities metaphor. When you use this metaphor, you say, "Here is what I can do."

The portfolio demonstrates, through work and through portfolio interface, your talents and specialties. It organizes material around work categories. Capabilities port-

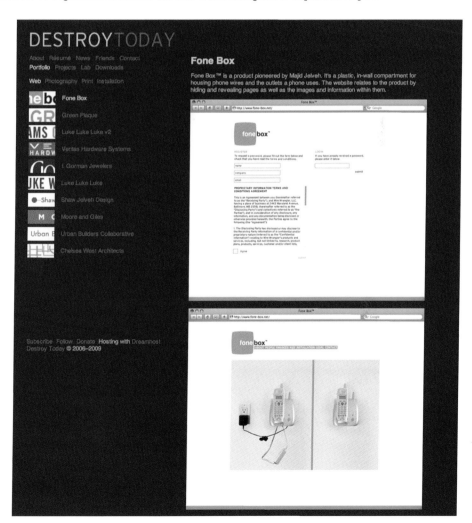

DESTROYTODAY.COM/V2
Ace programmer and web designer Jonnie Hallman emphasizes his capabilities. He has two connected sites: this one explicitly for his design work, and another for his programming projects.

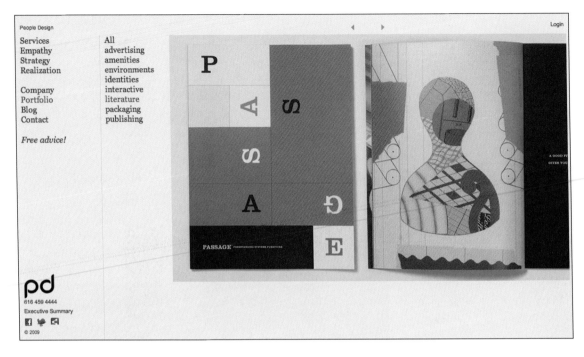

WWW.PEOPLEDESIGN.COM

People Design is very outreach focused. Their portfolio work is accessible in a variety of overlapping categories. They designed their site by asking two questions: "What do our prospective clients want from us?" and "What can we give them?"

folios are usually web-based, and at least minimally interactive. Visually, they often contain more than one way of looking at a project, highlighting details the way a spec sheet for a product might highlight its best features.

Outreach

An outreach portfolio is client-centric. It can superficially look like a capabilities portfolio, but it differs from the spec sheet concept by offering integrated services rather than skills. It says, "This is what I can do for *you*."

The client-centric portfolio is almost never sequential. Work is organized by relationships. The portfolio is usually distinguished by fairly complex navigational linking and overlapping categories of information. Client-centric portfolios reflect the target audience more than the portfolio maker, and they are frequently (though certainly not always) visually conservative and technically sophisticated. They make it as easy as possible for the viewer to navigate the space.

Diary

A diary portfolio is the opposite of an outreach metaphor. It often feels intensely personal, and may give the impression that it was created more for the portfolio maker than for any client or prospective employer. This format is good for an artist, a student, or for someone who wants to explore new ideas without necessarily waiting until a project comes around to pay for the time. These sites say, "This is my work and my work is me."

In one respect, diaries can end up being very effective marketing tools, because they can become capabilities-oriented without the formal, programmed feel. Diary portfolios are almost by definition web-based, because they require frequent

LIONINOIL.NET
Blog-based portfolios lend themselves most explicitly to the diary metaphor. They encourage experimentation and feedback, and are deliberately less permanent, more fluid work records, as John Locke and his partner Jackie Caradonio's diary-based portfolio blog attests.

updates. As a result, they require either a strong command of technology or a lot of free time. Because of their personal nature, they are often less hierarchical and more broad than other portfolios.

What do I look for in a portfolio? Good organization and, even more important, good storytelling.
—Michael Borofsky

Narrative

In a narrative portfolio, the portfolio tells a story through its sequence and organization. Narratives are not necessarily stories in the sense that they have a plot, but they do have a clear order. They may even have a formal beginning, middle, and end. A narrative portfolio says, "My work is about something specific."

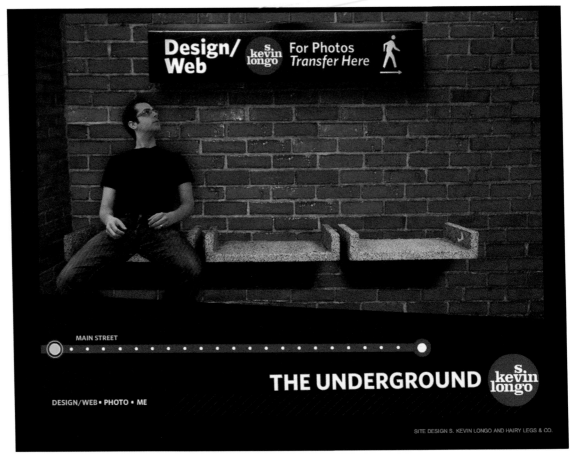

WWW.SKEVINLONGO.COM

Kevin Longo's subway metaphor provides a useful reason to engage his portfolio story in his preferred order, while still allowing random exploration. It provides an engaging beginning for a journey and ensures that his viewers will visit at least one or two "stops" along the way.

Narrative portfolios usually contain a few very carefully chosen works, because it's important that the viewer experience the entire portfolio for it to deliver its message. A large narrative portfolio only works if the narrative is contained in "chapters." These chapters, like case studies, can be experienced as individual modules. No particular format is required for a narrative portfolio, although Flash presentations lend themselves to this metaphor because they allow more control of page access.

Experience

Experience portfolios take you for a ride. They differ from diary portfolios by their emphasis on entertainment. These portfolios are almost always visually or technologically rich, and frequently are a humorous outlet for the portfolio maker. Always interactive, they say, "Play with me."

Although brilliantly memorable when handled with a sure hand, this is an extremely difficult portfolio metaphor to carry off successfully (see the section, "Concept versus style," below). It can just as easily put people off as suck them in. Experience portfolios sometimes have experimental interfaces and are often complicated to create. They lend themselves to Flash presentations.

> I think the worst thing is a site that works against you and becomes annoying. If I have to look for hidden corners to click and reveal a concealed menu that doesn't explain what and where I can find things, that browser window could get shut just as quickly as it was opened.
> —Layla Keramat

HOW YOU USE A METAPHOR

A metaphor can be applied literally ("Welcome to my gallery") or simply be a way to think about your portfolio site map. For example, a capabilities portfolio requires you to think about which of your projects best demonstrates your skills. Perhaps you'd highlight a project and show how you applied your knowledge through process sketches.

You are not limited to a single metaphor. These ideas are flexible enough that some can overlap. For example, large studios frequently combine the spec sheet with outreach. However, you should mix and match with care. Don't combine metaphors with radically different objectives. Outreach and diary simply don't mix, and will leave you ping-ponging between pleasing yourself and pleasing others—ultimately pleasing no one.

CONCEPT

A metaphor is also useful to start you thinking about your concept—and to keep you from mixing too many ideas. But it is only a starting point—the good bones that you flesh out with a concept. The concept is the visual way you express how you think about your work.

We first figured out the best way to present the work and then built a site around it. This sounds obvious, but my general impression from many sites is that the designers set out to build a website, rather than an online extension of their portfolio.

—David Heasty

A concept is much more than figuring out whether your buttons are green or blue. It is the reason you make that decision in the first place. At the very least, the design concept should not get in the way of the work. It is much better to create a very simple, barely noticeable interface design than to create an interface that overwhelms your projects. At best, the design concept should enhance your work, so the two engage in a pleasant visual conversation.

A good concept is easily identified by the fluid experience it offers. It works with your work, not against it. It emphasizes the things that you do best. It is consistent on all pages. Navigation is easy to find, and easy to figure out. On a site with a consistent concept, elements are related to each other visually and functionally. You should be able to tell the difference if you move from one designer's concept to another, and you should be able to recognize the look and feel of each concept when you return.

Concept versus style

Don't confuse concept with style. Concept is an idea that you apply consistently because it fits your work and your site's architecture. Style, on the other hand, is a collection of attributes that create a surface look. For most people, style is what's hot. If you find yourself thinking of your interface in terms of using a cool effect or type treatment you've seen in an annual, you're letting a style dictate your concept, not the other way around.

PUTTING IT ALL TOGETHER

It's not easy to develop a really brilliant portfolio design, but almost anyone can manage a decent one. Don't be afraid to look at portfolios by other people. In fact, look at as many as you can, so you won't be tempted to copy anything specific. Ask yourself what makes some of them really memorable and attractive to you. If you select a technology you can master, choose an organization scheme that fits your work, and design an interface that keeps the viewer interested and focused on what you do, the portfolio that results will be one you are proud of.

CLASSIC CONCEPT BLUNDERS

What can go wrong in a concept? Plenty. Here are some that even well-schooled designers occasionally fall into:

- **I'm too flashy for your job.** Avoid a portfolio interface that is so intricate, it feels like you've forgotten its purpose for existence—your projects. The more bells and whistles you have that don't connect to the work itself, the more impatient the viewer will become.

- **Hide and seek.** Lots of really interesting work is being done on experimental interfaces. Unless you are an interface god, don't experiment on your portfolio. Make your navigation easy to find. Why would you want to put barriers in the way of people seeing your work?

- **Low contrast.** Because of the difference between Macs and PCs, two colors that may seem quite different on a Mac may be perilously close to each other on a PC. Check your color combinations on different computers and monitors before you commit to them.

- **Glass ceiling.** All portfolio designs should be modular from the beginning—easy to update and replace. Don't design a site that cannot be changed without breaking the page. Before you finalize your concept, ask yourself, "What if I had to add three projects or a new category here?"

- **In-jokes.** Something may be very cool to a small number of people in the know, and totally pointless or even ugly to those who are not. Show anything you're not sure of to your mother (or someone like her).

- **Johnny one note.** In most cases, it's a mistake to make your portfolio look and feel exactly like a project in it, unless that project is a self-promotional piece. Besides the lack of variety, it implies that you are a creative wannabe.

- **It's all about sex.** Well, it isn't. Unless you want to work for porn sites, avoid suggestive comments or images in your concept. That doesn't mean that you need to eliminate all racy content, particularly if you are a game designer or animator. But the wrapper for such work is more appropriately brown paper.

PORTFOLIO HIGHLIGHT:
CLOUDRAKER | EXPERIENCED DESIGN

WWW.CLOUDRAKER.COM

There is no formula for an unforgettable portfolio. The only common denominators among portfolios whose tastes linger are that they display exciting work, and that the structure that wraps that work is implemented perfectly.

Many of these textbook-perfect sites are polished marketing tools or beautiful client-centric outreach. In the outer limits are those that use the structural metaphors of narrative or experience. Requiring good storytelling skills and an intensely personal style, they should not be attempted lightly. They require such a fine balance in order to avoid being so self-absorbed or functionally irritating that a single false step opens them to portfolio fail. Obviously, these professional high-wire acts are rare. Montreal-based CloudRaker has brilliantly executed one of them.

> **We founded CloudRaker on a simple but critical belief: We wanted to create a place that would make our kids envious — an agency that they would dream to work at one day.**
> **—Thane Calder**

CloudRaker set an ambitious goal for its current site. As Thane Calder, co-president, says, "Going forward, we wanted the site to position CloudRaker as a digital branding agency. We wanted the new website to reach potential clients and influencers. But, first and foremost, we—the CloudRaker team—had to love the site."

Simply meeting the online design standard of a sleek, clean interface would miss the mark. They needed to show their total command of the online experience—providing unique solutions that go beyond effective to memorable.

Navigation and architecture

Discussing navigation on the CloudRaker site requires several deep breaths. The site visit takes place in a snowy Canadian landscape. You use arrow keys to interact with the guide, a bearded, hygiene-challenged Sherpa who leads you around and up a forested mountain. Signposts that match the nav bar headings orient you as you travel.

CloudRaker offers multiple ways of navigating their site and all of its elements. There is an exploratory narrative for viewers with the time to accompany a Sherpa guide on a tour of the CloudRaker world. For those who can't linger, there's an easily accessible standard nav bar with links that jump to the main site topics. Have even less time? Select the HTML version of the site. No interactivity, but all the basic information is available in text form. Intrigued, but no time at all? Viewers can download the company PDF fact sheet and read at their leisure.

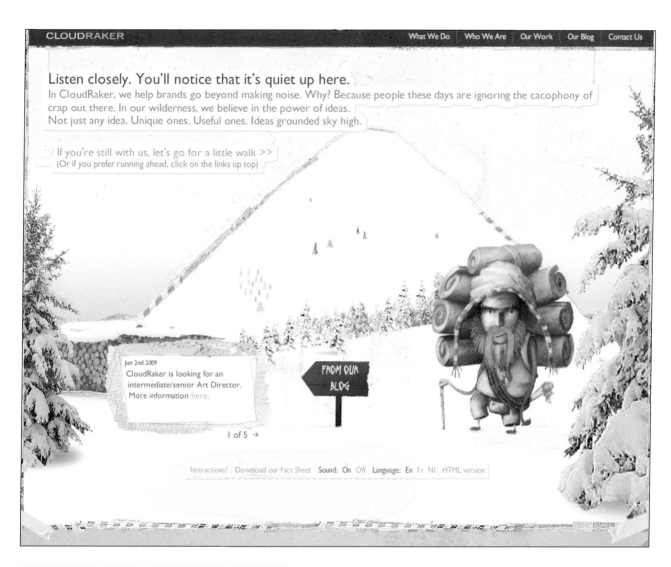

The CloudRaker splash page looks rich and potentially complicated, but in fact only the first of those impressions is true. Menu bars are in obvious places: the top of the screen and centered toward the bottom of the screen.

The animated navigation is intuitive, but doesn't force you to guess how it works. You can simply click on the Sherpa to prompt him to move, or, as the instructions helpfully suggest, you can have more control over him by using the arrow keys.

It's kind of like watching a movie for the second or third time; you inevitably notice details you had missed the first or second time.

—Thane Calder

The point is that CloudRaker thinks deeply about how visitors might need to navigate their site, and doesn't insist on the long way home. But those people who are seduced into exploring the Sherpa interface are amply rewarded.

In fact, the more time you spend on the site, the more tidbits you're likely to discover. For example, informational texts give new meaning to the phrase "drop-down menu." They literally fall from the sky and hang from wires. Resize the window, and the hanging signs respond, shaking back and forth as they slowly settle back into place.

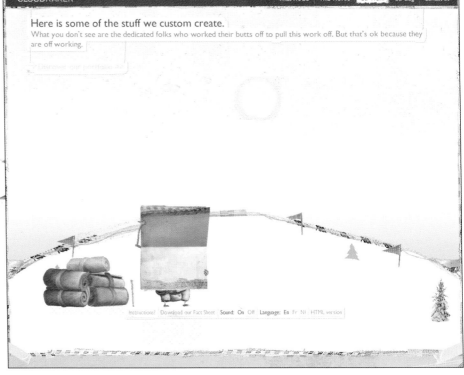

The Sherpa is a real personality, not just an animated cursor. He looks at you, interacts with the environment, and takes an active part in the portfolio presentation.

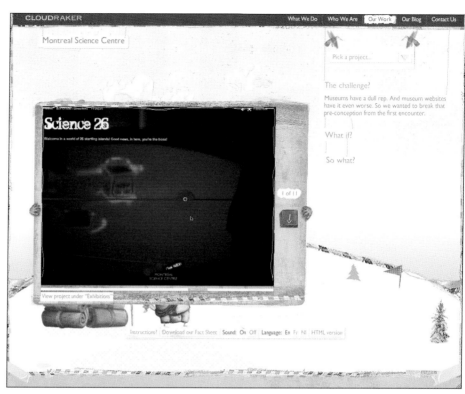

The project menu is held by two birds with frantically beating wings. Select a project and the menu closes. A case study drops from the sky on wires.

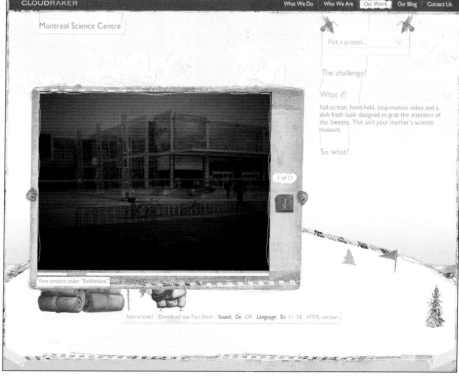

Select from three options—the challenge, what if and so what?—and the hanging text is hauled up. The selected paragraph opens and drops down to replace it.

Content

The entire site is a portfolio project, as well as a site to hold the company's portfolio. It demonstrates all aspects of CloudRaker's talents. The onsite text is compelling. The interface is fun to navigate, and the illustrated animation is engaging. Instead of a routine fast clickthrough, you tend to hang around. As a result, a visit to the CloudRaker site is a guilty pleasure that can easily fill up a lunch hour.

The goal of CloudRaker's portfolio was to show our work in motion; to make it a part of the site experience. Looking at multiple screenshots of a website is like looking at a piece of print advertising.

—Thane Calder

But the work is always the most important part of a presentation, and CloudRaker's portfolio section emphasizes creative solutions, variety, and technical mastery. Select a client project from the menu and the foldout display screen held by the Sherpa plays a video walkthrough of each site. The video is designed to show you highlights from the client site's navigation and decisions, not just static screen snaps. You might think that would obviate the need to see the site itself. However, one idle check on a client site shows you that the inventiveness that characterizes CloudRaker's site is put to good use for their clients as well. Although every client's web presence is unique in both branding and structure,

The site uses sound as well as it does sight. In this scene, the Sherpa intones each client service in an invented language, making the experience feel a bit like watching a movie with subtitles.

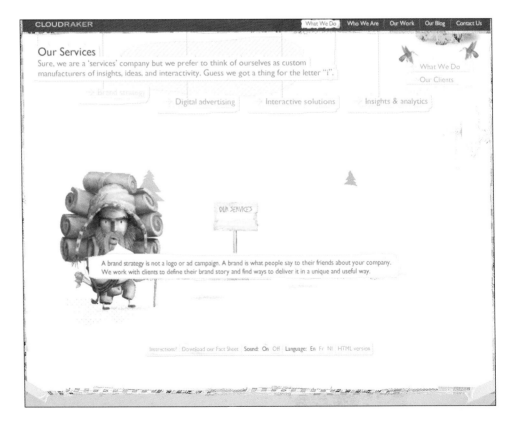

The text on signposts, on menus, and inside the "cave of beliefs," is delightfully clever and brief, occasionally dipping into vocabulary seldom seen in promotional copy.

all share a taste of the CloudRaker style: sleek, stylish, animated and smart. Each one is as much fun to experience as the CloudRaker site itself.

Future plans

The CloudRaker team is its own sharpest critic. They see elements of their site that can still be improved. Most likely they will change the presentation of their portfolio videos. As Calder says, "We've realized that our current presentation poses a challenge because the portfolio videos are set apart from the explanatory texts on the right-hand side. It's pretty hard to convey both at the same time because the user is focused on one or the other. We are looking to produce case studies in video where all the text is integrated to ensure that we can convey all the importance of the project in one unified story." Story is certainly what this expressive, experience-based site is all about, and its fans—inside and outside of the firm—look forward to its change and evolution.

CHAPTER 10

Designing a Portfolio Interface

Chapter 9 provided a conceptual framework for thinking about your interface and how it's organized. This chapter is all about process—what you need to know to move from concept to implementation on a portfolio interface. What follows is critical if you've never made an interface before—or have only done so by the seat of your pants.

Process can sound boring, especially when you think you have a brilliant idea for the way your interface should look. In fact, a good, honest process can be the reason a brilliant idea remains sparkling when it's finished. Without it, your interface can turn into an unattractive, haphazard, or frustrating experience.

Interface design is a specialized discipline that is still changing rapidly. Even seasoned graphic designers learn new skills and ways of thinking to master it. To build an exceptional interface, you must study user interaction, have a special talent for organizing data, and be a good visualizer. You must also know a lot about complex technology and adhere to many arcane rules so the largest possible audience can access your material.

Fortunately, your portfolio, having a very specific and limited purpose, requires a subset of interface design. You don't have to know everything to create an interface that won't frustrate your visitors or unknowingly cause you embarrassment.

THE SCREEN IS NOT A BOOK

One of the first things we learn about onscreen content is that each file or screen is a "page." That sounds like a book or magazine, doesn't it? There is only one tiny problem—it's a very inaccurate metaphor. Although both physical book pages and online pages contain text and image content, the way we experience that content is completely different in each medium. In fact, the same set of content, if presented onscreen in exactly the way it would be in a book, will frequently fail to deliver its message accurately and effectively.

What makes us pass on a portfolio when we see it? A clear lack of understanding of the digital world. You don't want to scratch your head and wonder if you're looking at a print or web portfolio.

—Thane Calder

The most important difference is obvious, yet it's the most frequent cause of badly designed portfolio interfaces. Except for references—like a dictionary or encyclopedia—you experience books sequentially. It is not possible to faithfully mimic that experience with digital content. If you design your interface the way you would a book, you will drive your audience berserk. We need different metaphors to think about a portfolio interface.

How is your digital portfolio "page" not a physical portfolio book page?

- **Multiple entryways.** Experiencing a physical book is like walking down a hallway. You start at one end, and finish at the other. Experiencing an interface is like walking into an atrium, with multiple doors around the walls, the floor, and the ceiling.

- **Linear versus dimensional thinking.** A book is meant to be experienced in a straight line. An interface is more like a deck of cards. You can pull out different pieces of information, randomly or with a purpose, and experience them in any order. In fact, you can jump back and forth from one deck of cards to completely different ones. As a result, the interface designer can never be sure what each visitor's experience with their work will be.

- **Visual control.** When you design a book, you control all decisions that affect the reader: order, legibility, style, texture, color, position, size. When you design an interface, there are many contingencies you can't control. You can't know your audience's monitor size, resolution, or brightness; their type of computer; or their browsers or plug-ins.

Some Flash sites are designed to make their windows automatically fill the screen. Unless the site is programmed to scale up when it does this, the result on an Apple Cinema Display or the like is to fill the browser window with whatever was placed in the background while the active portfolio section stays at its fixed size. The result: wasted space and an irritated viewer, who can't see anything else on his computer while the portfolio window is active.

To avoid this, set the window to open to the exact pixel dimensions of your design. Don't lock the screen, and provide the full-screen view as an opt-in choice.

INTERFACE DESIGN PROCESS

How do you design around the constraints of the digital medium? For your audience to see your work in the optimal way, you need to figure out the pathways through your work that will create a positive experience. Like many other stages in the portfolio design process, planning and organization are key. As we work through the stages of interface design below, remember that these steps are not separate from the design. They are as much part of it as layout and graphics are.

Modularity

Designing a good portfolio is such a major project that it's hard to contemplate doing it again. Eventually, you'll have to redesign, but it would be nice to put that day off for a little while and just update. Unfortunately, many portfolio sites that simply need updating don't get it, because doing so would be almost as much work as recreating the original.

To avoid finding yourself among the group of people whose portfolios are never current, try to approach every step of the interface design process with the word "module" at the top of your mind. It's particularly important to think of modules when designing a Flash site. If you are not yet an expert, you can fail to group interface elements together in timeline layers, or make one-off objects instead of creating reusable symbols. Your site may look great and run fine, but it's frozen—out of date before its time because you can't add a new link to your main nav bar.

PROCESS STAGES

Stages are modules as well. They break a long and complicated event into discrete pieces—maybe not bite-sized, but at least meal-sized. They are sequential, but they are also iterative. That means you may get through a couple of them, discover something you hadn't realized before, and have to return to an earlier stage and rework it. That may seem awful when it happens, but in fact it's a good thing and you should be glad you've caught the problem before you start production.

The interface design process can be summed up as four stages:

- Group
- Map
- Schematic
- Look and feel

These stages should be approached in order, because in good design the schematic layout and the look-and-feel design are dependent on your earlier decisions. It's impossible for a visual person to completely ignore visual considerations while working on the first two stages. (That's like being told not to think about pink elephants.) But self-control will save you time and much reworking later.

Group

Some people skip this stage, thereby dooming their design process. Their unhappy sites list every artifact—brochure, political poster, web banner, annual report—without organization, hierarchy, or criteria. Other sites have an inappropriate grouping scheme that seems selected by dartboard—alphabetical, for example. Or the main group types are mixed. Mixing creates a haphazard experience and makes it hard for people to see the work that's relevant to them.

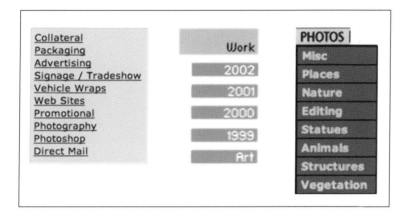

These examples of poor grouping choices have been pulled from online.

Moving left to right, the first mixes category and discipline (collateral and photography). The second mixes date with discipline, as well as automatically time stamping the website. The third equates image editing with photography topics.

But for every bad portfolio grouping scheme, there are many good alternatives. You might find yours by returning to the way you've organized your work after reading Chapter 5, "Organizing Your Work." If the way you've organized your archive feels natural, it might be the best choice for your portfolio interface.

If your archive's organization doesn't feel right for the work you'll use in the portfolio, here are a few grouping scheme ideas to get you started:

- Date/employment history

- Discipline/area (design, illustration, photo)

- Category (collateral, packaging, editorial)

- Technology (print, interactive, moving image)

- Medium (traditional, computer, 2D, 3D)

- Process (sketches, modeling, character animation)

- Client

- Client industry/market

- Difficulty/size of project

- Visual interest

WWW.SANDSTROMDESIGN.COM

Sandstrom has a very creative grouping scheme. From the "our company" nav bar, you can reach a traditional client list that indicates case studies. From the "your company" nav bar, you'll find case studies organized around client challenges.

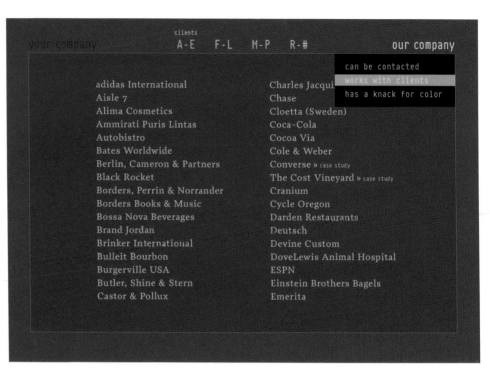

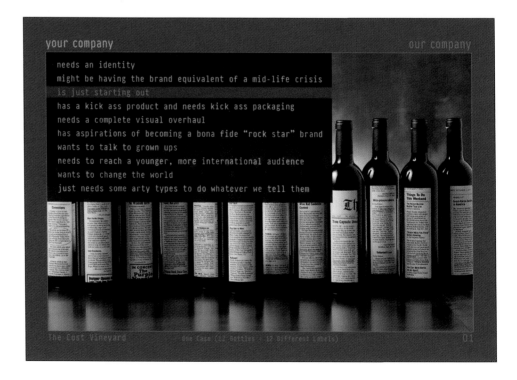

Look at the work you've chosen through each of these filters to see where it fits. Or find your own. The way you think about your work, the type of work it is, and the audience you are targeting are all considerations that should drive your grouping scheme. If you can't come to a decision easily, make a spreadsheet with the name of the project along the left and each possible category at the top. Put checks next to a project when it fits a possible category.

Examine the spreadsheet for patterns. Is there a cluster of checks under one category and very few in others? If so, those categories are bad ones to use. The thin ones will telegraph that you don't have enough experience. The fat ones are fat because you have not yet found a grouping scheme that is sufficiently granular.

You may look at these groups and discover that you could organize your portfolio equally well in more than one way. That's wonderful! It means you can offer alternative paths for people to experience your work. Just remember to provide distinctly different ways of navigating to match the different types of grouping. Perhaps you'll have a main nav bar with technology types, but also have a client list that allows people to see how you worked with the same client in multiple media.

Not categorizing your projects or having too many categories can be frustrating. People shouldn't have to guess which category to choose.
—Layla Keramat

Projects	Logos	Branding	Posters	Pub Design	Web	Ads
MMS expo			2		1	
Gordon	1	1	3			1
LOHP	1				2	
DCFG			1			
Brain Trust				1		
LDBC	1					1
Left Bank	1	1				1
Thayer			1			
Sager	1	1				
Rockport Homes	1	1			1	1
RGD movie series			4			
Italian designs					1	
Attrillo					1	1
DM					1	5

This spreadsheet shows a pattern. This designer is strong in web projects, advertisements and posters. There is only one entry under publication design, but if it was an important project, the categories will have to shift to include it. This person might want three categories: identity, print, and web.

Map

Once you have groups, you're ready to impose a hierarchy on them. Will you go directly from the home page to your work, or will you have a second level of pages for each group? Will all the work in a group be equally available, or will you want people to see some pieces in a specific sequence? These are big decisions. That's why you need a *site map*.

A site map is a flowchart representing every page in your portfolio. This chart will enable you to recognize links within your pages, and links out to other sites. It will also help you to organize your ideas logically, so visitors to your site won't feel lost as they explore it.

A good site map shows three things at a glance:

- **Grouping:** How you've broken out your work.

- **Hierarchy:** Where each page fits within the site.

- **Connections:** What links to and from each page.

There is no standard form for this chart, although you'll find a flowchart in this chapter's Portfolio Highlight on page 221 that will help you get started. A small site can start as a sketch on paper or Post-its, and then become an Illustrator file as it solidifies. Flow-charting software can make the process easier, particularly if you anticipate a complex site. On Mac OS X, I can recommend OmniGraffle (www.omni-group.com), an inexpensive and fun tool. Many Windows users work with Microsoft Visio (office.microsoft.com), which is comprehensive but expensive if you don't plan on doing many maps. On either platform, the best free selection is VUE (vue.tufts.edu), an excellent open source option.

No matter what physical form your site map takes, make sure that you leave enough room on it to insert items. You may discover as you work that you need to move things around, or add a major project that develops while you're still designing your portfolio.

What will your chart contain? A home page, of course, and perhaps an opening page for each group. Every group should branch from one of these types of pages. Remember to account for single pages that aren't part of your work groupings.

After you've accounted for every page, move them around to make sure that you've got their hierarchy correct. Pages that are only accessible from a main page should be drawn beneath that page. With your pages in position, draw lines to document your planned links. Remember to consider outside links too. For example, if you have a link to a client's site or a secondary portfolio site like Flickr or Behance, document that.

> People often forget the importance of persistent elements. A friend of mine was showing me his site. After the home page, there was no link to email him.
>
> —Layla Keramat

If you have embedded any video or animations on your site, they qualify as links as well. You'll also want to provide links to any plug-ins they require, and consider how people will see them. Will you open a new window for your clips? Will they play in a frame inside your portfolio window? Will you provide a download link to a high-resolution version?

Keep your chart on or near your computer, so you'll be able to name your actual files and directories to match your documentation. Don't rename files or move them. If you do, you'll break the links you've made to them. Troubleshooting broken links is frustrating, and avoidable.

Schematic

You'll have a feeling of accomplishment after you have a completed site map. Seeing the bones of your portfolio will make it feel more real. Next, step down one level and do the same kind of planning for your pages by creating a schematic.

A *schematic* is basically a page layout grid. You create one for each level of your site map hierarchy. On it, you determine where you'll place repeating material, different types of navigation, and variable content. When you prepare your schematic, you'll begin to visualize the following decisions:

CHOOSE A PAGE SIZE

How big should your web page be? Consider your target audience. Will you be showing your work on a laptop, where the screen will be smaller than most desktops? If so, design conservatively, keeping your window small. It is better to allow a viewer to enlarge a window than to force a person with a smaller screen to constantly scroll back and forth, either vertically or horizontally.

Many people currently specify a portfolio screen size to fit 1024x768. This dimension will inevitably increase with technology. But no matter what size becomes the norm, you don't have the entire screen to play with in your design. All those pesky icons and taskbars at the top and bottom of the browser window decrease the active area—sometimes considerably. To be safe, use a maximum that's at least 60x60 pixels smaller than your target screen size. That margin will leave enough wiggle room for browser variation, and allow someone working with smaller displays to still click on the desktop if they need to.

OUTLINE A GRID

Some people deal with varying content by creating radically different page layouts for it. That's a mistake. When you carry a traditional portfolio, you arrange everything so it fits in the case, upsizing the case or downsizing the artwork. You use the same type of matte board for mounting, and you use the same rules for positioning work on your boards or in sleeves.

WWW.PEOPLEDESIGN.COM

Looked at as a group of pages, you can see how People Design approached their page grid. Each page is designed to the same proportion, although the content of each page determines how much of the page fills up vertically.

The farthest-left column is the main navigation. It is always in the same position and fills the same width on every page.

All other pages have an underlying grid made up of many small columns. It allows for flexibllity—not everything is exactly the same width on each page, because different types of content need different amounts of space.

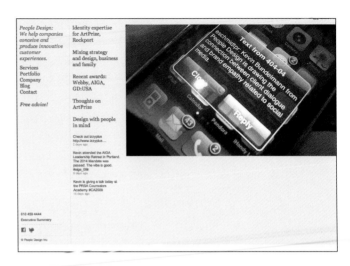

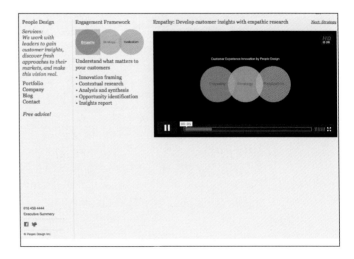

You present a better impression if your page architecture is equally consistent. Every page should be the same size, with all major elements in exactly the same place on the page. If your page will scroll vertically, the width of the layout should not vary. If your page will scroll horizontally, the depth should be locked instead. Every page's content should reflect an underlying grid. Images should appear in the same area, even if their dimensions vary.

After you have dimensions in mind, divide the page into equal-sized columns. Use these columns to help you position your elements, and to make sure that they all line up. Use combinations of these columns to help you determine how much space to allow for each type of thing.

LAYOUT FOLLOWS CONTENT

A portfolio site usually contains three types of material: unique page content (images, captions, explanatory text), navigation (links to main groups, secondary navigation to get you around inside a group), and global information (branding, contact info). Your portfolio might also include tutorials, news, a section for experimental work, or a portfolio highlight. You'll want to account for all of it.

When you actually start to design, use real content instead of *greeking* (gibberish placeholder text). Find your largest image, your longest caption, your deepest description. Draw outline boxes representing the image dimensions and the approximate text block sizes.

LINKING DECISIONS

Before you can lay out your navigation, return to your grouping decisions. If you were able to see a method of grouping your work in more than one way, your navigation and linking will be affected. In most cases, you can't combine the two groupings in the same nav bar area. Maybe one version should be reflected in your main nav bar and the other available as links from a separate page.

Make it easy to back up a level in your hierarchy, and jump between branches. Visitors shouldn't have to hit their browser's Back button to return to the beginning of a section.

NAVIGATION MENU LAYOUT

Use the same strategy for planning your navigation space as you do for your content. Account for all navigation levels so they won't extend into the portfolio content. Roughly sketch out how your navigation will be arranged when it's at its most expanded state. Try both vertical and horizontal orientations. You'll discover that one will probably work better than the other.

THINKING ABOUT TYPE

If you've had some formal design training, you know that typography is an important element. In fact, many people think it is the single most important factor for how they judge a design portfolio. Although non-design portfolios don't have to meet as rigorous a standard, truly bad type usage can reflect poorly on good illustration and art.

Here are a few suggestions tailored to the needs of a portfolio interface. These suggestions are no substitute for true knowledge, but they will keep you from making the most obvious typographic mistakes:

1. **Legibility is everything.** If you can't read the information, you might as well not put it in. Type is not necessarily more legible when it's bigger. If the font you've chosen seems hard to read, change the typeface before you upsize it.

2. **Use Cascading Style Sheets (CSS).** No matter what your text design, style sheets will keep your decisions consistent. If you define your type with pixels, not point sizes, you will gain the most consistent type size across platforms and browsers.

3. **Audience age matters.** Type can be slightly smaller for young eyes, but should be slightly larger for older ones.

4. **Don't type in all capital letters.** That goes for headlines, too. Unless you space them properly, words in all caps are hard to read.

5. **Avoid horsy type.** Most people make headlines too big, and then end up with text that's also too large. Really bold and large type doesn't communicate—it screams.

6. **The smaller your typeface, the narrower the column.** Don't run captions the full length of your window. Specify an area for text in a web layout program, and use the HTML tag ‹blockquote› to limit your line widths. For short caption text, break lines manually.

7. **Don't center headlines. Ever.**

8. **Avoid Times Roman.** It was designed for newspapers, not computer screens. If you need a serif typeface, try Georgia.

9. **Don't use italic, at any size.** Because of the way a computer monitor displays, italic fonts can break up or get jagged in a browser. You must be very familiar with different typefaces to select an italic that will display well onscreen, and it's better to avoid the problem all together if you don't have that knowledge.

Interested in knowing more about type? You'll find that *Stop Stealing Sheep & Find Out How Type Works*, by Erik Spiekermann, is a very good, and very visual, introduction.

Look and feel

By considering your content and creating quick sketches of your page and its elements, you've started designing the look and feel of your portfolio. Your sketches should suggest the size of your navigation elements and their placement. Now you have to think about what style or theme you'll use, as well as how people will interact with your design decisions.

Even if you are using the wrapper as a portfolio project, it shouldn't be fighting with your other work for attention. That doesn't mean that your interface can't be visually arresting. It means that it should be appropriate to who you are, who your audience is, and what your work is about.

AVOID DISTRACTIONS

Once you concentrate on your look and feel, it's easy to forget the rigorous way you've approached your process and give way to well-known portfolio excesses. If you adhere to your basic schematics, the portfolio will still function. But you want a portfolio that is both functional and visually satisfying. In order to ensure this: remember to KISS.

KISS stands for Keep It Simple, Seriously. Simplicity is the most important virtue in portfolio design. You'll find it easier to create a clean and simple interface by keeping these guidelines in mind:

- **Look for a design idea that will be easy to create.** If you will have to spend hours making your navigation elements, they are probably too eye-catching for a portfolio.

- **Keep animated actions small and discreet.** Even better, limit your actions to ones that happen when a mouse rolls over a button. There is nothing more distracting than buttons that flash or change color or shape when a visitor hasn't done anything to activate them.

- **Limit your color palette.** Especially if you don't have a lot of experience in design, select two colors plus black and white. Make all your interface elements variations of one color. (Start with the pure color at rest, make a brighter version on rollover, and a darker version when you click.)

- **Don't fight with your artwork.** It's the reason you're making a portfolio, isn't it? Keep it the focus of each page.

- **Think twice about your background.** A good designer can integrate a subtle texture or photograph into their presentation beautifully, but there are more wrong ways to do this than right. Do it wrong, and your background, not your work, becomes the main event. If you're new to interface design, and

Portugal photos: 1 2 3   5 6 7

Praca da Vao, commissioned for Nuevas Portugal magazine, 2002

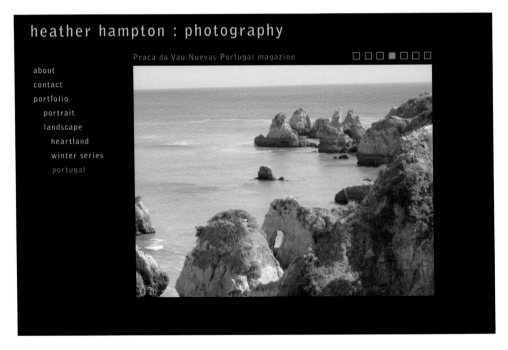

Here are two versions of a portfolio page. They contain exactly the same amount of material, but the first one feels cramped and busy, while the second one is more spacious. In the second, you can focus on the art.

particularly if you've had little or no formal design training, stick with a solid color, preferably black or white.

- **Don't fill up the page.** For a portfolio, you almost can't have too much white space. You can have too much stuff on a page, however.

- **Limit your page size.** A portfolio viewer should never have to scroll to see artwork. Use a horizontal format (they're easier to control) and keep your page size consistent.

- **Arrange your navigation in groups.** Keep all your navigation together. Put any captions and other text all together in one place. Always show your work in the same place on the page.

MOVING TO PRODUCTION

After you've finished your design, you're ready to create your website, CD, or DVD. Although production will take time, it will fly by compared with the hours you've spent in preparation to this point.

Because there is no one right application to build your portfolio, and every application handles the process differently, it makes more sense for you to reference a good hands-on, step-by-step book for this next stage. In Appendix A, you'll find resources covering each of the major software methods of producing your portfolio.

PORTFOLIO HIGHLIGHT:
LAYLA KERAMAT | THE MASTER PLAN

WWW.LAYLAKERAMAT.COM

Like most good work, effective portfolios exist as a fait accompli. You can only imagine how they got that way. The most fascinating and difficult aspects of the interface design process are hidden from view. Wouldn't it be exciting to sit on the shoulder of a master as she steps through her thinking about design development, organization, and process? It would indeed, and it might even influence your own ideas. Layla Keramat offers us a window into her process.

Why create a portfolio now? To get short-listed on a recruiter's search. To show hiring managers that I'm qualified for an interview. To share my experiences.

—Layla Keramat

Keramat is an interaction and corporate designer who has worked for and with some of the biggest brands worldwide. And she has a potential problem to solve with her portfolio. Although she has an enormous body of work, in a world where everyone expects to find a neat package online, she can't share. Most of her best projects were done under rigorous client agreements. She can present a digital portfolio on her laptop, but it would violate copyright and contract to distribute it online.

So how does she approach the conundrum? We follow her thinking as she creates the map for a comprehensive laptop presentation, with a unique grouping approach. Then she isolates aspects of that presentation to create "tastes" for her specific audiences. Last, she uses the power of connectivity to build an online personality that enhances the tastes. The result: a comprehensive development process that meets her unusual needs.

Content

Organizing a mature and diverse body of work is a mixed blessing. There are so many ways to group this work. Keramat could group by category of project: user interface design, e-commerce, packaging, or concept. Or she could separate the work into print versus interaction. Yet as her work changed over time, she kept coming back to simple chronology.

The more she tried different options, the more Keramat began to notice that she had made a major change in how she approached design. In her opinion, it was so striking that it was a better way to group her work than brand or chronology. Her intensely personal way of grouping her early work is by intuition—emotion, enthusiasm, gut feeling—and her more recent

My first ten years were driven by intuition. I still subscribe to that enthusiasm, and I want to preserve that impression. But I also enjoy understanding a client's corporate communication needs. I realized that I could categorize these two features in my portfolio as "designed by intuition" and "designed by process."

—Layla Keramat

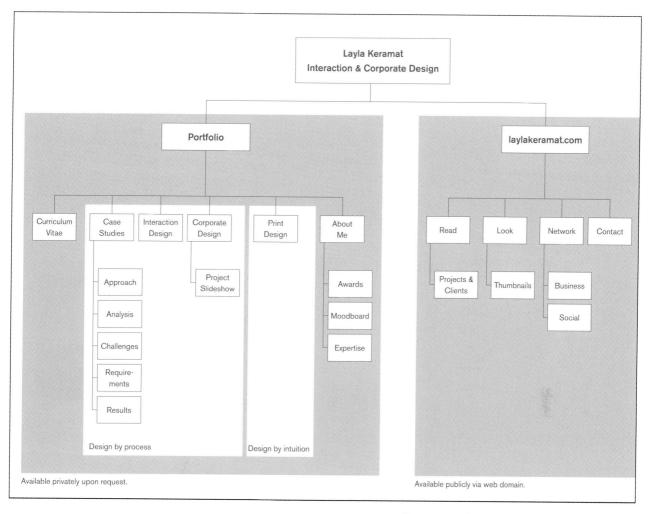

Layla Keramat
Interaction & Corporate Design

Portfolio

laylakeramat.com

Curriculum Vitae

Case Studies

Interaction Design

Corporate Design

Print Design

About Me

Approach

Analysis

Challenges

Require-ments

Results

Project Slideshow

Awards

Moodboard

Expertise

Design by process

Design by intuition

Available privately upon request.

Read

Look

Network

Contact

Projects & Clients

Thumbnails

Business

Social

Available publicly via web domain.

Keramat needs two related portfolios, but each needs a different grouping and map, since their goal and audience are not the same.

Her main laptop portfolio, on the left, is grouped by intuition and process, with a case study to indicate how an idea by process develops. Her web portfolio, on the right, is organized by action. Its content, and by necessity that content's presentation, will have to be radically different.

work by process—a holistic methodology of designing not just for a single project, but with the total brand personality in mind.

Having determined the main way to organize her work, Keramat moved forward with her Keynote laptop presentation. Fortunately, her process and documentation made it easy to compile and sequence the work. She based her overall design on the elegant hand-bound physical portfolio, with her signature silver ink, that she had presented with for years.

But unlike its predecessor, the laptop portfolio is a living work, and a tribute to modularity. Each time she presents it, she customizes the presentation to the audi-

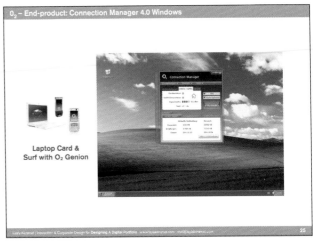

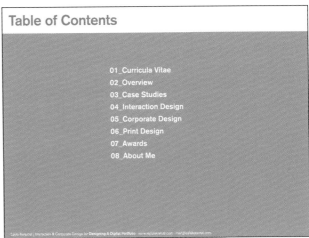

Keramat's portfolio presentation has no long bullet lists. She shows her images in their full glory and walks her audience through each of the slide builds with her narration.

ence. Some are more interested in her packaging, others in the transaction websites, others in seeing a balance. As Keramat says, "Your pages must be practical, easy to update or add. I shift my focus from case to case. I change my Keynote presentation every time—no one ever gets it all."

Her scheme also works for a critical version of the laptop portfolio. Each time a recruiter or corporate hiring manager asks for a taste of her portfolio to show around before her presentation, she sends an 11-page PDF with a cover page identifying it as "Extracts" from the portfolio. She wants to whet their appetite, not steal the show from herself.

Navigation and architecture

The online portfolio is the latest addition to Keramat's arsenal. Although everything she designs has elements of her two grouping themes, they are not an explicit element online. This is not an omission. It is a smart acknowledgement that the online portfolio has a different purpose.

Since she can't show most of it there, her work itself doesn't affect the navigation directly. Instead, her site content is organized under four active verbs: read, look, network, and contact. Read provides highlights from her career: awards, client list, working process. Look provides a peephole tease of her work while identifying its scope and breadth—everything from the formality of stocks to entertainment packaging in leopard skin. Network connects her site, and interested visitors, to her assertive footprint in the virtual world. Contact is a straightforward mailto address.

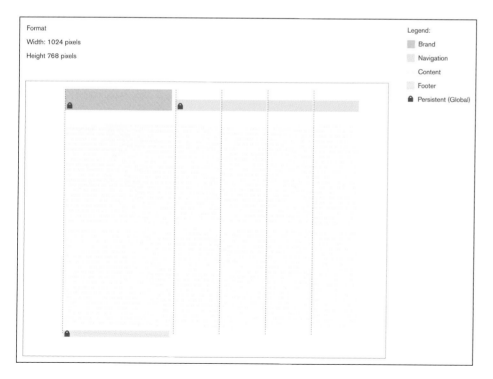

Format
Width: 1024 pixels
Height 768 pixels

Legend:
Brand
Navigation
Content
Footer
🔒 Persistent (Global)

This grid is the schematic for different types of site pages. Information is color coded. Besides the content itself, in yellow, navigation areas are in green, while persistent elements—name, contact info, and footer—are globals that will appear unchanged on each page.

Layla Keramat
Interaction & Corporate Design   Read   Look   Network   Contact

Whether you are interested in
connecting with me for business
or keeping an eye on my digital
footprint, you can connect with
me on any of these networks.
Or write me directly **via email**.

Business: Social:

LinkedIn   Digg
Xing   Flickr

www.flickr.com

Facebook
Plaxo
Last.fm
Twitter
YouTube

© Layla Keramat | Interaction & Corporate Design

Layla Keramat
Interaction & Corporate Design   Read   Look   Network   Contact

Welcome and thank you for visiting my website.

You can get a quick **read** of my professional history here,
look at an overview of thumbnails from my visual vocabulary,
or **connect** with me through various social networks.

If you are interested in viewing my portfolio, please **contact** me directly
for individual case studies or a personal presentation where I can give
you insight on projects and user experiences beyond graphical interface
and brand appearance.

I look forward to exploring new creative opportunities with you.

© Layla Keramat | Interaction & Corporate Design

Layla Keramat
Interaction & Corporate Design   Read   Look

Tireless curiosity has proven to
stimulate my mind. Ideas rotate
around brand, business and
user needs. I challenge my own
intuition with process, strategy
with appearance, innovation
with usability and emotion with
rationale.

I focus on delivering creative solutions for
the user that are empathetic, charming to
experience and simple to grasp despite
complex demands.

Designing for more than twenty years, I
have worked equally both client-side at
global corporations as well as at
renowned design consultancies based in
New York, Frankfurt, Amsterdam, Berlin
and Zurich.

Employment: Adjunct Professor:

Sony Music   School of Visual Arts
frogdesign
BlueMars
TimeWarner/
Sony CHC
MetaDesign
Blast Radius

Recent brands: Recent awards:

Aura Science   World Summit Award (WSA) 2007 e-Culture
Barnes & Noble   Design Preis der Bundesrepublik Deutschland
Best Western   2006, Nominee
Deutsche Telekom   IF Communication 2006
(T-Online)   Deutscher Design Club 2006
Cyworld Europe   One Show Interactive, 2006
Hessischer Rundfunk   Annual Multimedia Award 2006
General Electric   Grimme Award, Nominee
Maytag   Deutscher Multimedia-Award 2006
Nextel   Eurocreative 2005 Bronze Award
O2   New York, Festivals 2006
Nissan   WebAward 2006, Outstanding Website USA
Sony Electronics   Internationaler Medien Preis 2006
Thomson Financial   Eyes & Ears of Europe 2006
Vodafone   MKN-Awards 2006

© Layla Keramat | Interaction & Corporate Design

Keramat's layout tightly follows her
schematic. The bright orange text for
links adds visual interest and lends a
less formal touch to the pages.

Mouse over a thumbnail and its border expands to show the rest of the image, identified by type of project and client. In this way, Keramat maintains her client confidentiality and contractual obligations, while giving a hint at her broad range and high-level experience in brand devlopment.

Future plans

Keramat will maintain the look and feel she has developed for her overall package. It has become a personal brand that she can use to balance her client-focused body of work. She will keep her laptop presentation updated to spin off her customized PDF extracts for the hiring managers, recruiters, and clients who are teased by her online presence. By keeping her virtual presence active and pointing her networking tools at her online portfolio site, she will continue to generate interest in her work.

CHAPTER 11

Portfolio Reels

The demo reel holds a special place in the portfolio pantheon. It can be both content for a portfolio or stand on its own as the portfolio.

In either case, the reel is an object whose form, format, and rules of play are very different from that of the normal web or disc-based portfolio.

The exact purpose of your reel—content, audience, artistic specialization—affects its guidelines for planning and development. A reel for an animator interested in game development will probably contain different content than one interested in 3D modeling and lighting for feature films. And the reel of any animator or game artist will be different from that of a game developer, and radically different from that of a video or film editor or director.

Although the specifics for each artistic discipline can trip you up if you aren't aware of them, there are many guidelines for designing and developing that all reels share. In this chapter, I explore what makes a good portfolio demo reel, how to tweak reel basics for your own type of content, and how to avoid the things that guarantee your reel a home in the circular file.

REEL POSSIBILITIES

Unlike other portfolio artifacts, the reel is sequential, just like the tape reel (and then the VHS cassette) from which it takes its name. A viewer might fast forward, but usually won't skip back and forth. The linear format offers much more opportunity for control—and showmanship—than other digital portfolio forms.

The reel format can also be the proverbial rope long enough to hang its maker. The standard of excellence has risen steeply with the move of the portfolio reel to a digital format. If the reel presentation is just adequate, it will devalue all but the most extraordinary work because it will be up against reels that actively support their individual project clips.

The single most important thing to remember as you build it is that the demo reel is not just a nice collection of clips. It is an exercise in personal branding. Here's where your soul-searching from Chapter 1, "Assessment and Adaptation," must pay off.

YOUR REEL AND THE MARKET

A trained graphic designer may specialize in corporate identity, but can express that specialization in more than one medium, as great portfolios containing both print and online projects prove. But in the moving image professions, there is much more granular skill specialization.

Particularly when it comes to animation and gaming, technology has taken what was already a highly-segmented set of jobs and sliced them even thinner into hundreds of niche production jobs. If you're a 3D animator, you'll first be confronted with a selection of major job categories: character animator, modeler, compositor. From there, you may have to parse finer, into some combination like 3D modeling and lighting, or lighting, texturing, and rigging. The game world is even more complicated, since it encompasses not just game artists, but game designers and game developers who may be visually talented as well.

But the irony of these narrow job descriptions is that all but the biggest studios use them to specify what they need in a freelancer for a single project. For a full-time position, the most desirable person is the generalist—someone who can wear several hats equally well: model a character one day, light a building another day, and design a new character the following week. So the ideal portfolio reel—particularly for someone who is just starting out—has to demonstrate deep proficiency in at least one important skill while also indicating broad creativity and talent in related ones.

That's a tall order, and hard to nail perfectly. Talented graduates from the same program in game art and design may have radically different experiences in landing a job, depending on the mix their reels display.

Obviously, the deck is stacked in your favor if you are a multitalented generalist because you can fit yourself to a wider range of positions. However, if you're significantly better at one role than most of the others you could apply for, it doesn't matter if there are more jobs for generalists. Narrow your emphasis to your strongest suit and you'll increase the chances of getting your foot in the door.

> Most stuff that goes into any animation is fairly mundane. So when big studios see an absolutely gorgeous, beautifully modeled, textured, and lit highly-detailed, pixel-tight ottoman, they'll just drool. You know that if you hire this person and you say, "I need this living room done. Go!" that they can do it.
> —Terrence Masson

DEVELOPING THE REEL

The reel has many of the goals, limitations and requirements of a movie trailer. In a very short time, it has to pull in the audience, keep them engaged, and make them want more. Even a momentary lapse of tension can break the spell.

You'll need to plan your reel carefully to make it past the levels of gatekeepers to the people who will actually make a hiring decision. You have a better chance of hitting that sweet spot if your material is unbelievably great. But few people are so amazing that they'll be hired no matter what. For the larger number of people who are good or really good, the goal is to create a reel that will move the perception of their work up a notch.

Reels are probably the most time-intensive type of portfolio to design and develop, including the portfolios of multimedia specialists. Even when you take that as gospel, chances are that you will spend infinitely more time creating your demo reel than you expect. No matter how organized you are, set aside several weeks before your due date to have the luxury of recutting and tweaking as you get feedback and rethink your decisions.

Reel length

As with a regular portfolio, the first questions anyone asks are how many pieces to include, and how long a reel should be. The number of pieces is less of an issue than length. Unless you have a remarkable history of high-profile projects, your demo reel should not run longer than two minutes. Arguably, even that is too long; some great demo reels are considerably shorter than that. You have a maximum of 30 seconds to excite, and even less if the viewer sees anything—even something minor—that they strongly dislike.

Selecting highlights

Like any other portfolio, the rule is: only your best stuff. However, the format of the demo reel gives you the opportunity to cherry pick. Maybe you have a fairly early project with flaws, but that also included some great short bits. In a demo reel, you won't have to show anything but the little gems. The same is true for a piece you've been working on in your spare time but haven't finished. No one will wonder whether the project the clips came from was complete, unless they are so impressed with your reel that they start searching your portfolio site for it. And by that time, you've probably grabbed them anyway.

> **The vast majority of demo reels don't get past the first 20 seconds. I'll hit play and five seconds, 10 seconds tops, if I'm not totally enthralled I'm already on the fast forward button.**
>
> **—Terrence Masson**

Go through your work looking only for the highlights, particularly those that support your expertise in your chosen area. If you are a film editor, for example, you should highlight the way you juxtapose two types of material, maintain perfect continuity, or cleverly recut a scene to create a subtext. If you are looking to break into 3D animation, you'll want to show proficiency in texturing and modeling. For work in game animations, clever workarounds in low-poly environments and good 2D work are important.

But these are only broad categories, and can change year to year as new features are added to software packages. One of the best ways to figure out the types of skills that are currently in demand is to look at the reel submission requirements for companies you'd like to work for. In many cases they will be quite specific about what techniques matter to them. Of course, you always have to remember that such guidelines will only give you a sense of in-demand technology, and that everyone who pays attention will have seen the same lists. It's still your game to find the expressive and creative ways to meet the technical basics that will make your reel memorable.

Variety

Within the highlights of your best work, look for variety. Part of what makes a good reel is a broad mix of styles, types of projects, and subject matters. Variations in pacing can be particularly useful, because they can help you establish a rhythm and

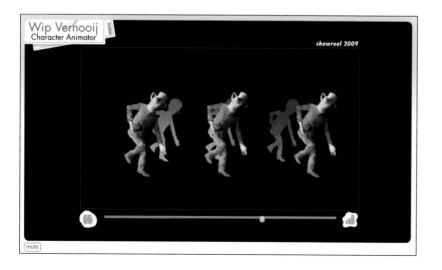

WWW.WIPVERNOOIJ.COM

Vernooij is a 2D character animator who shows his variety in style and character type with his demo reel choices. The first clip is from a claymation project, the second from a personal 2D animation, the bottom, a character designed for a Flash game.

prevent visual sameness from overtaking your reel. If you are working with documentary film, for example, you should look for places where you've captured strong emotion or facilitated a great dialogue between two people so you can mix up lively, external moments with intimate scenes. Nothing is more deadly in a reel than pieces of six projects that are good individually, but that when excerpted and strung together feel like a wall of gray sameness.

Variety is important, but not all clips are equally appropriate for your reel. As with any other portfolio, avoid explicit violence, sex, and bathroom material.

Unifying idea

As you rethink your work as a series of short moments, you should be looking for ways to smoothly connect your clips. There is no single right way to do this. Some people concentrate on visually linking to and from each clip in the sequence. You can make those links with subject, position of main objects in the frame, color, and direction of movement. Or more subtly, you can use pacing and music to create a mood. All the great cinematographers and directors find ways to cut between two disparate shots while maintaining continuity, and so should you.

> **We look for game artists and animators who can bring an original personality to their work. It's a plus if they can tell a good story. The more multitalented the person, the happier we are.**
>
> **—Jay Laird**

If you are a good storyteller, you have a powerful plus in developing your reel's structure. You can create a unifying idea and use it as a thread to sew your reel together. Some refer to this unifying reel concept as a theme. However, many people misunderstand the term and take that to mean a visual style, like a desktop skin. That's the opposite of a concept theme, because it is an unrelated element grafted on top of the work rather than having a true connection to it. A real theme helps to put your work into perspective by making disparate projects feel that they belong together.

You can find a unifying theme from within the clips themselves. For example, you can use a character or object as an MC. Or you can create playful opening and ending screens that place the viewer in a frame of mind or environment: an airplane, a beach, in 1920s Paris, or in an alien dinner theater.

STRUCTURE

Your reel structure is really very simple. The reel is "just" a collection of clips drawn from a variety of material, techniques, and challenges. Your objective is to mine your body of work and provide the viewer with an expansive impression of your imagination, knowledge, and abilities.

WWW.WIPVERNOOIJ.COM
Vernooij unifies his reel
presentation by creating a little
character who introduces his
portfolio reel, then returns at
its end to wrap up and provide
his contact information.

You can really add another level of appreciation and excellence in the bumpers, the head and tail, and the reel's overall packaging.
—Terrence Masson

The opening is a very important part of your reel, no matter what your specialization. It sets the mood and gives your audience a moment to focus their attention. You can provide that settling-in moment with something as simple as a nicely designed static titling screen, or something more ambitious, like a bumper.

Bumpers are pretty much what they sound like: a little something that protects two different things from uncomfortably smashing into each other. They are a very short sequence of frames—one to three seconds is sufficient. If you are having problems transitioning between two otherwise disparate clips, creating a bumper as a transition and sandwiching it between the two might solve your problem. Bumpers can

TRANSITIONS

Most animators or game artists graft their clips together with straightforward cuts. In most cases this is wise, as a badly used transition will detract from the impression of a seamless flow and draw attention to the seams between clips.

However, intelligent use of transitions can actually enhance the sense of continuity. For example, if you are following a character moving from right to left on the screen, a fast wipe in the same direction with a new scene's character following the direction of the wipe can have the same serendipitous effect as matching two objects in the same approximate position in two consecutive frames.

WWW.HERCFERN.COM

These three consecutive frames in Herculano Fernandes's reel are unified by the style of animation and the direction of movement. When the character who is the main focus of the first clip looks up as the type moves from behind him, the text that begins the next animation wipes down. The man's focus prepares the viewer for something dropping from the top of the frame.

after effects

also be a lifesaver when you are cutting your work to music and you are just a few frames off hitting a downbeat or the end of a musical phrase.

Sequencing and flow

Sequence your work by placing all your clips into one place, and select two of the very best as bookends. You want to start with something terrific to capture the viewer's attention and get them on your side, and end with something astonishing or moving that can reverberate in the mind long after they've viewed your reel.

The devil is in the details, and that's the big center area. Don't put anything mediocre between the two gems. Padding hints that the first great clip was a one-hit wonder. But you can ratchet the intensity up and down. A great example of a wireframe from a low-polygon model may not be exciting, but the quality of your craft

Transitions are also useful if you want to graft some sections from different parts of one project together. They require a careful frame matchup, but they can be a great way to indicate the passage of time in the same physical space.

For a film reel, short visual breaks between each clip are a plus, since each clip is likely longer and slower paced than those on an animation reel. A simple transition, like a fade down to black, a hold, and a fade up or a cut to the next work's title screen is usually more than enough.

after effects

after effects

Each cut, each frame, has to be really tight. It's a little subjective, but when you watch the reel in front of a class, there's usually a consensus: That cut is 10 frames too long and it hangs a bit.

—Terrence Masson

may be just the right counterpoint to lead into your next fully rendered clip. For a video artist, use your selections to create an umbrella narrative arc, with an opening, a couple of rhythmic changes, and an impressive closing piece to bring it all together.

Keep each piece of content just long enough for the viewer to get the gist of the action. The mix of types of work should be as unpredictable as possible: Jump as quickly as the material allows from one clip to the next. It's often better to use different parts of a single project as glue over the course of the reel than to graft long pieces together. If you have a great long piece, you can graft a few cuts back together as a mini-trailer segment, or use pieces of this work as a thread throughout the reel to support other material that may not be as exciting but that illustrates an important skill.

Once you have a sequence in the rough stage, play it through and examine it critically. It's unlikely that you've nailed your sequence at first try. Treat your clips like playing cards in a game of solitaire: Swap them in and out for the best visual transitions.

Music and timing

In many ways, music may be the most important single element in your reel. Every director from Hitchcock on down has demonstrated how critical sound is to a movie experience. It's likely to be a major contributor to your portfolio reel as well. The right piece of music will provide you with a mood or attitude that perfectly captures your work's personality.

Music also helps you through that critical last point after sequencing: timing. One of the most obvious failings in a reel is clips dragging on too long. And in a reel, too long can often be measured in fractions of seconds. The rhythm and punctuation of music gives your clips a structure to follow. Music is a form of narrative, with a convenient beginning, middle, and end. Combine a brilliant flash of light with a sudden, crashing guitar chord and both effects are amplified. Because music has phrases, clips can be cut at exactly the point where one phrase ends and another begins. Your end result is stronger, more dynamic, more magnetic.

That being said, music is also a potential red herring. Because it can smooth over rough spots and create enormous energy, it's very easy to gloss over deficiencies in your reel simply because you don't see them...you're too busy bouncing along with the beat. You can only hope that your audience is, too.

Music is tremendously important to me. It can be mood setting and moving and really tell you a lot about a person. I personally put a lot of time and effort into the type of music, the track, the timing or the pacing. It can make a huge difference.

—Terrence Masson

ONE-WAY TRIP TO THE LAND OF NO RETURN

Unfortunately, many people who want to spend their life creating new worlds never even get an interview. Most likely, that's because there is something about their demo reel that bars the way. What says that a reel has gone down the wrong path?

- **It's my world and welcome to it.** Everyone has private fantasies, whether it be winning the Indy 500, meeting Prince Charming, or feeling The Force. And it's OK to express those in your reel now and then. But there is a difference between a mild interest and an obsession. When everything in a reel centers on one era, one object category—like unicorns, busty maidens, or weapons—or one fantasy world, that reel is history. And that is true even when the work is technically impressive. Mono-topic reels imply unsophisticated, uncreative thinking.

- **It's like World of Warcraft, only better.** Well, probably not. Some aspiring game- or movie-makers interpret the idea of customizing their reel for a potential employer to mean that they should slavishly copy a company's style and story. That company probably has plenty of people with years of experience who have that style nailed. They are looking for something that they have not seen done before, to help them develop the next great thing.

- **Draw? Someone else will do that!** Many aspiring game designers assume that a game company will only look at their game mechanics, so they use stock art and videos to illustrate their work. If aspiring gamers were in short supply, that assumption might be true. But in the real competitive world, few people looking at a game reel will sit through bad graphics to figure out whether or not the developer understands gameplay. If the idea is good enough to put on a professional reel, it is good enough to find an illustrator or animator to partner with first.

- **I want to make you think.** Film and video reels, particularly those from fairly young practitioners, can be filled with artistic slow moments with ambiguous cinematography. In the kind of environment in which most reels are reviewed, abstractions are wasted. Each short clip in a film reel should communicate its purpose clearly, with good storytelling and sharp editing.

- **Canned? Sweet!** Showing a cool effect can be nice, but only if you created it from scratch. If it's a canned effect that merely shows that you know how to use an application, don't highlight it. No one wants to watch a software demo on a portfolio reel. Accomplished professionals are very aware of the plug-ins for major software packages, from Adobe Photoshop to Autodesk 3ds Max. Drawing attention to a premade filter or effect may devalue your reel.

Problem is, they may not be hearing the music at all. In large companies, the first people to vet your reel will probably be those in the HR department. People hired for these positions are chosen specifically because they have experience with creative departments. They aren't expected to make final decisions, but they do have enough sense for what the final decision-makers want that they can be trusted to handle the first cut. By and large, they do that by gathering in a conference room and watching the reel with the sound off. If your visual presentation isn't good enough to stand on its own, it will become obvious to them quickly.

The only way to ensure that the music doesn't blind you is to turn it off yourself. If you've used it well, the sense of rhythm and the build in pleasurable tension should have transferred itself to the reel. You'll miss the music, but not enough to ruin the enjoyment.

The other time when dependence on music can hurt you is when you use a self-publishing site as your portfolio reel's home. Unlike on your own address, where it's unlikely anyone will notice or care, these sites are big enough to be sued. YouTube, for example, will take down a video that infringes on a company's copyright if they complain, or if someone else points it out. That's most likely to happen if you use a popular idol's music for your reel. Or perhaps they'll simply block the sound portion of the feed. For some reels, that's not much better than being blocked entirely.

AUDIENCE SWEETENERS

After you have your clips sequenced and timed exactly as you want them, it's time to consider those seemingly small details that wrap up the reel package and telegraph that you are an experienced pro—even if you aren't quite that yet. Adding the following elements to your reel shows your sensitivity to who will be viewing it, and under what circumstances:

- **Sound level test.** Every reel with sound should contain a brief audio test tone at the very beginning. This tone may be a nicety for funky jazz, but a necessity for heavy metal. Every playback device for your reel will be set to a different volume, and the last thing you want to do is explode the eardrums of a potential employer. Sure, they'll adjust the volume when your music begins, but it's a guarantee that they will utterly miss whatever is actually onscreen for that time. Since its likely to be one of your best bits, you want them totally focused from the beginning.

- **Color bars.** Like the sound test, placing SMPTE color bars at the beginning of a reel is a leftover from the days of tape, and many digital reels no longer include them. That's a shame, because they're just as necessary now as they were then. Not all viewers have a calibrated monitor or projector, but they all

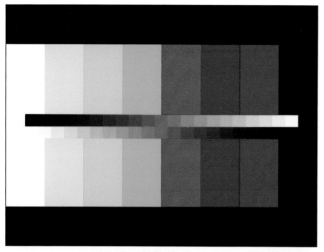

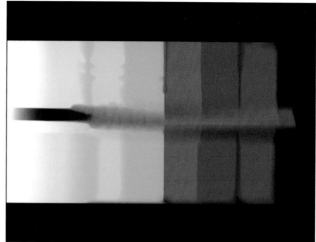

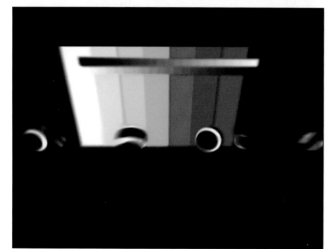

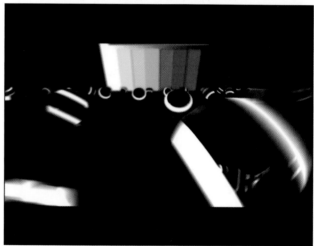

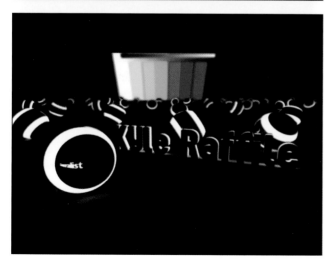

WWW.COMFORTKYLE.COM

Kyle Raffile turns the color bar into a clever bumper animation. Finding a way to make even a dry requirement into a visual treat is one strategy to make a jaded reviewer sit up and take notice.

know what a color bar test should look like. If the colors they see on the bars before your reel are off, that's a good hint that they will not be seeing the reel as you designed it. Hopefully, they'll make adjustments. But if not, at least they'll be aware that those orange faces are not the result of your visual limitations.

- **Credits.** As you'll see in Chapter 12, "Copyright and Portfolio," claiming only your own share of a project and giving explicit credit to others is non-negotiable. Identify clearly any collaborators or team members. Credit the music and any other elements you did not create yourself.

- **Labels.** A discreet MTV-like label in one corner of the screen can serve many purposes. Because it travels with and is seen at the same time as the clip itself, it can immediately end-run the question, "What part of this project was her responsibility?" If the answer to that question is too complicated to

WWW.FISTIK.COM/CEMRE_WEBSITE/

Cemre Ozkurt identifies the work category in this clip—character modeling— with a brief label in the lower left corner. He also prompts the viewer to match the code number on the right against his reel breakdown. This clip was part of LA-based Blur Studio's 2006 animation "A Gentlemen's Duel."

fit on the screen without distracting from the work, at least use the space as a key matched to your reel breakdown.

- **Contact Info.** Most people do remember to put their name on their reel's title screen, but a significant number fail to put their contact info there as well. How will anyone reach you without it? In fact, your contact info should be both at the beginning and the end of your reel.

- **Reel breakdown.** Even if you label your clips, you'll still want to provide a reel breakdown. That's a separate document that identifies each clip that you used in the order in which you used it. The reel breakdown is also the place where you clearly identify exactly what you were responsible for, in whole or part. For example, if you only modeled one character or a few objects, you need to identify and claim credit only for those elements. Ideally, you'll want to brand your reel breakdown to match the reel itself, using the same typefaces and general design feel so it's clear that the two pieces belong together.

REEL DELIVERY

Once you have designed and sequenced your reel, you need to finalize it in player form and get it out into the world. See Chapter 7, "Repurposing and Optimizing," for some technical suggestions on encoders and players, and Chapter 13, "Presenting Your Portfolio," for how to disseminate and present it.

Creating multiple reels

As recently as 2005, you slaved over one perfect reel as your calling card, and sent it everywhere. That has begun to change. In the current marketplace, you can miss an opportunity just because your title screen and lead-off clip appear to put you in the wrong category for a freelance project. This is easily avoided by planning for the eventuality. We live in a world where the gods have given us non-linear editing tools, and it would be a pity to ignore the gift. Use your time in Adobe After Effects, or in Apple Final Cut Studio to build reel variations for the alternate job positions you can imagine yourself being qualified to fill.

Multiple versions still require advance work, and they are admittedly easier for a film/video person to develop than for an animator, whose clips need to segue seamlessly. But as you work on more projects, you may find that you have two or three stellar projects that display different aspects of your talent. If so, you can create two similar, but not identical, reels with different emphases.

herculano fernandes
maya generalist | compositor

reel breakdown*

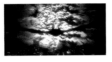

Burger King Endtag

Maya particles and instancing for bats.

DirecTV/MLB

Lighting for 3D elements.

Dominoes Endtag

All modeling, shading, lighting, rendering, and compositing. (no 2D work)

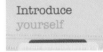

The Art of Hello

Concept, Animation, Type

Burger King/Indiana Jones

Modeled and shaded the crates and and positioned the money.

Attack!

Know Your Rights

Quote

Ice Road Truckers/Nascar

Attaching shaders/toon lines and setting up render layers; rendering

Sprint

Shaded rubber back, lens, and chrome sides of the phone

DirecTV/MLB

Lighting for 3D elements.

The Art of Hello

Concept, Animation, Type

Capstone Short

Compositing; modeled dog, young and old woman; character lighting in some shots, shading object

The Pig

Modeling, shading, simple rigging of objects, castle animation, light - ing, compositing

*all work by me unless otherwise stated

WWW.HERCFERN.COM

At the very least, your reel breakdown should provide a title for the work, a legend or image to help people match the pieces up, and as exact a statement as possible of what part of the project was yours.

The other way to handle the challenge is to create and maintain a wrapper portfolio that clearly defines your different skills and allows the audience to download the reel, or view the section, that is relevant to them.

Wrapping the reel

Creating a wrapper for your reel is essentially the same thing as creating a regular disc or online portfolio, with your reel as the jewel at its center. The wrapper allows multitalented people the opportunity to show their ability to handle another visual medium, and is particularly useful for, say, a 3D animator or video pro who wants to be seen as the perfect jack-of-all-trades for a small animation studio or game developer. If you are not such a person, don't wing it on the wrapper. Read the section on Partnering in Chapter 1, "Assessment and Adapation," and find a graphic designer.

If you are planning on a DVD menu, be sure to create a structure with submenus, as covered in Chapter 10, "Designing a Portfolio Interface." You'll find that you have to consider many of the same issues for a DVD menu as you would encounter for a website, from grouping to a site map.

Either way, make sure you have a reel version that is small and fast enough to play on your website, and link it to a downloadable high-resolution version. Provide full-length versions of the best pieces in your reel if you own the rights to them, and if you do not, provide links to the studio that does own the rights.

PORTFOLIO HIGHLIGHT:
METAVERSAL STUDIOS | REEL LIFE

WWW.METAVERSALSTUDIOS.COM

Portfolio development isn't easy. Although great portfolios project a beautiful inevitability, you're still conscious that there are calculated decisions behind them. In fact, in the design professions, part of the project is to make other designers and potential clients sufficiently aware of the site decisions that they want to claim that creativity for their own. Reels are different but equally exacting. Even those that are focused on technical prowess have to be perfect gems of entertainment.

While we want the site to have our signature wacky sense of humor, we also need it to be professional, to make it clear that we know what we are doing.

—Jay Laird

Now imagine putting both of these development challenges together, and add the requirement that both site and reel have to exude that elusive element: fun. That pretty much describes the requirements for a game developer's site. There's a lot of pressure to hit that mark, but Metaversal Studios seems comfortable batting cleanup. Their reel is a nonstop adventure with textbook-perfect pacing and variety.

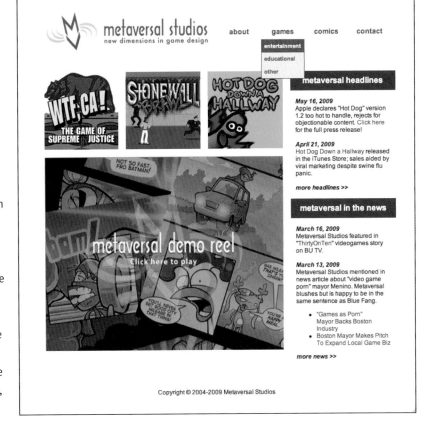

Metaversal's site navigation is simple and unobtrusive. Shallow dropdown menus make all major categories available, and a click on the Metaversal logo brings you back to the homepage. Always on this page are the demo reel and three game links, selected to showcase their newest, most popular, or most topical offerings.

Navigation and site content

Jay Laird, Metaversal's lead game developer and founder, knows that people come to the site for two things. The nonprofit and corporate clients come to check out their reel, and avid casual gamers visit to play an online game. Their site meets the both demographics' needs by putting these most important elements on the home page. The visual tension between the nerdy goofiness of their games and the cleanly corporate neatness of the interface is notable.

Their text plays the balancing game as well. Much of the site is devoted to detailed case studies for corporate clients, but it is extremely easy for the casual game player to avoid these sections completely. The areas that are likely to be read by both types of visitors are just a little tongue-in-cheek—toned down for the gamers, but a lightly entertaining break for the clientele.

Our site is special because it offers a combination of good clean fun and good clean site design not often found in non-Flash-based game portfolio sites.

—Jay Laird

James Mullen
Vice-President and Lead Programmer

A graduate of Northeastern University with a dual degree in Computer Science and Multimedia Studies, Jimmy Mullen has been a Metaversal programmer since July, 2006, becoming Vice-President and Lead Programmer in July, 2007. Jimmy's coding skills include ActionScript 2.0 and 3.0, PHP, SQL, JavaScript, Java, C++, and XHTML and CSS.

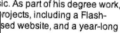

Before working at Metaversal, Jimmy was a technical support agent at Teletype GPS and a PHP/MySQL web developer at Harvard University ITIS. Since joining Metaversal, he has been lead programmer on projects for MIT, Fidelity, Boston College, Northeastern University, and Berklee College of Music. As part of his degree work, ... rojects, including a Flash- ..... sed website, and a year-long ....

my is also a talented musician
to a variety of Metaversal

James Mullen
Vice-President and Lead Programmer

A graduate of Northeastern University with a dual degree in Computer Science and Multimedia Studies, Jimmy Mullen has been a Metaversal programmer since July, 2006, becoming Vice-President and Lead Programmer in July, 2007. Jimmy's coding skills include ActionScript 2.0 and 3.0, PHP, SQL, JavaScript, Java, C++, and XHTML and CSS.

Before working at Metaversal, Jimmy was a technical support agent at Teletype GPS and a PHP/MySQL web developer at Harvard University ITIS. Since joining Metaversal, he has been lead programmer on projects for MIT, Fidelity, Boston College, Northeastern University, and Berklee College of Music. As part of his degree work, Jimmy participated in several long-term group software engineering projects, including a Flash-based single player educational puzzle game, a C# and ASP.NET based website, and a year-long rich media database project based on discovering local college music.

In addition to contributing to many of Metaversal's game designs, Jimmy is also a talented musician and an excellent editor who lends his sound design and writing skills to a variety of Metaversal projects, including Stonewall Brawl and Jerk of Art.

A serious bio turns playful if you roll over the portrait photo. The new image reveals the true cartoon essence of each member of the Metaversal staff.

The crowded gaming marketplace means that we always have to be one idea ahead, and that we have to implement that idea quickly.
—Jay Laird

Game developer sites have to be very sticky. The idea is that, the longer you spend playing, exploring, and enjoying, the more likely it is that you will become a client or a dedicated user. A variety of content is key to making this happen. Metaversal is known for the range and diversity of their game topics and gameplay, and for their quality visuals. They combine traditional word games with wryly topical quizzes. Their special event games, from the Halloween ZombieDrop to the Thanksgiving game pitting turkeys against Pilgrims, are visually adept, fun to play, and display the kind of twisted humor that many game developers reach for but seldom grasp.

Reel structure and content

Metaversal's demo reel is not very long, but it feels very rich and packed with content. The first images blast the message that the reel will take you on a fast-paced journey as you speed by planets and dance through musical clefs before being introduced to the first of many beautifully-conceived and rendered game animations.

One of many delightful time-wasters on the Metaversal site is T-Day, which sends turkeys back in time to try to prevent the Pilgrims from landing and bringing Thanksgiving Day into existence. The turkeys, being turkeys, neglect to bring any weapons, so you use a slingshot to throw them into the air toward their targets. You fight on the seas, fight in the air, fight on the ground, and turn into roasters if you fail. The inevitable result is made palatable by the smooth and responsive gameplay and the rich illustrations.

Hit a glowing boat and a power-up hits your plate. Something different happens to the Pilgrims for each special icon that is put in play. Select the snowflake icon, and winter descends, freezing all the Pilgrims in progress.

The segues between each clip in the demo reel are smooth, with a strong emphasis on transitions that connect the dominant motion of each clip to its predecessor. In the ZombieDrop game, the coffins shift left and right, so following that clip with a giant robot striding left feels natural.

To show the beautifully rendered detail of Metaversal's characters, one clip elegantly steps through the technique of bringing a character and scene to life.

One game clip is tightly cut through time lapse to display several layers with a similar layout but brilliantly different graphics. Another walks through an educational interface game for learning the formal language of music. All impress with their visual range and diverse subject matter. They end, literally, with a bang, and a wag of the tail from a bomb-defusing dog created for an engineering project.

Our demo reel and most of our games also feature original in-house music, showing that on top of our artwork and game design, we also rock — and we rock well enough to have landed Aerosmith for a brief gig!

—Jay Laird

When you think about the reel afterwards, you realize that it does more than just show the reach and variety of Metaversal's work as it bounces between different types of games and interfaces. Each individual clip has a different point to make about what they do and how. It's a fun reel to watch the first time, and it brings a smile even on repetition as you pick up on more of their subversive humor.

Future plans

Laird and crew view their current website as a work in progress. The demo reel is updated when groups of major projects are completed, since it needs to be carefully rethought before adding anything new that would change the flow and tempo. Laird is extremely conscious of the Metaversal brand, and wants the site to continue to be seen by the typical gamer as slightly subversive while not alienating corporate clients. Changes are constant, but are mostly incremental. As Laird says, "Word of mouth has been our best source of business, and our website has proven to be the best calling card for our work."

CHAPTER 12

Copyright and Portfolio

Not too long ago, it was easier to call an artist and ask for permission to use their work than it was to appropriate it. Now that so many projects are digital, there is a smorgasbord of ways to borrow, sample, copy, alter, and out-and-out steal creative work. It is also harder to stay within the law, even when your intentions are honorable.

How does this affect your portfolio? In more ways than you might imagine.

A few examples: The website you designed may be copyrighted by the company that paid your fee. The photos from the royalty-free CD you used may have reverted to the copyright of their original creator. A print project that's perfectly legitimate to display in a traditional portfolio might get you into trouble if you put it on a website if your contract says that you can show, but not distribute, the work. It's also easy for you to be the victim of a copyright violation. Your work could turn up in someone else's portfolio—with another person claiming credit for it.

You can't cover every possibility without becoming too paranoid to show any work digitally. This chapter will help you become more aware of your rights and responsibilities, suggest ways to minimize your risk, and prevent you from making assumptions that could get you into trouble later.

TERMS OF OWNERSHIP

Intellectual property: A unique or new intangible asset created by the human mind.

Copyright: Exclusive rights to an identifiable expression of intellectual property, as defined specifically by the government that grants the copyright.

Trademark: Something that visually and/or verbally distinguishes one individual's or organization's product from its competitors. A trademark can be a logo, an advertising phrase, a symbol, a brand name, a design, or some combination.

Public domain: Another way to describe intellectual property that the law sees as public property. Works enter the public domain when their copyright expires (see copyright.cornell.edu/resources/publicdomain.cfm for a chart of when that takes place in the U.S.), or when their legal owner declares them available for use without reservation. A work's copyright expiration date is determined by the year it was initially copyrighted. However, after 1921, different blocks of dates have different minimum copyright lengths.

Infringement: The improper use of a legally recognized piece of intellectual property. Trademark infringement is limited to the misuse of an identifying symbol, like incorporating Mickey Mouse ears into a logo for a company called Mouseworks Design. Copyright infringement is broader, since copyright protects most original artistic and intellectual expression.

Fair use: The doctrine that some forms of expression that use another's copyrighted intellectual property do not infringe the copyright.

Cease and desist order: A legal order that forces a copyright infringer to immediately stop using infringed art or pay fees that are usually steep and accumulate daily.

UNDERSTANDING FAIR USE

Most copyright problems arise from a misunderstanding about *fair use* (see the "Terms of ownership" sidebar above). Whether your use qualifies as fair use is determined by a combination of subjective factors. Issues like intent, type of work, and the profit motive are all considered. In all cases, interpretation is key. But this interpretation is usually made with a bias toward protecting the original copyright owner. Assuming that something is in the public domain, or relying on the principle of fair use without checking on the status of a specific piece, causes trouble.

What is the work you're planning to use? Just as some nudity is protected under the idea of "redeeming social value," some source material—like a Matisse—is considered more worthy of protection than a less socially or creatively valuable item—like a mass-produced velvet painting.

Why are you using the work? Fair use frequently protects free speech, like when an artist excerpts a piece to make a political or social statement. Claiming free speech rights won't protect you, however, if you use the copyrighted work of another artist whose work has nothing to do with your intended target. (See the section "Collage" later in the chapter.)

Whether you intend to profit from the use makes an enormous difference. Violating copyright of a commercial item for nonprofit or educational purposes is generally seen as being less serious than if the violator profited handsomely (or at least hoped to) as a result of the violation. For example, in 2009, Woody Allen sued the American Apparel company for using a still from his movie *Annie Hall* in a billboard. The owner claimed fair use, arguing that he was making a statement in solidarity with Allen. Eventually American Apparel paid Allen $5 million in a settlement. No matter what the claimed intention, the result was infringement of a well-known artist's work in what looked suspiciously like an ad.

What about work that you've used "just a little"? The law considers the percentage of the piece you're using, and how critical that piece is to the original.

Finally, will the owner of the copyrighted piece lose money, or the ability to market the original piece, if you use it? If your work could prevent someone

When you borrow a generic piece of sky from a photograph, it's likely that no one will notice, even though you have still violated the photographer's rights. But if you use an image like this one, the sky is central to the concept, and your violation will be clear to anyone who is familiar with the original, or who sees the two works together.

from buying the original—or even a reproduction of the original—you could be in trouble.

Note that there is a big difference between copying an actual artistic creation and using the idea behind it. Neither ideas nor facts can be copyrighted—only the specific way that they are expressed.

One final consideration: Even when your piece meets all the legal tests for fair use, if it moves to the wide visibility of a website you could find yourself challenged in court by a company with a large legal department. Even if you win, it could be an expensive victory. When in doubt, don't do it.

RESPECTING OTHERS' RIGHTS

Young creatives are accustomed to YouTube parodies and illegal but ubiquitous music downloads. They know that there are plenty of sources for media online, and that, most of the time, infringement means little more than a wrist slap. So sometimes it's hard for them to swallow the message: Using assets that aren't yours without crediting them in your portfolio can get you into trouble. The creative community is small enough that, eventually, people who fail to respect the rights of others feel the consequences. And it's worth considering: A person who is willing to borrow or appropriate the work of others shouldn't be surprised if someone else returns the compliment. If your intentions are honorable, you should make an attempt to reach the copyright owner to get their blessing. Nolo Press (www.nolo.com) offers *Getting Permission,* a book that explains the permission process in detail, and includes any and all forms you might need to do it right.

The easiest way to go wrong with copyright issues is through incorrect assumptions. Like icebergs, a project element that looks insignificant at first glance can actually have surprisingly large issues attached to it. The following are standard creative situations where copyright issues can sneak up on you.

"Orphan" projects

An orphan project is one where the client no longer exists. There is little chance that the client is going to rise from the dead, grasping for rights with its mummified hands. But photographs or other artwork in these projects may have been purchased for limited or one-time use. Showing such work on a disc or at high resolution on a web portfolio is chancy.

Design comps

It isn't ethical to use another person's work in a comp without requesting permission, but it's accepted professional practice to do so if you end up hiring the artist for the project or paying their licensing fee.

But what if you didn't end up hiring the artist? Sometimes, a designer develops a concept, but their idea isn't the one the client picks. Unfortunately, if the comp

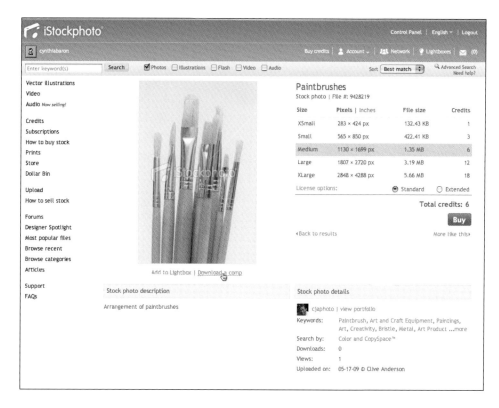

You can download a comp from a stock site that will be exactly what you see in the preview: a low-resolution JPG with the stock company logo watermark imprinted on the image. But the cost of replacing the comp with a usable and legal photo is usually very modest from all but the most prestigious sites. In this case, a good-sized image for a portfolio—about 1200 pixels at its longest dimension—would cost less than $10. Some images and smaller sizes are even less expensive.

artwork wasn't licensed, you can't show the ad concept in most digital ways. If you feel the idea was fabulous and shows your creativity well, you can contact the artist directly for their permission to use it in for the limited purpose of your portfolio. You can also search for a similar image through a stock-licensing site. Prices for low-resolution versions of images are often extremely cost effective.

Clip art and stock sites

Most download sites state their usage policy explicitly, but not necessarily in big bold print. Usually there is a link to the fine print on usage. Read this material before you get your heart set on using a piece. There are some sites that offer completely copyright-free art. However, with a couple of notable exceptions (see the sidebar "License to share"), most provide small images meant for web page backgrounds and clickable buttons. This is low-quality art, and it shouldn't find its way into a creative professional's work. The general rule for a stock image: If it's good enough for you to want to use it, it's probably someone's licensed work.

Usually, your license-free rights on a stock image are limited to low-resolution versions of the work. Otherwise, there is a payment structure based on the size and resolution quality. What if the downloaded work is presented on a project that was clearly just a comp? If the work came from a stock site and you are only using the comp-sized version, there is no reason not to use it in your portfolio. Of course, that

LICENSE TO SHARE

Although most artists are zealous in protecting their work, others are happy to share it freely, without even a small licensing fee. Those who feel this way can become members of Creative Commons (CC) (creativecommons.org). Then, they can publish all or some of their work with licensing rights that range from unrestricted public domain to free usage only under specific circumstances.

Unlike low-quality clip art, many of these images are in print-quality resolution, and can be used in the same contexts in which you might use a regular stock photo. Unless they have opted for public domain, the owners retain their copyright, and require explicit credit in any project in which the work is used. Many owners allow the work to be used for profit, not just for fun or portfolio. Other content owners allow you to edit and adapt the work, an option that opens up a host of possibilities for the right project. For example, CC licensing can solve problems for animators who need sound for their reels and want to post them on a public site like YouTube. Such sites will block a project's soundtrack if it is found to contain appropriated music.

CC-licensed work can be found among the media on many sites, such as Flickr. CC also has links to many works that have entered the public domain through copyright lapse. For example, many such works are used to illustrate entries in Wikipedia, with links to downloadable copies of the art.

There are other sources for license-free work. A comprehensive list with thumbnail descriptions can be found at meta.wikimedia.org/wiki/Help:Public_domain_image_resources.

comp version probably has the stock source's watermark prominently displayed across the image. If you don't want that as a distraction on your work, you will have to pay at least the minimum cost of licensing to replace it with a clean image.

Bear in mind that this book's discussion of copyright is geared toward the use of these stock images in a personal project, or for a typical client project that you would eventually want to display in your portfolio. For anything else, be sure to read the fine print on usage. You'll discover that most of them explicitly prohibit using their images on products for resale. You can't use them in a logo, or put them in any form on a T-shirt or self-promotional piece that you might offer for sale on sites like Cafe Press (www.cafepress.com) or Zazzle (www.zazzle.com).

Collage

Collage involves not just the collection of images, but their careful extraction, composition, and alteration. It doesn't seem fair that practicing a respected form of art could get you in hot water. But even without the added complication of a digital image, collage can run afoul of copyright laws.

For example, in 1991, Robert Rauschenberg incorporated a photo of a car from an old *Time* magazine into a collage, and was sued by the commercial photographer who took the photo. Mistakenly, he viewed the decades-old work as "found" material. Students often do the same, scanning elements from magazines and books. The sources frequently are an important element in their composition. Anyone who appropriates materials from magazines and design annuals could someday present their portfolio to the very person who created the source art.

> People come into the industry having done very well in school, but they don't know how to draw. If they had some reasonable level of drawing skills, they could have put down an idea in less than a minute. Instead they spend hours going through found photography, trying to find precisely the right photo. I don't think that's healthy for our industry.
>
> —Stan Richards

Derivative art

"Derivative" art is work that is based on someone else's creative output. The Copyright Act clearly states that only the original work's copyright owner can copy, duplicate, reprint, alter, or adapt it.

What about the "gray area," where you think you've altered the piece to such a degree that it qualifies as new art? The law takes a commonsense approach to these actions. If you pluck a person off the street and show her both images, would she recognize them as being similar? If so, no matter how you've changed the work, you have violated the law.

Sometimes the medium you select for your derivative art affects its usage. Many artists use art classics for inspiration, or as a starting point from which to comment on or satirize the work. When appearing in a painting or other one-of-a-kind work, the use can be perfectly legitimate. But a reproduction of the same artwork that could be downloaded and printed—like a piece of your online portfolio—might fail the rights test. Even if the work is supposedly in the public domain, it may be owned and licensed by the museum where it's displayed. See "Terms of Ownership" above for information on how to determine the status of a work you want to use.

Derivative style

There is a big difference between adapting an existing artwork and working in the style of another artist. Working in someone else's style can be an homage, particularly if the artist has historical relevance and the work is not a copy of any existing work. It can also be a way to get the superficial benefit of a distinctive look without having to pay the original creator. Copyright law has no way of protecting the original artist or designer in either case.

For example, one of the best-known graphics from the late '60s is Milton Glaser's Bob Dylan poster. If you scan a copy of his poster, change the colors in the hair design, and straighten Dylan's nose, you have done more than use an idea. You have created a work to replace the original and have violated Glaser's copyright.

On the other hand, if you came across Glaser's work and it inspired you to create a totally new graphic combining a solid color form and strips of curved, stylized lines, a savvy viewer will recognize that you are working in Glaser's style, but you are legally clear.

Creative influences

Unlike derivation or collage, there are no negative ramifications if you have been influenced by the ideas and work of another. Even Einstein gave homage to those who came before him by saying that he "stood on the shoulders of giants." In fact, acknowledging your influences in your portfolio, although still rare, is becoming a way to show your awareness of your creative domain's history and heroes. A shout-out or short mention of an influential teacher or mentor can even be a way to start a dialogue with potential collaborators or employers.

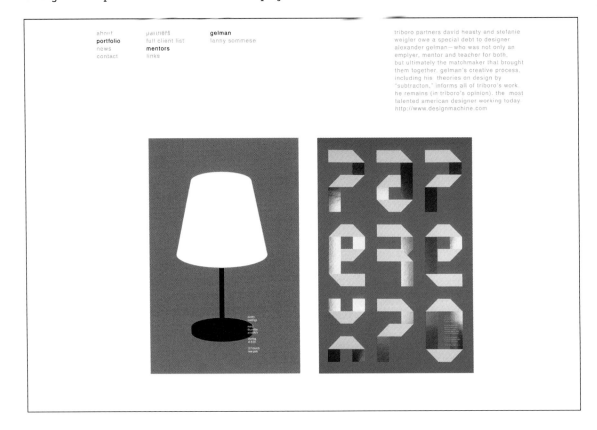

WWW.TRIBORODESIGN.COM

Triboro's partners feel they owe designer Alexander Gelman a particularly important acknowledgment for being their mentor. They show examples of his work and link to his site. In their About section, they also acknowledge their collaborators. As David Heasty says, "I think these full disclosures of influences are very interesting to people. I would love to see more designers embracing this transparency."

ROLES AND LARGE PROJECTS

It can be very exciting, when you have worked on a project for a well-known brand or taken part in a major campaign, to include the project in your portfolio. Before you do, be honest with yourself about your share in the work. Were you the art director, or a junior designer? Did you develop the concept, or only execute the production?

It's always better to present your share of the project honestly. Everyone knows that major projects are the work of many minds and hands. If a project is great, taking credit for only your share will reflect well on you. Giving credit to those who earned it will prevent confusion when more than one team member applies to one firm or deals with the same placement agency. Not only will you be better prepared to speak about the portion of the project that you know intimately, but you will be spared the embarrassment of being confronted with any gap between reality and your presentation. See Chapter 11, "Portfolio Reels," for ways to specify your roles and to offer credit to others on a team.

OWNING YOUR WORK

In a surprisingly large number of cases, even when you create all your own material, you don't own the copyright to it. The circumstances under which a work was created determines who owns and gets to license it. This can have profound implications for a digital portfolio, which by its very nature involves copying and adaptation. It has particular financial implications for illustrators and photographers. If you maintain rights to your work, you can recycle an image into the stock-image market, making your portfolio a potential income stream.

If you have created an image on your own time, for your own purposes, it remains yours to duplicate or change. Even if you sell the original artwork, you can retain the right to show copies of it in your portfolio, no matter what form that portfolio might take. If you choose to make a series of unique images in the same style, on the same theme, or with elements from the original, you are still free to do so.

On the other hand, work you do might conceivably belong instead to your employer, your client, yourself in combination with one of the above, or a third party entirely. One key to this distinction can be your legal working relationship with the other parties.

I hired a woman who had been designing and art-directing for multiplatinum-selling artists. About six months later, I received another book with one project that was also in her book. I finally said, "We hired so-and-so, and that same project is in her portfolio. She says she did it." He was defiant, but his body language told me that he was lying. He was good, but I did not put him forward to the creative director.

—Cynthia Rabun

Employee or independent?

Were you an employee when you created the work? Did you do the work while having taxes deducted? Did you have a supervisor? If so, the work belongs, and will continue to belong, to your employer. You can certainly claim that you did the work, and probably show a printed copy of it, assuming that trade or non-disclosure contracts are not in effect. But you can't copy it, sell it to someone else, or adapt it for a freelance job. If you want to use the work in a digital portfolio, you will need to get permission in writing from your employer to do so.

A freelancer is considered an independent contractor if you use your own materials and computer, work at home (or not regularly at the client's office), set your own hours, and get paid by the project, not by the hour. Unless there is a contract stating otherwise, the freelancer retains copyright on the artwork, and the client simply has rights to use it. The nature of that use (how extensive and broad) should be negotiated at the beginning of the project. The independent contractor has every right to reproduce this type of work in portfolio form.

You (or your employer or client) can't have it both ways. If you want to retain rights, you can't also get the benefits of employment—sick days, health insurance, overtime, and so on. Conversely, your employer can't deny you these benefits by calling you an independent contractor unless they also let you retain your copyright.

Work-for-hire

In a work-for-hire arrangement, an independent consultant is paid to design, create, or produce something for a fixed sum, selling their rights to the work to the person or company who pays them.

Work-for-hire is a growing problem for creatives, who can end up with large chunks of their creative output belonging to someone else. An old-fashioned portfolio —where one copy of a finished work was carried around, shown, and returned to its case—almost never prompted a legal action. The existence of digital artwork—infinitely and immediately duplicable—has changed that, and made the work-for-hire provision in a contract an increasingly ugly by-product of doing business.

What qualifies a commissioned freelance project as a work-for-hire? A surprisingly broad category of work:

- A contribution to a "collective work"—a large corporate website, a newspaper or magazine, or an encyclopedia.

- Something that's part of a motion picture or other audiovisual work—like character animation, modeling or lighting, or contributions to an interactive CD or its storyboards.

- A translation, a test, or answer material for a test.

- Instructional text—a textbook or training package.

Independent Contractor Status

The contractor is an independent contractor, not the client's employee. The contractor and client agree to the following rights consistent with an independent contractor relationship.

The contractor has the right to perform services for others during the term of this Agreement.

The contractor has the sole right to control and direct the means, manner and method by which the services required by this Agreement will be performed.

The contractor can perform the services required by this Agreement at any place, location or time.

The contractor shall perform the services required by this Agreement; the client shall not hire, supervise or pay any assistants to help contractor.

The contractor is responsible for all applicable income taxes. The client will not withhold FICA and other taxes from the contractor's payments, or make state or federal unemployment compensation contributions on the contractor's behalf.

Intellectual Property Ownership

To the extent that the work performed by the contractor under this Agreement includes any work of authorship entitled to protection under the copyright laws, the parties agree to the following provisions.

The contractor's work shall be deemed a commissioned work and a work made for hire to the greatest extent permitted by law.

The contractor's work has been specially ordered and commissioned by the client as a contribution to a collective work, eligible to be treated as a work made for hire under the United States Copyright Act.

The client shall be the sole author of the contractor's work and any work embodying the contractor's work according to the United States Copyright Act.

To the extent that the contractor's work is not properly characterized as a work made for hire, the contractor grants to the client all right, title and interest in the contractor's work, including all copyright rights, in perpetuity and throughout the world.

The contractor shall help prepare any papers the client considers necessary to secure any copyrights, patents, trademarks or intellectual property rights at no charge to the client. However, the client shall reimburse the contractor for reasonable out-of-pocket expenses incurred.

The language in this contract clearly states that the artist is selling the rights to his work on this project.

- A "supplementary work"—everything from maps and tables to indexes and bibliographies.
- A compilation—like a database or bookmark list.

If you've been looking for a common thread, you may have noticed that the law assumes that the work would not have been made without the larger project, and that the work would not necessarily stand on its own. On the other hand, both parties have to agree in writing that the project should be considered a "work made for hire." Any item that both parties put their names to that calls it such is considered a binding contract. The phrase has, therefore, been known to be tucked into a work contract and printed on the back of payment checks.

Assignment of rights

As a freelancer, try to avoid being pushed into work-for-hire. You are being asked to give up more than the time you spend creating the work, without any employee benefits and protections. At the very least, negotiate for rights to display the work in your portfolio when you and the client draw up a contract. The contract should state your intent to assign the rights to the client after the work has been completed and paid for in full. This differs from a work-for-hire because the two of you can write the specific provisions necessary to give your client the rights they need to use their material without denying you the right to claim your contribution.

A perfect example of why an explicit exemption for portfolio purposes is so important is the animation portfolio reel. By and large, unless the animation in question was designed, developed, and executed by and for one person, or by one team of creatives with no third party (like an ad agency) involved, getting rights to display your work after the fact is likely impossible. There are too many layers of individuals and teams of lawyers between you and the final client.

Almost every animator puts excerpts of these projects into their reels with the probable assumption that no one will chase them. That is true...until you place the work on YouTube or another public site. Some large corporate clients—exactly the

If you stamp a big copyright C over the image,
you are certainly safe, but you also degrade
the quality of your work, often to the point that
people fail to look at it carefully.

companies whose work it would be valuable to show—are the most vigilant in maintaining their rights.

Teamwork and individual rights

With the growing need for groups of people with different roles to work collaboratively, it becomes more important for the artist or designer to document such involvement. From the beginning, your contract should clarify the scope of your involvement. If you will be responsible for a project section, or a specific group of illustrations or layouts, keep copies of your process work. If, as sometimes happens, you are called upon to handle more material than was originally planned, make sure that the change is also documented, not just to make sure that you are appropriately paid, but so you can ask for rights to show the material.

> **I made a distinction between my work as a Designer/Art Director and my work as a Creative Director. CDs are less hands-on and rely heavily on the talent of other designers and art directors. I wanted to make sure the right people got credit for the work.**
> **—Ken Loh**

PROTECTING YOUR WORK

Any time you provide an image at a resolution or in a format that would allow the work to be edited or printed, you could become the victim of art piracy. Besides threatening to sue, and then really doing it, what can you do to protect your work?

Copyrighting

In the U.S. and Europe, copyright is implied without the need for a symbol or any registration. However, you can't sue for copyright infringement without registering the work. In the U.S., you have five years after you create something to register. If you register before a copyright infringement—particularly if you did so within the first three months of the work's creation—your chances for winning a case are higher. You can register your work online for $35 (www.copyright.gov/eco/index.html) by filling in the form and uploading a copy of your work in an acceptable file format. There is a complete list online, but it is exhaustive and covers all major formats in a variety of media types. This is by far the fastest and easiest way to register, and the one with the shortest government processing time. Although it will still take from two to six

---

DETAILED COPYRIGHT PROTECTION INFO

If you are hoping to use your portfolio to license your artwork, need to hire illustrators for your design projects, or are a freelancer hoping to protect your creative rights, check out Nolo Press's aptly named, "Protect Your Artwork" (www.nolo.com). It includes detailed copyright information and several useful contracts and agreements.

months to receive a certificate, you are covered as soon as the Copyright Office receives a complete and correct form.

A U.S. copyright is valid in most other countries, so you don't have to worry about taking out additional copyrights to show your work on the web, or to send it to people in other countries. If you are in the U.K., copyright is considered automatic and you don't have to fill in a registration form. However, there is a useful PDF with relevant copyright information at www.ipo.gov.uk/types/copy/c-about.htm.

Using the copyright symbol with your name can stop innocent appropriation. The proper format for doing this in the U.S. is:

Copyright © 2010 Your Name. All rights reserved.

However, any statement on your web portfolio that clearly states your copyright is considered valid.

Luke Williams displays his copyright in shorthand as part of his nav bar. It is present at all times, and on all pages of his site. Jonnie Hallman, who programmed his site, used code to make the copyright for his portfolio update automatically when the year changes. That way, as the portfolio is updated with new work, the most recent edition of it is recognized.

LUKE WILLIAMS
©.09
ABOUT
DESIGNER
MICA: DATA SURVEYS
PCB PAPER SHOW LETTERING
THE FIRST AMMENDMENT

PROTECTION TECHNOLOGIES

The most common way to claim copyright on a digital image is to simply add the copyright symbol and information directly to the piece. Although more than adequate warning for the well-intentioned, this is not much protection against anyone with a good eye and a cloning tool, especially since you can't put the notice anywhere that is critical to viewing the work.

One compromise between paranoia and laissez-faire is to provide low-resolution images. An image large enough to represent your work onscreen but well below printable threshold prevents someone from easily "borrowing" your work. However, this is a less useful solution than it used to be. It doesn't prevent a determined or clueless violator from copying your image and using it in low resolution. And it negates one of the most critical reasons for putting your work online in the first place: to display it in the best possible way. Most portfolios are showing big, beautiful images, but they do so safely by making technology work for them. There are several options to help show your work in all its glory:

- **Adobe Acrobat PDFs.** PDF files preserve font, format, and color decisions for artwork that combines type and image. (See Chapter 4, "Delivery and Format," for more about PDFs.) If they're not password-protected, anyone with Acrobat Professional can extract text and images from them. Fortunately, it's easy to lock your PDF in Adobe InDesign, the software that most designers use to create multi-page portfolio PDFs. After selecting File > Export and clicking the Save button, you'll see a small column of options on the left side of the dialog. Select Security from this list of options. In the Permissions section, check the check box to require a password, and type a password in the field. Uncheck "Enable copying of text, images, and other content" to prevent your work from being copied or extracted.

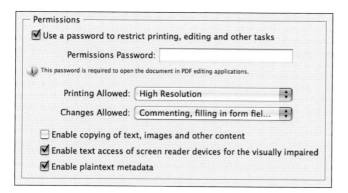

You can prevent the materials in your PDF from being copied or extracted by changing the defaults in the Permissions controls. To be even more secure, you can limit the changes allowed to Commenting. That way, team members of a potential employer can still share one copy of your work and point out specific projects that interest them.

- **Player software.** Players make your work portable. Although it is possible to extract material from a player file, it is very difficult, and usually far more work than it's worth. Flash SWF files are the preferred players for interactive portfolios. If you are concerned that someone might download one of your SWF files from your site and repost it elsewhere as their own, you can easily disable the right-click context menu. Before you create the SWF file, just visit File > Publish Settings and select the HTML tab in the dialog. Uncheck "Display menu" in the Playback section.

- **Watermarking and digital "signatures."** Some programs allow you to imprint sound and image files with invisible digital watermarks—methods that hide identifying content inside the digital data of a file without changing the look or sound of the file. This embedded data makes it possible to prove ownership of an image, even if someone makes major alterations to the original.

DEALING WITH INFRINGEMENT

Anyone who has ever found their work passed off as someone else's, or has seen a portion of their art looking back at them from an unknown source, knows the feeling of personal violation. The reaction, after the shock passes, is to DO something about it. But what?

Your legal rights

Copyright law states that you are "entitled to recover the actual damages." This means that you can get the money you should have been paid, including any net profits that the infringer made through the use of your art. Though it may be tempting to overestimate the damage, assign a realistic dollar value to your artwork and the effect of its loss. If you have been getting a few hundred dollars an image, suddenly claiming $10,000 for one won't be believable.

If your work accounts for only a small portion of the piece (one design element in one screen of a CD, for example), the profits will be prorated accordingly. Even so, if the project was lucrative, you could be awarded statutory damages, in addition to your legal fees. Statutory damages can punish a deliberate infringer more seriously than actual damages.

On the other hand, few infringers nowadays are major corporations. Large companies have departments responsible for tracking and getting releases for art, precisely to avoid this type of issue. Most likely, your infringer is not making any money from your work. If there is little or no financial impact and no damage to your reputation (particularly if the violator clearly thought they were operating under fair use), your time might better be spent educating the infringer.

Acting effectively

Even if you have access to unlimited free legal help, try to deal with the situation yourself first. The law can be unsympathetic to an action that might have been settled amicably out of court. Send a certified, business-like letter (not a hot-tempered set of empty threats) to the infringer. Let them know that you've discovered that they are using your copyrighted artwork without your permission. Describe the work clearly and give the date the violation was discovered. If the violation took place on a website, make it clear that the infringer must stop displaying your work immediately. Then send them an invoice with a realistic usage fee, and a deadline before you take action. You may receive a shocked and contrite phone call, a request to work something out, or an apologetic note with a check attached.

If the violation was online, you can bolster your case with solid documentation by visiting the Internet Archive Wayback Machine (www.archive.org). They have archived websites from well into the Internet's prehistory (1996!). Search your site for the first instance of the violated work. Do the same for theirs. With luck, the archive has the page or pages in its database that will allow you to prove that your work existed first, and that theirs is the copy.

Assuming your documentation is in hand, and the infringer is not responding, you can up the ante by contacting their Internet service provider. They may find it in their best interests to exert pressure on the violator by shutting down their site. Under certain circumstances, Google may come down on your side by removing access to their site from their search engines—tantamount to taking down their site, since, without search access, in practical terms they will no longer exist.

If you've decided that legal action is your only option, search for a lawyer who knows intellectual property issues. If your infringer stonewalls, or you receive a corporate "up yours" letter—and if you've decided that the $1,000 or more cost is worthwhile—your lawyer will file a cease and desist order against them. Make sure your lawyer makes every effort to settle the case out of court. Even if you get less money than you think you deserve, anyone who has ever spent time in the court system will tell you that the wheels of justice turn slowly, when they turn at all.

You may decide that you can't afford to go to court. If the infringer is a professional, and they have chosen to stonewall rather than apologize or negotiate, call in your social and professional networks. Speak to relevant guilds and associations. Some of them have funds set aside for copyright actions. If the work has been used to create a commercial product, contact the client directly. Send a cover letter with a clipping of your stolen artwork. Ask them to compare it to the non-original art and judge for themselves. Sometimes public shame will do what good conscience will not.

PORTFOLIO HIGHLIGHT:
NOA STUDIOS | FAIR SHARE

WWW.NOASTUDIOS.COM

A portfolio is one place where you can unabashedly trumpet how good you are. Sometimes that freedom leads people to claim more involvement or input in a project than they actually had. They fail to mention that their input was a team effort, or that some artwork they used was created by someone else. Critics tend to blame the young for the worst of this lack of attribution. And yet, the portfolios of young artists and designers are where you most often see overt collaboration, along with exuberant pages of thank you's and shout-outs to those who have shared their work.

I've done a lot of collaborative work with other artists. It makes you look at the work you've done in a different way.

—Pascal Vertegen

One of the most delightful examples of this open handed, go-for-it attitude is the Netherlands-based Noa Studios portfolio site. The result of a pairing of creative opposites—project director and artist Pascal Verstegen and web designer and Flash programmer Emin Sinani—the site bends many a standard portfolio rule, and does so with enthusiasm, *élan*, and some serious skills.

The Noa site opens with a short 3D animation of their logo, establishing their aesthetic and their major visual elements. Although you are welcome to skip the intro, at normal cable speed it is barely 3 seconds long, which is very impressive given the window size of the video.

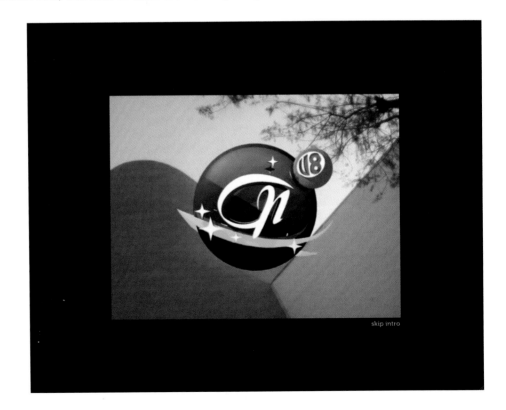

Architecture and navigation

With so many creatives posting their work online, it's a constant struggle for newcomers to find ways to be noticed. Noa's site was the result of its partners being challenged to enter the 2008 edition of the annual May 1st Reboot web design contest. Despite having never entered before and being among its youngest participants, they walked away with top honors. Not knowing the "right" way to do something, coupled with boundless energy, can sometimes lead to surprising results. In a contest that looks for innovative new ideas in web design and interaction, Noa stood out.

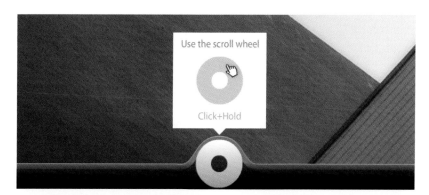

The scroll wheel begins as an iPod clone, in an environment where mimicking a rotatable physical wheel is extremely difficult to do. The wheel performs elegantly at any scrolling speed as it acts like a radio dial along the linear bar to bring up each of the main navigation choices.

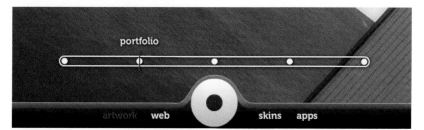

The white iPod skin morphs into a stylistic echo of the Noa logo when you use it to navigate through a portfolio category. As with any video player, clicking the arrow starts a video slideshow of each portfolio group. A counterclockwise white marker provides visual feedback.

Our working styles are different so we disagree all the time on details. But I think this is healthy, since it mostly leads to the best results.
—Emin Sinani

The most striking element on the site is their main navigation: the iPod-like scroll wheel at the bottom of the frame. Using it moves you fluidly between their main portfolio areas with an effect that is surprisingly realistic.

Stylistically, the scroll wheel drives the look and feel of all other components: their portfolio thumbnail build and even their site's version 8 logo are driven by circular motion. Although Noa provides alternative navigation (a small standard nav bar at the top of the window and selectable menu text at the bottom), everything on the site is readily available from the scroll bar, which requires very little arm and mouse movement. The click and hold navigation is just as smart on the website as the original concept is in Apple products.

Content

From the beginning, Verstegen and Sinani viewed the site as an exploration in user experience. They wanted to provide designs for a wide range of applications, from logos to websites to desktop skins. However, although they definitely appreciate each other's work, they come to the table with very different instincts and talents. Verstegen has mastered Flash programming, but is most interested in graphic art,

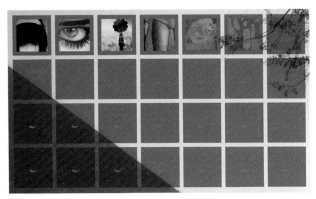

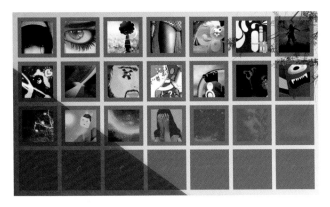

Select a portfolio area, and a grid appears onscreen. Images in the first stage of loading are indicated first with Noa's signature counterclockwise circle. They are quickly replaced by transparent thumbnails of the work, whose resolution and substance increase until the grid is fully populated.

Select the Info button at the top of each framed portfolio piece, and a balloon appears to the right of the work identifying the main partner involved, or specifying that the work is a Noa Studios collaboration. In these two representative projects, Sinani (nicknamed Zunamo) was responsible for the top project, a website, and Verstegen (nicknamed Enkera) was responsible for the bottom project, a desktop skin.

The biography section not only introduces
Noa's partners, it thanks people who helped
them add features, like the streaming video
and site music. The map to the right offers
thank you's to contributors, pointing out the
global reach of their collaborations.

trendwatching projects, and "useless" but richly entertaining interaction. Sinani is a
devotee of minimalist design and functional interaction. The result of their creative
push-pull is, as Verstegen says, "the middle path that makes something everyone can
enjoy and that we both love." You can easily see that in their website. They compete
and collaborate equally well, and with the same intensity.

Unlike most studio sites, they clearly label each work as a Noa Studios effort,
an individual project of one of the partners, or a piece created with an outside collaborator. This labeling makes it easy to recognize what each one brings to the table
when they combine forces.

Future plans

Although they are both basically happy with their current site and feel that it met their goals, it won't be long before Noa Studios morphs again. They have received a tremendous amount of feedback on their site, far more than they would have without putting themselves so boldly into the online mix, and it has helped them toward new ways of thinking about their futures. In addition Sinani and Verstegen are excited and enthusiastic about the addition of new features, like a blog and new video options.

Noa's principals are students, at the beginning of their careers and with a long creative life ahead of them. They see every iteration of their joint portfolio as an opportunity to apply the new things that they are learning. Because their work is driven by a desire to hit new technological levels, their new site will be redesigned and rewritten from scratch. The one thing that is certain is that the two partners will continue to use their web presence to bring them a bigger network of collaborators and more recognition.

Could this be the new version of the Noa Studios site? Their site is always a work in progress, full of possibilities and connections.

CHAPTER 13

Presenting Your Portfolio

Planning, design, and production are the major stages in digital portfolio development, and they are certainly the ones that take the most energy and time. But uploading files or burning a disc doesn't mean your work is done. In creative endeavors, exquisite presentation is not a bonus— it's the required last step in designing and producing a portfolio. It matters tremendously how you present your portfolio to others, both when you are physically present and when the portfolio must speak for you.

This final chapter considers the presentation as part of your portfolio design. When your artwork, your product, and your presentation are in harmony, you make a powerful statement to a prospective client or employer: "This person loves and cares about their work." That's exactly the type of person anyone would want to have on their team.

TESTING YOUR WORK

When you discover a bug while you're using a program, you get irritated and angry. Well, digital portfolios are software, too. It is much better to find a problem before it reflects badly on you and your work.

You may not think you need to test your work if your portfolio isn't interactive, but sometimes even in the simplest projects you can let something silly slip through. If you've made PDFs, or created a simple slideshow, or even used a template on a sourcebook site, you should still spend the time to verify that everything works, looks good, and reads well.

How to test

If you don't have one already, make a spreadsheet list of each page. Compared with most commercial websites, your portfolio is a small project and it's absolutely possible to test everything. As you test each page, check it off on the list. If you find a problem, either fix it immediately or carefully write down what's wrong on the spreadsheet. Don't depend on your memory!

A successful procedure is thorough and complete, and includes the following:

- **Test against your site map.** If you made a website or integrated disc presentation, you should have a good site map to refer to. (See Chapter 10, "Designing a Portfolio Interface.") Are the pages linked from the places you planned, and are the links from those pages correct?

- **Test on different computers.** Open your project on a different computer. You may have browser default settings on your working machine that you take for granted, or you may discover errors in a style sheet or a font. You may also notice, on a more- or less-powerful computer, that some animations move too slowly or are much faster than you thought that they would be.

- **Test on different platforms.** If you designed your work on a Mac, test it on a Windows computer, and vice versa. Fonts, colors, and browser elements may look different or not work properly.

- **Test on different browsers.** Not only are there visible differences on different platforms, there are a surprising number of formatting differences on the same platform with different browsers. You must at least test on Firefox and Safari on a Mac, and on Firefox and Microsoft Internet Explorer on a PC. Even better, once you have a URL in place, visit Browsershots (browsershots.org). Not everyone makes a point of updating their operating systems and browsers when new ones are released, and a quick check will let you know if a major browser has problems displaying your work as you've designed it. If your test page doesn't pass muster, you know exactly which browsers you'll need to test it against after you've researched the problem.

Screenshot request group 1 [+] BOOKMARK ...
Javascript enabled, Flash 9, 1024 pixels wide, 16 bits per pixel
Submitted 50 minutes ago
Expires in 20 minutes (Extend) (Cancel)
23 browsers selected, 8 uploaded

MSIE 7.0 Windows XP | Safari 3.2.1 Windows XP | MSIE 5.5 Windows 2000 | MSIE 6.0 Windows 2000 | MSIE 8.0 Windows XP

Download 8 screenshots (3.1 MB)

Firefox 1.5 Windows 2000 | Navigator 9.0.0.5 Windows XP | Firefox 2.0.0.4 Windows 2000

Request new screenshots?

BROWSERSHOTS.ORG

Browsershots submits your URL to the collection of servers you specify. As they load, they appear as thumbnails that link to the full screenshot. Not all failed loads are serious—your portfolio is not an e-commerce site. As long as all of the browsers that are likely to be on your target audience's computers load correctly, your page passes the test.

- **Test at random places.** Unless your work is in one Flash SWF, people could gain access to your site through a chance link or Google search, not from your site's homepage. If you open your site randomly, does all your navigation still work?

- **Test with other people.** Watch someone else look through your portfolio, preferably not someone who's been working on the computer next to you while you developed it. Do they click in places that you never intended? If they do, does anything unexpected happen? If your guinea pig seems confused by your interface or slow to understand your environment, rework the difficult sections.

- **Test your media.** Particularly if you have created a DVD player interface, you must verify that your disc will work, not just in your own computer or player, but in many player and platform combinations. Use brand-name DVDs: Generic brands are often incompatible. A visit to an electronics megastore can provide an opportunity to pop your disc into a range of players.

What to test

Test everything, really—every page, every image, every interactive state. In particular, watch for the following:

- **Fonts.** A bug may cause some fonts to be replaced with one that is incorrect or has an incorrect weight.

- **Links.** When you update, links can break, especially if you retype file names. If you have links to launch an email program, or links that open new windows, make sure they all work. Use *absolute links*—ones that contain the entire URL (such as http://www.outsidelink.com/folder/mywork.html)—for all external links.

- **Images.** Images should all be in one image folder, and accessed through a relative link (such as "images/mypix.jpg"), so they won't generate broken links when you upload your files to a server.

- **Downloads.** When you download a video clip, does it play on both Macs and Windows? How long does it take to start? Does it play correctly?

- **Coding.** Different versions of browsers, and browsers on different platforms, can read your code in a variety of ways. Layers, for example, don't always work on older browsers. You may need to change your code so it works in more browser versions.

- **Speed.** How long does it take your homepage or Flash preloader to finish? How long does it take each of your artwork images to show up? Are these acceptable times for your target audience?

GETTING FEEDBACK

Once you're confident that your portfolio is in good shape technically, get some feedback. The more interviews and reviews you can get, the better. Even an accomplished professional can miss things that a fresh eye will notice. Trusted, discriminating friends are a valuable source. But sometimes, especially when you have created something in a new format, objectivity is very valuable.

It's easiest to get feedback if you're a student. In fact, enrolling in a professional development or certificate program at an art school or university can give an older professional access to some of the school's faculty and placement services—and their portfolio reviews. Don't be shy about asking a favorite professor for an appointment to discuss your portfolio. How well you do reflects on them, and on the school.

Local professional organizations also sponsor portfolio reviews, often in the spring. They offer the opportunity to get feedback from faculty and professionals from different schools or companies—offering a new perspective on your work.

No matter what your position, look for opportunities for informational interviews. Many design studios, for example, offer a specific process on their website for portfolio feedback. Another great place for feedback is a placement agency. You'll get unvarnished reactions from a place that sees hundreds of portfolios in your area.

Of course, the online community offers endless feedback. Too endless—there are lots of critique sites. Unfortunately, I can't recommend one in specific that consistently gives good creative advice, although you are likely to get a better quality of response by posting on a professional portfolio site like Behance or Coroflot than on most technical forum sites (they're best for software tips and feedback on site function). To figure out if a site will be useful to you, look for three warning signs:

- **The site's design.** Even blogs and forums can be designed with taste or without. If they're using an off-the-shelf look and feel, the feedback they provide may be just as generic.

- **Anonymous posters.** Do you really want a critique from someone whose handle is "stinkyfoot"?
- **Rated reviewers.** Except on purely technical advice sites, high-rated reviewers get there by being supportive, not by being effectively critical.

You might have better luck joining—or starting—a local community of creatives who critique each other's work. Again, professional organizations can be good sources for such a network.

One last consideration about critiquing: You may not always like what you hear. Any professional who is offering feedback should be polite and offer constructive criticism—you shouldn't have to take tantrums and abuse. But they are doing you a favor if they honestly point out that a project doesn't belong in your book, tell you that your portfolio needs work, or give suggestions on improving your presentation. Even if you disagree, don't argue. If you really think that they are wrong, ask someone else. Second opinions can be as useful for portfolios as they are for medical decisions.

> I'm much less inclined now to be opinionated about a portfolio in front of a student. Because when, in the past, somebody asked for my honest feedback, I would actually give it to them.
>
> —Bill Cahan

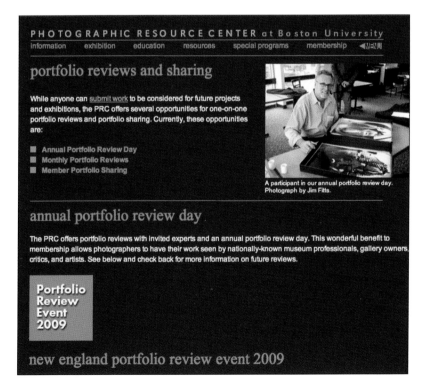

WWW.BU.EDU/PRC/PORTFOLIO.HTM
Boston University's Photographic Resource Center offers free monthly portfolio reviews to its members. It also provides a fee-for-service portfolio review for the entire photographic community.

Packaging a portable portfolio

If you've designed and produced a disc portfolio, you'll probably be sending it out for review. Almost any place you target probably gets scores of other portfolios in a month. You want your work to stand out from that crowd. Generic-looking material could easily be tossed in the trash in a fit of end-of-project house cleaning.

Designing a disc package

There is a difference between adequate and excellent portfolio packaging. Design creativity is of course critical, but good process will help you maintain quality and produce a better package. Consider these issues as you develop your design:

- **Maintain design consistency.** Connect your physical materials visually to your online portfolio. You might be surprised by how many people begin their package design from scratch. Packaging, like your portfolio, is part of a self-branding process. You should reinforce that branding whenever you can.

- **Aim for legibility.** You want your package to be distinctive, but your design should never sacrifice legibility for effect. Make sure your name, and the word *portfolio* figure prominently in your packaging and related materials.

- **Design all elements.** If you are using a jewel case for your CD, make sure to design all surfaces: front, back, and the side. The side is particularly important, since discs are often stored standing up.

- **Design a leave-behind.** In addition to having a digital portfolio, it's always a nice touch to have another form of portfolio leave-behind to accompany it. It offers a way to show your work in tangible form, and can double as a great way to advertise your site. (See "Mailings," later in the chapter.)

- **Print on stiff stock.** Your jewel case cover and insert should be printed on (or constructed with) heavy paper. If you're lucky, it will be opened and closed multiple times as people pass your disc around. You don't want the design to look shopworn after a few people have handled it.

- **Design your print portfolio.** You may still be maintaining a print portfolio for pieces that can't be shown, or don't work well, digitally. It should be organized and designed to match your digital presentation. The absolute best book on developing a stellar print portfolio is Sara Eisenman's *Building Design Portfolios: Innovative Concepts for Presenting Your Work* (Rockport Publishers, 2008).

> I know folks who won't even open the package if it's sloppy and handwritten in marker. Places like ILM get thousands of disks a week. It's a lot of volume and you can't be bothered if someone doesn't put their time into it.
>
> —Terrence Masson

DISC LABELING DO'S AND DON'TS

It's important to label your work, but not all labeling is equally good:

- **Burn your CDs before you label them.** Chances are that the disc will not burn properly after the label is on.

- **Don't use tape, glue or pre-stick labels.** Most labels, including many laser-safe brands, are made with an adhesive that eats away at the disc coating. Glue dries out and loses its ability to hold, so labels will begin to curl, crack, or bubble. Anything that isn't absolutely flat can ruin a CD player if it gets caught inside.

- **Don't send a disc without a sleeve or case.** CDs and DVDs may be long-lasting media, but if you scratch them, they may not play.

- **For one-time disc printing, use a local or online service bureau.** There are many short-run printers that specialize in disc duplication and printing. Use the same company to print your disc sleeve or case insert as well and you should have consistent color matching and an integrated presentation.

- **For multiple mailings, consider your own printer.** For about $100, you can buy a color inkjet printer that has the ability to print directly onto a disc, as well as act as your daily quick-print color option.

To raise the odds that your work will be viewed and retained, your digital portfolio should be attractively packaged. At the least, you should design a disc label. Even better is to add a matching sleeve or case and a mailer insert.

GETTING THE WORD OUT

Promotion is not a dirty word. True, there are people whose tireless and egotistical self-flogging give the practice a bad name. But if you believe in your work, you should be prepared to be your own advocate. It's easy to get discouraged if you don't have an immediate response once you've posted your portfolio, but if you feel your work has value, you must be persistent.

Advertising your site

Publicizing your portfolio is the other side of researching your audience. Take advantage of all the connections you made in lists, forums, and other groups to help your portfolio rise above the noise. In particular, be sure to contact everyone who critiqued your portfolio and send them a personal thank-you with the URL of the final site. If someone was particularly helpful, you might even add a line of thanks or credit in your online portfolio. It may prompt them to send people to see your site, but even if it doesn't, they'll appreciate the public thanks.

> We all know that the art world is about relationships. Artists have to get their portfolio together, but with the same zeal they have to learn the relationship game.
>
> —Ellen Sandor

Add your URL to your email signature, along with a line about your site's content. Be descriptive, short, and subtle. If you're good with words, try to include a teaser that will draw people in.

Redo your business card and put your URL on it. Never leave the house without carrying a few business cards with you. Go to art and design events, and offer your card when you can. Both the creative and business worlds run on networking. Contacts in the community can lead to recommendations and referrals later.

Linking and Web 2.0 sites

A finished portfolio is a cause for rejoicing, and considerably more interesting to look at than the results of some Facebook contest. Make sure all your online friends know the address. Add it to your LinkedIn updates. Post work samples with the portfolio URL on appropriate self-publishing sites. Twitter. This is not the time to quiet and modest. Generally, you will get the most mileage out of your new digital portfolio within the first month of its existence, and it would be a shame to waste its shiny, fresh status. If people like your site, they will link to it, extending your network and visibility, and ensuring a small but steady march through its pages for weeks to months. Some of these visits will just be well-wishers. Others will be people asking you for help. But if your work is good, this barrage of connections will also lead potential employers and clients to you. Some of the featured portfolios in this book were found in precisely this way.

Luke Williams has explicitly designed an elegant mailer to use as a leave-behind and as a prequel. Its style evokes the personal writing style he uses to speak directly to his website visitors.

Online contests

To keep traffic coming to their own addresses, many professional portfolio sites, blogs, and even software giants like Adobe sponsor contests for creative work online. Some of these result in actual prizes, like software, web hosting, free upgraded subscriptions, printing, and, yes, money. But all of these goodies are beside the point. What they really offer is priceless: an immediate ticket to professional viability. If you are both talented and lucky, they may help to catapult you into your future career.

Obviously, like winning the lottery, you really can't base your life on taking first place in a contest. But even gaining a mention will drive traffic to your portfolio and result in invitations to join useful public and private networks. Particularly if you already have work in the wings that might fit the contest's rules or have time to make the extra effort, you lose nothing from entering the arena. Should you actually gain notice, you have the kind of news that gives you an excuse for mailing and posting.

CONTACTING INDIVIDUALS

You spent a lot of time researching target audience possibilities. Now is the time to pull that material out. You know who you'd like to work with and for, and now that you have a portfolio, it's time to let them know about you.

Email

If you found the name of a specific person, email is probably the best way to contact them. Even if their email address isn't on their website (although it probably is), it's usually pretty easy to figure it out. Look at the email addresses for other site contacts. Chances are they're all in one of these formats:

j.jones@firm.com	jjones@firm.com	Janine_j@firm.com
JanineJ@firm.com	Janine@firm.com	Jones@firm.com

Try them all, one at a time. The incorrect ones will bounce back to you, and the contact person will never know that you tried them. The correct version will hit their inbox.

Be sure to have a subject in the email that describes what you want. Good possibilities are "informational interview request" or "interested in your studio." Don't use subjects like "Hi!" or "want a job." Besides being unclear, they are headings that spam software reads as junk mail. The body of your email should also be clear and direct. Look at Chapter 8, "Creating Written Content," for suggestions on how to compose an appropriate email cover letter.

If the contact person doesn't reply, don't give up. Wait a few days, then politely acknowledge that they might be very busy, and ask if there is someone else at the firm to whom you might direct your email. You want to strike a balance between showing your interest and being too persistent.

> I interview all of the creatives that join us. I want to be sure that they're people who will fit well in this culture. I've always figured that if I like everybody who works here, they will like each other.
>
> —Stan Richards

Including your résumé

When you send email, of course you'll include your résumé with your samples. You'll also include it on a CD or DVD. But these portfolio forms are most useful when you have a personal contact or know of a specific hiring opportunity. With an online digital portfolio, you can choose either to include your résumé or replace it with short descriptive text and contact information.

Some people deal with the résumé question by creating a download link to their PDFs. This approach has many benefits. It ensures that your name will find its way into a paper file and encourages viewers to find out more about you while your portfolio is still fresh in their minds.

In some situations, it's better to use the bio plus contact approach. Separating your résumé from your portfolio can be useful for these reasons:

- **Confidentiality.** When you put your résumé on a static web page, its text will be searchable. This might seem to be a plus, but remember that few people will search on your name. Instead, your site will come up most frequently

WWW.CEFARATTI.COM

Mike Cefaratti makes his living as a freelancer. Although he doesn't include a bio on his site, his résumé is readily available for viewing or downloading to encourage potential clients to examine his impressive experience.

when they look for information on your prior—or current—employer. If you are actively looking for a new job while you're still employed or have had issues with a former employer that might come up in an interview, this information might be better left less accessible.

- **Contact.** Handing out your résumé without requiring any contact takes a possible point of control away from you. After all, your résumé is only important to a company if they are already intrigued by your work. If they email to request the résumé, you have instantaneous feedback on your site. You also have an opportunity to present yourself in a less formal, more personal way—and gain a contact name for future mailings.

- **Confidence.** A résumé online can imply less skill and accomplishment than you have. A recent college graduate in photography or illustration may already have a solid collection of work from commissions, co-ops, and internships or personal projects. Drawing attention to your youth may imply inexperience to a potential client, when your work says "professional."

- **Customizing.** Waiting to send your résumé on request also allows you to customize it slightly to each query. You can create alternate résumés for different situations, sending the most appropriate one when asked. Or you can use it as an opportunity to gain points. After you know who wants your résumé, you can visit their site to find out more about them. If you've done a project that's directly relevant to their clientele but isn't in your digital portfolio, a PDF along with the résumé can show not only what a good fit you'd be, but that you think fast.

Cold-calling

If you don't have the name of a person to speak with, call the company. Be straightforward about what you want, don't make them guess why you're calling, and, above all, be polite. Ask if you can send your résumé and a PDF, or your portfolio URL. Describe succinctly and clearly the kind of work you do and why you think you might be a good fit with their firm.

Even if your contact says that there are no positions available, or that they're happy with their current suppliers, send a short follow-up note thanking them for giving you their time, and enclose your résumé and URL. Situations can change quickly, and your information could arrive just as an employee unexpectedly leaves.

Mailings

If you are trying to get as much coverage as possible, one of the best ways to do that is through old-fashioned snail mail. Do not send a copy of your portfolio... send a printed example of your work. One way to do that is with postcards.

Your postcard should be extremely simple: an example of your work on one side, and your name, contact info, URL, and what you do (illustrator, interface designer, photographer, and so on) on the other. Check out www.modernpostcard.com for good-quality, reasonably priced custom postcards.

They're inexpensive to send, and you can produce them yourself.

Each time you update your site with new work, mail postcards again. If you finish an exciting new project, particularly if you are a creative who lives on freelance work, invite people to visit. That way, your prospects know that you are still around and available. Every fresh and new interaction resets the clock and wipes the dust away from the memory of you and your work. Many studios keep a file of prospective freelancers and collaborators. When a new project comes in that requires a new hire or outside help, that file is one of the first places they look.

> **You can have the best reel in the world and send it to 100 companies and get no response whatsoever. It doesn't mean give up your career and go ditchdigging. It's just a matter of timing.**
> **—Terrence Masson**

THE PERSONAL PRESENTATION

With any luck, between advertising, job listings, and your network, you'll get the chance to present your work—and yourself. You want to bolster that positive impression you've given by doing the same in person.

Rehearsal

After you set up a date for a personal presentation, go through your portfolio and prepare what you are going to say about each piece, and about your work in general. Rehearsal doesn't mean memorization, which leaves no room for personality or spontaneity. Nor does it mean developing a sales pitch. That turns other creative people off. It does mean having a plan and feeling prepared, which should make you feel more confident.

WHAT TO PREPARE

Good presentations, like good portfolios, have a story behind them. You need to grab your audience's interest immediately, support that positive first impression, and end on a strong note. Because an online presentation isn't linear, your emphasis until now has probably been on the overall experience of your portfolio site. But in a personal presentation, the sequence in which you introduce your ideas and present your work is critical.

You've already limited your portfolio to your best work. For your presentation, look for the best of the best, and lead off with it. Pull out the extras, the supporting elements of a project, and any work that you couldn't put online because of contractual issues. You don't want your presentation to be exactly the same as your site if your site is how you got the interview in the first place.

> **What shocks me is that so many designers will work so hard on their individual pieces in their portfolio but then throw them all together with little energy devoted to creating a well paced and entertaining experience for the viewer.**
> **—David Heasty**

Layla Keramat makes a point of customizing every presentation she makes with the name of the company or client. She continues this customization by reviewing her presentation and shifting the balance of her work toward material that will be relevant to the audience.

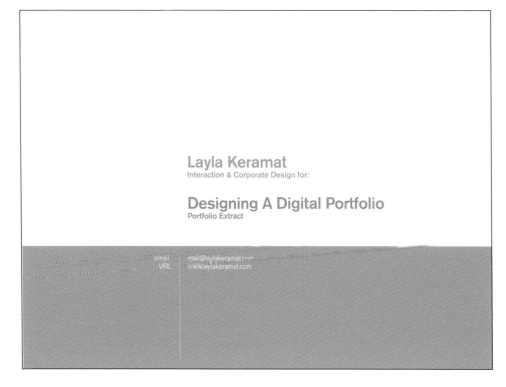

HOW TO REHEARSE

Don't just rehearse in your head—speak out loud and act the process out. If you are bringing a traditional portfolio with you, go through the physical act of presentation to make sure that it's easy to pull out mounted boards from a case, and that you can access each individual element without rummaging around for it.

If you'll be presenting with a laptop, consider customizing the presentation for your audience. Nothing does a better job of telling a group of skeptical listeners how serious you are about their job than an opening screen with their firm's name on it. If you've done a great job in organizing your portfolio, you should already have categorized all your work. Cull through it before the presentation to emphasize the type of projects their firm specializes in.

Ask in advance if you'll be projecting your work. Most projectors are a generation behind desktops in screen resolution. Make a special version of your presentation to run at 800x600 resolution so you'll still be able to access your interface if the projector is an older one.

A good portfolio is going to get you in the door, but it's how a person talks about their work and how they express their ideas that's a large part of it. I remember hiring someone who had only one piece to show me, but she had such energy, and the piece that she showed me was good. I hired her on the spot.

—Bill Cahan

BE PREPARED

You can't know in advance exactly who will be present at your interview, or how much knowledge they may have. Even if it's "just" a screening meeting at a placement agency, bring your portfolio materials.

You'll want to clarify your role in creating the work, especially if you played more than one role. Did you design, but also create the illustrations or write the copy? Did you do the programming for the prototype? Was the work completed in a very tight time frame? Remember the issues of attribution and honesty in Chapter 12, "Copyright and Portfolio," and claim only your fair share of the work you present.

Know why you made your creative decisions, and find words to describe them. "It just came to me," will sound as weak as it is. How can you be hired as a client problem-solver if you can't describe the problem? If appropriate, bring process materials that aren't part of your regular portfolio to help you describe how you think.

Talking about your work can also involve listening. I once attended a presentation by a midcareer design professional who turned every query about how he approached a specific client problem into a lecture about how good he was at addressing client problems. Despite his reputation, this introduced doubts in his audience about whether they could work with him. He projected his agenda too clearly.

Think about the personal assessment that you completed in Chapter 1, "Assessment and Adaptation," and allow yourself to be who you really are. Your chemistry with the interviewers is something you can't control—either it's there or it isn't. But if you're prepared to field questions about how you deal with deadlines and your experiences in collaborative situations, it will be easier for you to loosen up and let your personality come through.

> People were never prepared to talk about their work with me, because I'm a recruiter. They were sometimes taken aback when I wanted to rip apart the portfolio and talk about their design approach.
> —Cynthia Rabun

> If you're hiring someone, you're looking at their personality and their demeanor—even their vocabulary in some cases. Are they going to be nice to be around? Are they going to take direction? And are they going to be capable of handling a client relationship or directing other people eventually?
> —Nancy Hoefig

Dress code

Even if you have very strong opinions about style and dress, avoid extreme clothing, and cover your tattoos. Even if your daily wardrobe is a T-shirt and torn jeans, have one outfit that is clean, ironed, and ready for the public. Being unwilling to adapt your style implies that you are either clueless or inflexible, as well as being someone who would have to be insulated from many clients. Your work had better be astoundingly good to balance these negatives.

Dressing appropriately doesn't mean that you should show up clad in a corporate uniform. Clients expect a creative person to "look" creative. Sharp, good-quality clothes that telegraph a personal style are very acceptable for professionals in the arts.

Presentation do's

There are too many books and job sites that offer hints on interviewing well to list them here. One whose style and approach I like is *The Interview Rehearsal Book* (Berkley Trade, 1999), by Deb Gottesman. However, you don't need to read 100 pages to make it through an interview without embarrassment. These commonsense hints will help you support your portfolio with the presentation it deserves.

- **Face your audience.** Be familiar enough with your material that you can concentrate on the people you'll be presenting to, not your screen. Avoid turning your back while you present.

- **Speak up.** If people ask you to repeat what you've said, you are probably talking too softly or quickly.

- **Make eye contact.** If you want to know whether you can work with them— as well as whether they can work with you—try to catch your interviewers' eyes occasionally as you speak.

- **Show interest and enthusiasm.** Energy and good humor can be infectious. So can whining. Don't complain about your previous experiences, talk about how hard it's been to find a job, or introduce any negative topics about your past work experience.

- **Be proud of your portfolio.** Above all, never apologize for your work. You can discuss design, financial or branding constraints, your client's specific requirements, or problems and solutions, but never point out what's wrong with a piece or with your skills. That isn't perfectionism—it's suicide. Besides, by this time you should have eliminated from your portfolio anything that doesn't reflect well on you.

- **Hand out a leave-behind.** Whether it be a disc copy of a portion of your work, a PDF extract, or a small, printed sample that evokes one of your most impressive projects, you are more likely to be remembered at the end of a series of interviews if there is something tangible in your wake. Come prepared with multiple copies...you never know who might have missed the presentation and might appreciate the chance to see what everyone else in the office is talking about.

Luke Williams is committed to doing everything right, and it shows. To prepare for major portfolio presentations in his graduation year, he printed up small flyer cards that remind the people he presented his portfolio to of his most important projects and the design story behind them.

FOLLOWING UP

If you are interested in the assignment or position, you should make that clear. The form you use will depend on the nature of the interaction and the position. For job or informational interviews, a thank-you note, particularly on your own letterhead or a nicely designed card, can make a big difference. But if time is important, it's better to send an email than to take the chance that they will decide before the snail mail arrives. If the interview was for a full-time job as opposed to a freelance opportunity or a potential client, it's also legitimate to make a follow-up phone call before you have to move on.

Finally, don't get discouraged if the presentation doesn't result in a job or assignment initially. Your style may not fit their current concept, or they may have found someone with more experience. Stay in touch. If you have a new collection of work in a few months, send it off to your contacts with a cover letter reminding them of who you are. Make phone calls on a regular cycle (once every six to eight weeks is reasonable) to see if there's something new available, or if they'd like to see more work. Keep the conversations short and upbeat. If you had a PDF and have now added a website, or have significantly updated the website they saw originally, send a note to announce the URL and invite your contacts to visit it. If your work is good, persistence will be rewarded.

THANK-YOU NOTE

The text for a thank-you should be professional, short, and warm, but not effusive. It should be sent to the person who conducted the interview. Make sure you spell their name right, proof your work for spelling and grammatical errors, and don't refer to other people in the interview by name unless you are very certain of who they are. Do mention something specific about the interview, so they know your note isn't generic. Such a note could go something like this:

Dear Scott,

Thank you for the opportunity to present my portfolio to your group yesterday. I really appreciated the give and take, and I hope we'll have the chance to continue the process in the future.

Looking forward to hearing from you,

Linda Jones

STAYING RELEVANT

It's so tempting, once you finally have a portfolio in place, to treat it as complete. Many people who use their portfolio as a tool to find a new job throw it on their mental shelf once they start the new position. But very few jobs are permanent. You should clean house and freshen your portfolio on a regular cycle. If you ignore it and let it become stale, you hasten the day when your portfolio can no longer be presented. It becomes a major project once again.

The simplest chore is to check your links, if you have any. One typical boo-boo is to fail to update your mail-to link when your provider email address changes. If you link to any sites outside your own (friends, web-based projects you contributed to or designed), check every one to make sure that they haven't changed as well. And don't forget to check links to group portfolio or self-publishing sites. Something they think is old might be purged. Link-checking should go on your calendar as a monthly housecleaning task.

Of course, as you accumulate new projects, you should add them to your site, or replace some older ones. If you have created a modular design, inserting a new project should take very little time. The energy you invest in scanning or repurposing is small compared to the benefits of a lively, current site.

Many artists and designers include a résumé, vita, or biographical timeline as part of their portfolio. Every six months at least, you should look at these items again. Have you changed jobs, added a new, noteworthy client, or taken part in a group show? It's much easier to add new things while they are still fresh in your mind.

In general, pay close attention to places on your site that include specific dates. When you first put them up, they can be useful markers, and in some cases, as with annual reports, listing the year is almost obligatory. But as your site grows older, the lack of anything with the current year stands out as a signpost of a dead site.

> People shouldn't take it personally when someone doesn't follow up. Just because someone doesn't call you back after they said that they're interested in talking to you, it doesn't mean that they're not interested. It just means that they haven't had the time.
>
> —Bill Cahan

AND, THE END. MAYBE.

With luck and perseverance, your digital portfolio will do its job and get you the recognition and clients you deserve. Once it does, celebrate! You've worked hard, and smart. Start your new job, or your new projects. But don't forget the portfolio that got you there. If you've chosen to make creativity your life's work, you owe it to yourself to continue to show the world your best efforts—your latest concepts. Your portfolio may change form or purpose as your career advances, but it is never really finished until you stop creating. It's a stage in your constant journey to better work and a more satisfying career.

PORTFOLIO HIGHLIGHT:
KEN LOH | A HAND IN THE GAME

KENLOH.COM

Eventually, some creatives show a knack not only for creative concepts but for mentoring, managing, or directing the creativity of others. Their hands-on moments decrease as their responsibilities expand. What happens to the relationship between their career and their portfolio? Addressing that question says a lot about the individual. Some maintain a choice portfolio comprising every good project in which they've had input, perhaps feeling—with or without justification—that the work would have been a lesser thing without their touch.

> **I don't do much hands-on designing anymore. I miss it, but when you have a talented staff like I do, it's a lot easier to let some of that go.**
>
> **—Ken Loh**

Historically, those who felt uncomfortable with that approach, who felt that their staff of artists and designers really deserved pride of place, ended up with a frozen portfolio stashed in a closet. Case closed, zipped, forgotten.

Former ace designer Ken Loh has reached that career turning point. But luckily for him, the online world has redefined the concept of a portfolio, as it has nearly everything else. Being at the top of a chain has changed what he does on a daily basis. But in return, it gives him the freedom to turn his creative enthusiasms and connections into a different type of portfolio: one that advertises his continued engagement in visual issues, and provides a way to keep his hand in the game.

Navigation and architecture

Plug in Loh's URL, and his "Latest Updates" page appears. A literally "playful" opening displays one of a constantly rotating subset of Loh's truly staggering collection of toys. The highly organized top of the page becomes a cornucopia of content as you scroll down. At first glance it seems chaotic, but you quickly realize that the page is actually tightly organized in a multicolumn grid. Each column holds all the most recent updates of one aspect of Loh's busy online world.

Loh was not only a designer and art director; he was, and is, a master of website coding. His website has been featured on several blogs for its excellent design and CSS implementation. The site is built with CSS and JavaScript: a skillful compilation of feeds from all of his social networking sites, gathered in one place on the "one ring to rule them all" principle.

> **Each subsite has a particular purpose. Thing is, none of them do a good job of telling the visitor who I am on their own. It just made sense to integrate them all into one lifestream.**
>
> **—Ken Loh**

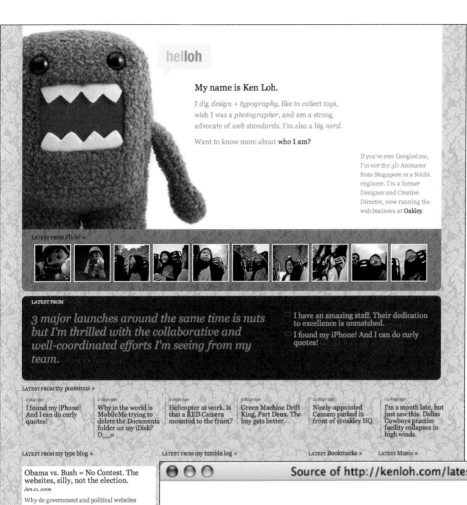

Loh's navigation on the Latests page is extremely simple, yet a simple View Source betrays his mastery. The source code is very short, as it has little unique content. He has created a grid with CSS that automatically gathers everything from his tweets to his Flickr images at one address. Now that it is set up, the site requires no additional effort to maintain.

Navigation is extremely unfussy and clear. Anything red is a link. Hover over a link and it turns white. Click the link and a new window opens to the source site for the column that the link controls.

Content

Content is not only king on Loh's site, it is the entire royal family. There are ten social networking feeds and five personal sites, each dedicated to a different facet of his interests and creative output. Like many good designers, he loves type. Among his subsites is, of course, a type blog. There's his Flickr feed, a fascinating collection of ever-changing bookmarks. There's even his old portfolio site, circa 2005.

This is the one place where I can do whatever I want, without having to take anyone else's opinions into consideration.

—Ken Loh

In many ways, the most impressive element is the "Who is Ken Loh?" subsite. Organized by human facets, each page explores one aspect of his life.

But page is perhaps a misnomer. What look like individual pages are really parts of only a single page of code. These uniquely styled, beautiful examples of graphic design have been designed with CSS. When each facet's text link is selected, a separate window for that portion of the page opens. If there is any question about Loh's continued interest in, and ability to produce creatively with, cutting edge technology, this subsite should answer it.

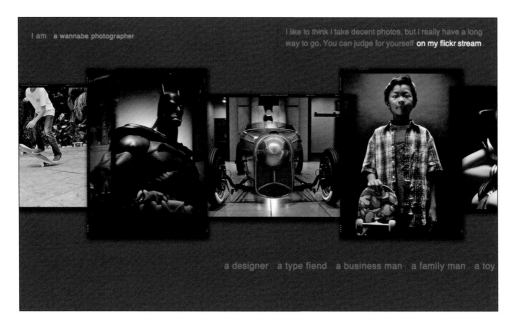

Loh captures the elegant feel of a professional photographer's portfolio site in his "wannabe photographer" window.

Each of Loh's nested windows has been designed separately to capture the flavor of each facet of his life, yet they are integrated by color. The splash page is a layered, typographic image that recalls his previous design aesthetic. The Designer window has a translucent layer that slides over a collage of his work. The business man page is crisp and geometric.

Loh proves his assertion on the type fiend page. The navigation for this window is made up of overlapping text, each line of which highlights in red when it becomes active. This piece of programming is impressive, but the real surprise is the type itself. Usually, when you blow up online type, you end up with a fuzzy, bitmapped mess. Loh's type retains its clean, crisp outlines, even at a 300 percent enlargement.

Totally in keeping with Loh's strong sense of modesty and fairness, he makes sure that every window in this subsite also contains a shout-out to designer Mark Jardine and programmer Bryan Veloso, whose similarly aggregated websites were his influences.

I'm a bit of a workaholic, so the lines between my personal and professional online profiles have pretty much blurred.

—Ken Loh

Future plans

Loh has reached a career point where the likelihood of having to develop a traditional portfolio again is slim. But he's happy with his online presence, and feels it meets his needs. Of course, when asked, he knows what he'd do if he had to clothe himself in the hands-on mantle once again. A self-proclaimed nerd, he'd experiment more with coding technologies. He has so much work, and it covers such a broad range, that he'd make a searchable online portfolio site that has links to projects by job. But most important, he'll continue to look for the best possible people for his design team, so he can continue to lead by example.

Appendixes

Resources

A bountiful collection of portfolio resources is just a few mouse clicks away. Although I've grouped these sites under headings for ease of use, you'll find that some sites, particularly those for associations, actually offer listings or information in other categories.

COPYRIGHT AND LEGAL ISSUES

These sites address intellectual property and the law. They're good places to check in for help with registering your portfolio content and keeping your nose clean when you're not sure what you can, and can't, legally do.

Copyright Website | BENEDICT.COM

This site is dedicated to intellectual property issues of all sorts. It has a copyright wizard that painlessly and quickly walks you through the process of filing a copyright on your work.

DigiMarc | DIGIMARC.COM

Digimarc is the developer of the best-known method of embedding watermarks in digital images. The site explains how the technology works, and allows you to enable the service plug-in.

IPG Art Law Center | WWW.ARTLAWS.COM

The Art Law Center offers intellectual property and other legal services to creatives. The site has a collection of standard legal forms, useful articles, and links.

Nolo | WWW.NOLO.COM

Nolo believes in the democratization of the law—anyone should be able to get the information they need on legal issues in clear, sane English. Their website and their publications demystify the sometimes Byzantine workings of law, and their copyright section is particularly good.

United States Copyright Office | COPYRIGHT.GOV

This is the site for the U.S. government's copyright office. It's a well-written, easy to navigate site for downloading relevant publications and registering your work.

GROUP SITES AND FORUMS

This group of sites is particularly handy for posting your portfolio for feedback (taken with a grain of salt, I hope), or for marketing to potential clients or employers. Some are specific to one or two disciplines; others are open to all creatives.

Animation and modeling

Animation World Network Television | WWW.AWNTV.COM

An animation-only competitor to YouTube, where you can submit a video of your work and hope to find it in the Featured Content section. This site is a cornucopia of every length and type of animated content. It has its own reviewers and an active community of registered kibitzers. Artwork is searchable by tagged descriptions, and theme-based playlists help you find your favorite type of content. There are also tips and tricks organized by category in the Channels section.

CG Channel | WWW.CGCHANNEL.COM/

This glossy site is dedicated to all forms of computer graphics. Besides providing news and interviews, it boasts a large and vital community that revolves around its forums. The Cool Links forum allows registered users to post links to their own sites or to others of interest, and then open them to critique and discussion. In addition, you'll find the CG Art portfolio area and a recruitment section with job listings.

CG Society | WWW.CGSOCIETY.ORG

The Society of Digital Artists runs this site, which is a hotbed of industry news, articles, workshops, forums, and galleries. The forum is very light on the flaming and heavy on useful feedback because they are moderated.

Gallery of 3D.com | WWW.GALLERYOF3D.COM

Less glossy than some of the other sites devoted to the 3D community, this site is exactly what its name implies. It displays member animations and 3D renderings. Anyone can become a member and post their work, but the site also profiles some members and places a few in the Cream Gallery. Among the forums is one (3Dartwork > Critique) dedicated to peer critiques.

InsideCG.com | WWW.INSIDECG.COM

The computer graphics community is full of enthusiasts, which may be why there are so many good sites and forums for them. Industry focused, this site has a large community following, in part because of a good jobs listing.

Flay.com | FLAY.COM

Flay has been around for, in Internet terms, a long time—since 1996. Similar in format to other forum-based CG sites, Flay offers a particularly strong Jobs section with the most recent (and most likely to still be unfilled), at the top.

Fine arts

Absolutearts.com and World Wide Arts Resources | WWW.ABSOLUTEARTS.COM and WWAR.COM

This is a marketplace and portfolio site for fine artists. It offers a mailing list of dealers and galleries for artists trying to get a show or representation, and it has a large gallery and portfolio database. The basic portfolio of eight images is free. They also offer a 40-image portfolio and a premier, juried version—a mind-boggling 3,000 images—for a yearly fee.

ArtistsRegister.com | ARTISTSREGISTER.COM

This site, run by WESTAF (Western States Arts Federation), positions itself as a marketing tool that connect artists with both art buyers and galleries, non-profit organizations, and participating state agencies. Membership is by application, and requires a membership fee.

ArtVitae | WWW.ARTVITAE.COM

A multilingual portfolio site used by artists in both the U.S. and Europe, the site boasts a substantial database of artists' CVs and their portfolios. For an annual fee, you can use their template to quickly get your information and a sampling of your work online, or you can design, create, and manage your own portfolio but use the site as a home address. One nice touch: Their ArtPostcards service allows both visitors and artists to email postcards of work—a nice way to do a cold-call email.

Art in Context Center for Communications | WWW.ARTINCONTEXT.ORG

This is a nonprofit site that creates a library of artists and organizations. They will put you into their searchable database for a small registration fee, that is renewable, for a small discount, annually. Because it's part of the art community and not a commercial venture, it attracts many academics and museum curators.

Game design

GamaSutra | WWW.GAMASUTRA.COM

The premier site for people interested in the game design world, whether it be for educational opportunities, jobs, opinions, or feedback. Friendly, informative blogs and a truly excellent job list put this site on the required list for anyone wanting to make a living as a game professional.

Gamedev.net | WWW.GAMEDEV.NET

The forums are the draw here. This site is dedicated to making you a better game developer, designer, or artist, with extremely active posting, particularly on the technical forums. The GDNet Lounge is a comfy gathering space for like-minded pros and wannabes. It is impossible to visit this site and not learn something useful.

Graphic arts and design

Behance | WWW.BEHANCE.NET

A strange grafting of social network, professional resource, portfolio site, and design magazine, Behance has quickly become a destination that rivals the more established portfolio options. You must be invited to join by another Behance member, with the idea that only serious creatives with a network will find their way in. Even without joining, the range of quality portfolios and the other online content makes this a good site to visit.

Communication Arts | WWW.COMMARTS.COM

Communication Arts is a magazine whose site includes one of the very best job and portfolio listings for the design professions. Jobs can be viewed by location, title, or discipline. In addition, using their template, you can create a portfolio of up to 27 images and a profile, and post for a fee in their Creative HotList section. The site also provides occasional articles of great value on career and other professional topics.

Coroflot | WWW.COROFLOT.COM

Coroflot is a cross-disciplinary professional development site for creatives, although it is most frequently used by people in the related areas of graphic design, interaction, and industrial design. It provides a comprehensive listing of design firms and organizations, a very good job board, and a portfolio site used by professionals around the world. You create a free portfolio by uploading your work into sets using their template, which includes a link to your own portfolio site if you have one. The site also has forums devoted to design careers and practice. Coroflot is also connected to *Core77*, a design magazine (core77.com) with informative and often fascinating articles on design issues.

PROFESSIONAL ORGANIZATIONS

Not at all comprehensive, this group of associations represents the best-known and most useful organizations for creatives. Most offer a variety of member benefits, including career help and job listings.

ACM (Association for Computing Machinery) | WWW.ACM.ORG

Far more than its name might suggest, the ACM is the home of the special interest group (SIG), known as SIGGRAPH. This group can be an extremely valuable networking resource for creatives in animation, modeling, and interactivity. Another good group for web professionals is SIGCHI, which covers areas of human-computer interaction and usability.

AIA (American Institute of Architects) | WWW.AIA.ORG

The defining organization for architecture, AIA has a site that offers extensive career and job search support. Their "Find an Architect" database allows potential clients to search the member listing with very specific criteria. Architects looking for a firm can post a résumé on the site. In addition, there are several articles and links for professional development.

AIGA | WWW.AIGA.ORG

AIGA, the professional organization for design, partners with Aquent to provide an excellent job posting area for graphic design and related positions in the U.S. Although anyone can search the listings, you must be an AIGA member to post a job-seeker profile. The AIGA site also hosts a lively collection of forums, and sponsors discussion lists on design theory and practice.

American Society of Media Photographers | www.ASMP.ORG

Professional photographers, particularly those who shoot for advertising and editorial clients, will find help with business issues, a listing of local chapters, and a friendly network of people at this site. They have a gallery where they feature members' work, and a good database for photo buyers.

BDA (Broadcast Designers of America) | www.PROMAXBDA.ORG

This site is the international resource for creatives in broadcast design and promotion, and marketing executives in electronic media, to connect with others through the message boards, create a link to their portfolio site, or search for posted jobs. You must be a member of either BDA or Promax International to register, to post, or to access the job board.

Graphic Artists Guild | www.GRAPHICARTISTSGUILD.ORG

A multidisciplinary organization for industry creatives, particularly designers (graphic, web, and so on) and illustrators. This site is particularly useful for freelancers and small studios, with Guild chapters in many cities in the U.S. In addition, the Guild offers a portfolio site for its members only. Areas range from cartooning to graphic design to video/broadcast design.

Industrial Designers Society of America | www.IDSA.ORG

IDSA is for industrial designers what the AIGA is for graphic designers. It covers a variety of disciplines related to ID: from furniture to consumer electronics to usability design. Included on the site is a listing of employment opportunities, as well as ID firms. The site offers links to each of the local chapters.

Rhode Island School of Design | www.RISD.EDU

Most art and design schools have websites, and offer services to their students. I single out RISD's site, however, because it is particularly full and rich. It provides a comprehensive list of extremely useful links—on topics ranging from a listing of job banks to company profiles—for its alumni, who must register to use the site.

Society for Environmental Graphic Design | www.SEGD.ORG

If your interests lie in the real world of three-dimensional environments—from exhibit design to architecture to ID—this site is what you need. It has a job bank with very detailed postings and a new referrals section where SEGD members can provide profiles for potential clients.

ADC (Art Directors Club) | www.ADCGLOBAL.ORG

By far the most important of the Art Directors Clubs that can be found in some major cities is the New York City flagship. It is a terrific international resource for professionals in advertising, interactive media, design, and communications, with a public job board of international postings.

SPECIALIZED RESOURCES

Google has become the default search system, both for its own directories and for those throughout the Internet. However, there are several independent sites whose databases contain specialized information for creatives on the research prowl: directories, listings, career information, and helpful articles.

InfoDesign | WWW.INFODESIGN.ORG

This international listing zeros in on resources for information designers. It has live links to an alphabetical listing of firms from the U.S. to Japan, links to information designers and information architects, and a jobs section.

CreativePro | WWW.CREATIVEPRO.COM

This is the mother of all directories for creatives. You can find every creative association in the U.S., as well as a comprehensive listing of agencies, firms, publishers, and suppliers.

The Firm List | US.FIRMLIST.COM

Looking for a web-design firm who might be looking for someone like you? If so, this is a good first stop. Listings are sorted by state, then by city/town.

CAREER SITES

With so many local or national career sites, it would be folly to try to list them all. Everyone is familiar with sites like Monster.com. But there are other, more targeted sites that are also worth a careful look. I've provided three very different sites from which to approach a job search: a targeted creative recruitment firm, a creatives-only company, and a large, extremely rich general site.

Roz Goldfarb Associates | WWW.RGARECRUITING.COM

Roz Goldfarb Associates is a recruitment firm in New York City specializing in creatives of all sorts. Most of the jobs listed on its site are for established professionals, not entry-level candidates. They are broken down into job categories, and the number of postings in each area is listed—a fast way to see what types of positions are generating traffic.

The Creative Group | WWW.CREATIVEGROUP.COM

The Creative Group is a staffing firm for marketing and advertising creatives. It has placement offices in a variety of cities around the U.S. The website allows you to search for opportunities by location and job description, as well as by keyword. Each local area posts a small portfolio for their featured artists on the main website.

Vault | www.vault.com

All careers, all jobs, all the time. The Vault is not a creatives' site, but it has research on over 3,000 companies (great for targeting an audience) and a daunting collection of message boards where you can read what people who are (or were) working at these companies have to say about the experience.

SOFTWARE SELF-HELP BOOKS

You'll need to master at least one software program in making your digital portfolio. There are many excellent books to choose from as companions in your learning process—and there is usually more than one that covers a topic effectively. What follows is simply my personal pick of books that I think cover their topics well.

AFTER EFFECTS FOR FLASH, FLASH FOR AFTER EFFECTS | Richard Harrington and Marcus Geduld

A particularly smart book for the motion or animation person who wants to be able to work with both Adobe Flash and Adobe After Effects to create a reel and portfolio.

The Zen of CSS Design: Visual Enlightenment for the Web | Dave Shea and Molly E. Holzschlag

A truly well-designed website needs formats and good typography. With style sheets, you can attain these goals. With this book, by the creator of the CSS Zen Garden and web guru Molly Holzschlag, you'll actually know what you're doing, and why you'd want to do it.

JavaScript and Ajax for the World Wide Web: Visual Quickstart Guide | Tom Negrino and Dori Smith

I'm prejudiced, because the authors are good friends. But I thought the book covered the subject beautifully even before I knew them. If you need a little website scripting, this is the book for you.

WEB DESIGN IN A NUTSHELL | Jennifer Niederst

A clear and concise explanation of how to make a website, from soup to nuts. The author knows what she's talking about, and she organizes it beautifully.

THE CREATIVE DIGITAL DARKROOM | Katrin Eismann and Sean Duggan

A book that takes you into the more complicated and creative realms of image editing. Particularly useful if you are looking for techiques to enhance your scanned printed materials or photographed 3D art.

DIGITAL CLASSROOM SERIES FROM WILEY

This is a great series for a relative beginner who wants to understand the basics of Adobe CS software. Each is a well-considered training package, particularly the books that cover Adobe Photoshop, Flash, and Dreamweaver.

VISUAL QUICKSTART GUIDES FROM PEACHPIT PRESS

The books in this series will help you master the software they cover. They are classics: inexpensive, well-organized, and easy-to-follow references.

Appendix B

Contributors

This book would have been far less rich, attractive, and exciting without the words and images of this international group of professionals, who so graciously allowed me to showcase their talents and ply them with questions. Some are at the beginning of their careers, and are certain to surprise and delight with their future great work and terrific portfolios. Others are well-respected professionals at the top of their game, who were generous enough to donate their time and thoughts to this project. My only regret is that I couldn't show more of their work, and include all of their insights.

RITA ARMSTRONG

Design Recruiter, Roz Goldfarb Associates   WWW.RGARECRUITING.COM

Since 1988, Rita Armstrong has sought out and placed talented designers and design managers in packaging, digital, and industrial design. She is passionate about encouraging designers to gain the business tools they need to promote their talent. She has spoken at conferences, given seminars at design schools, and contributed to articles and books, including a chapter in Roz's own book, *Careers by Design*. Before toiling in the fields of theater, advertising, and nonprofit communications, she graduated from Fordham University with a BA in Communications with a concentration in Journalism and Film.

THOM BENNETT

Graphic/Web Designer   WWW.TBGD.CO.UK

British designer Thom Bennett has always been equally drawn toward creativity and numbers. After studying art and graphic design, he pursued a degree in landscape architecture in an attempt to combine both interests, and because the idea of producing something physical (rather than pen on paper) was very appealing. After graduation, he again became involved in graphic design and secured a job at a local graphic design agency. He has stayed in this field ever since, moving more recently into website design.

MICHAEL BOROSKY

Creative Director, Eleven, Inc.   ELEVENINC.COM

Michael Borosky spent the first 15 years of his career working in the offline side of the design business for a variety of firms, including the San Francisco office of Pentagram. He started specializing in online media after joining CKS Partners (now MarchFirst). As Creative Director, he led interactive projects for clients ranging from MCI to General Motors, Visa, and Levi Strauss. As partner and Creative Director at Eleven, Michael oversees the online brand integration for a wide range of clients, including Kodak, Microsoft, and Williams-Sonoma.

RICK BRAITHWAITE

President Emeritus, Sandstrom Design   WWW.SANDSTROMDESIGN.COM

Rick Braithwaite co-founded Sandstrom Design in 1990 after 16 years in the advertising industry. He has three children, four grandchildren, and is an avid golfer, hiker, and reader. He grew up in Los Angeles, spent three years as an officer in the Marines, and has been married for 40 years. He is a former President of APDF (Association of Professional Design Firms), loves the theater and fly fishing, and is the only male in America who has not appeared on a reality TV show.

MICHAEL BRALEY

Art Director   WWW.BRALEYDESIGN.COM

Michael Braley is an Art Director and designer in Brooklyn, New York. His work has appeared in numerous publications and exhibitions including: British Design and Art Direction, Clio Awards, *I.D., Graphis,* Type Directors Club, CA, The Art Directors Club of New York, The One Show, Step 100, and *Print* and is in the permanent collections of the San Francisco Museum of Modern Art, the Chicago Athenaeum Museum of Architecture and Design and the Museum für Kunst und Gewerbe in Hamburg, Germany. Braley has taught typography at the California College of the Arts (CCA) and has lectured and led workshops at universities and professional organizations around the nation.

KEVIN BUDELMANN

President, People Design   WWW.PEOPLEDESIGN.COM

Kevin Budelmann studied computer interface design at Carnegie Mellon University before it was cool, while gaining his BFA in graphic design, and before pursuing further study at The School of Design in Switzerland and the Harvard Business School. His acclaim as a designer for a diverse roster of clients includes numerous awards in major design competitions from the AIGA, the Art Directors Club of New York, The Type Directors Club of New York, *Graphis, Print*, *Creativity,* and *Step*, as well as recent Webby Awards. He has been a speaker and judge at design events and institutions across the continent.

BILL CAHAN

Founder and Creative Director, Cahan & Associates

WWW.CAHANASSOCIATES.COM

Widely praised for its evocative annual reports, packaging, corporate branding, advertising, and web design, San Francisco-based Cahan & Associates has a diverse clientele ranging from Fortune 500 companies to consumer, high-tech, and biotech leaders to emerging growth companies. The company has won over 2000 awards and garnered write-ups in hundreds of periodicals and books. The Princeton Architectural Press book, *I Am Almost Always Hungry,* chronicles the agency's culture, process, and portfolio. Cahan's penchant for refreshing the stodgy world of annual reports has been chronicled in "Cahan & Associates on Annual Reports."

THANE CALDER

CoFounder, CloudRaker   WWW.CLOUDRAKER.COM

Thane Calder co-founded CloudRaker on Valentines Day 2000 in order to launch the no-bull digital agency of the future. After almost 10 years, he still feels like he's running a start-up, given the ever-changing nature of the industry. Thane oversees strategic planning at CloudRaker, and has a knack for asking a lot of questions (and spilling coffee). His creative, no-nonsense approach has led to the successful development of key Internet mandates with such clients as Air Canada Vacations, Bell Canada, eBay Canada, enRoute Magazine, Onitsuka Tiger (ASICS), Sympatico/MSN, and the Canadian Cancer Society.

MIKE CEFARATTI

Principal, Cefaratti Design   CEFARATTI.COM

In his many years in new media and broadcast design, Mike has created web-based solutions for agencies like Think New Ideas, Nicholson NY/IconMedialab, DePlano Group, Atmosphere, and Plural. He has played a critical role in the strategic development and execution of branded Internet solutions, CD-ROMs, television commercials, and music compositions. Most notably, he has created award-winning sites for both Avon and Rockport, and developed websites and banner campaigns for clients including AIG, Chase, Marriott, and Frito-Lay. Mike holds degrees in both marketing and graphic design. He currently works in New York City.

HERCULANO FERNANDES

Animator   WWW.HERCFERN.COM

Herculano Fernandes is a recent graduate of Northeastern University's Art+Design Department. He dual-majored in Multimedia Studies and Animation, emerging as a Maya generalist and compositor. Currently freelancing in the broadcast industry, he hopes to work in various cities creating amazing work.

HENRY FOSTER

Animator   TOADSTORM.COM

Henry Foster was raised in Foxboro, MA, a drinking town with a football problem. After getting his bachelor's degree in Multimedia Studies and Animation from Northeastern University, he worked as a Flash programmer and animator, and later as a freelance 3D artist and technical director. He currently lives in Los Angeles.

JONNIE HALLMAN

Web designer, programmer   DESTROYTODAY.COM

Jonnie Hallman is a web designer, programmer, and aspiring comedian. He is a graduate of the Maryland Institute College of Art, where he majored in graphic design. Throughout his four years at the MICA, Jonnie worked at the multi-disciplinary studio, Shaw Jelveh Design, focusing on "green" clients such as the United States Green Building Council. Under the name "Destroy Today," Jonnie won an Adobe Design Achievement Award for his Flickr application, DestroyFlickr. His Twitter application, DestroyTwitter, surpassed 150,000 installs within its first six months of being public. Jonnie plans to continue programming and hopes to someday find a hobby separate from the computer.

DAVID HEASTY

Co-Founder, Triboro Associates   WWW.TRIBORO.COM

Triboro is the husband-and-wife team of David Heasty and Stefanie Weigler. The studio excels both in building inspiring brands from the ground-up and in shepherding already established brands into new territories. The company's clients include Alfred A. Knopf, Andrew Roth, GQ, Johan Lindeberg, 4AD, P.S.1 MoMA, *The New York Times,* and William Rast. In 2005 David Heasty became an Art Directors Club "Young Gun." Triboro's work has been featured in numerous design publications as well as the *New York Times*, the *Wall Street Journal,* and *Lucky*. Triboro has been consistently awarded and recognized by the AIGA, Art Directors Club, *Print* and The Society of Publication Designers.

NANCY HOEFIG

Principal, Hoefig Design   HOEFIGDESIGN.COM

Nancy Hoefig brings more than 20 years' experience in brand-image campaigns and design systems to Fortune 500 clients, including BP, Charles Schwab, Ford Motor Company, and Visa. Before founding Hoefig Design, Nancy served as Creative Director at Landor Associates, an Associate Partner at Pentagram in New York, Executive Art Director at CBS in New York, Deputy Art Director at the *New York Times Magazine*, and as a Principal with The Richards Group in Dallas. Nancy holds a BFA in Graphic Design from Syracuse University and served as an instructor at The School of Visual Arts in New York. She has received numerous awards from AIGA, CA, Clio, *Graphis*, Mead Show, Potlatch Annual Report Show, Art Directors Club of New York, Society of Illustrators, Society of Publication Designers, and Type Directors Club.

ALEXANDER ISLEY

Principal, Alexander Isley Inc.   WWW.ALEXANDERISLEY.COM

Alexander Isley heads Alexander Isley Inc., a nine-person design firm with offices in Connecticut and NYC. He is also a partner in The Dave and Alex Show, an advertising and marketing communications agency. Alex is a graduate of The Cooper Union and the North Carolina State University College of Design. He is a visiting critic at the Yale Graduate School of Art.

LAYLA KERAMAT

Designer   LAYLA_KERAMAT@YAHOO.COM

With expertise in user interface and corporate design, Layla Keramat has led design projects on many digital platforms, including websites, desktop software, telematics, handhelds, mobiles, and touch screens. Her client roster includes Barnes & Noble, Coca-Cola, Deutsche Telekom, GE, Maytag, o2 Telefonica, and Vodafone. Layla's career began in 1987 with Sony Music, where she was responsible for designing packaging and advertising for European releases, including Bruce Springsteen, Pearl Jam, and Mariah Carey, as well as spearheading emerging technology initiatives. Besides design practice, Layla mentors design talent and is a former Adjunct Professor, School of Visual Arts, NY.

YANG KIM

Vice Presiden/Creative Director, People Design   WWW.PEOPLEDESIGN.COM

Yang Kim's fruitful client collaborations include efficient communications management for Southern California-based SitOnIt Seating, edgy retail brochures for Jaguar Cars, and landmark annual reports for Herman Miller. Yang's work has been recognized by major design competitions including the Art Directors Club of New York, the Type Directors Club of New York, *Communication Arts*, *Critique* magazine, the AIGA, *Graphis*, *How*, *ID Magazine*, the Mead Annual Report Show, *Print*, *AR100*, and *Creativity*. Yang has served as a judge in many international design shows and conferences. She has a BFA in Graphic Design from Carnegie Mellon University.

EMMANUEL LAFFON DE MAZIÈRES

Industrial Designer, Incase   WWW.EMMANUEL-LAFFON.COM

Emmanuel Laffon de Mazières was born in 1983 in Toulouse, France. He graduated with honors from Institut Superieur de Design (France) in 2006. After working for IDEO, One&Co, and Fuseproject, he freelanced for small consultancies and is now an industrial designer with Incase in San Francisco. His aim is to create iconic designs using symbols that reside in our memory, and to develop a special relationship between products and people. Emmanuel likes to picture himself as an antenna that catches trends and desires from the air to give them shape using the filter of culture.

JAY TAILOR LAIRD

Founder, Metaversal Studios   WWW.METAVERSALSTUDIOS.COM

Jay Laird is the Founder and Lead Game Designer of Metaversal Studios. A screenwriter and comic book author, his credits include the Roger Corman-produced film *The Strangler's Wife* and "Star Wars Tales" from Dark Horse Comics. He has been teaching writing, programming, animation, and design at Northeastern University for a over a decade, his career there culminating in his co-development of the university's graduate and undergraduate game design programs. He is currently completing his MFA in Creative Writing at Lesley University while producing a feature-length documentary and writing various articles and reviews in his spare time. He also still finds time to wash behind his ears, eat three meals a day, and occasionally, even, to sleep.

JOHN LOCKE

Architectural designer   GRACEFULSPOON.COM

John Locke lives in New York City. He received his M.S. in Advanced Architectural Design from Columbia University's Graduate School of Architecture, Planning and Preservation, where he was awarded the William Kinne Fellows Traveling Prize, the Lucille Lowenfish Memorial Prize, and the William Ware Prize for Excellence in Design/Saul Kaplan Traveling Fellowship. In 2005, John graduated from the University of Texas at Austin with a Bachelor of Architecture degree. Prior to attending Columbia, John worked as a designer with Randall Stout Architects in Los Angeles. He is also the co-founder of Lion in Oil, a graphic design and photography studio.

KEN LOH

Director of Web, Oakley   KENLOH.COM

Long before he understood what "marketing" meant, Ken was unwittingly building brands. Armed with his No. 2 pencil, he never left a Pee-Chee folder unadorned with surf and skateboard logos. At The Mednick Group, he developed advertising and design solutions for a diverse range of clients including Coca-Cola, NBA, NHL, Reebok, and Sega. Ken remained Creative Director when the firm transformed into THINK New Ideas, one of Omnicom's first interactive agencies. At Yahoo! Search Marketing he led creative efforts supporting the promotion of Paid Search. In 2006, those early surf/skate influences re-emerged when Ken joined Oakley to overhaul the company's web business; improving their e-Commerce platform and revitalizing their online branding and marketing initiatives.

KEVIN LONGO

Associate Art Director, RDA Food & Entertaining   WWW.SKEVINLONGO.COM

Kevin graduated from Northeastern University in 2004. At RDA Food & Entertaining (*Every Day with Rachael Ray, Taste of Home*, allrecipes.com), he helps oversee the in-book/online creative as well as their visual presence in the marketplace. He moved to New York City when, on a whim, he wrote to *Entertainment Weekly* to convince them that he was was their biggest fan—luckily they agreed and hired him. He currently resides in Manhattan with his wife and spends his spare time making music, traveling, and photographing it all along the way.

TERRENCE MASSON

Director, Creative Industries, Northeastern University   VISUALFX.COM

With 20 years of production experience, Terrence's work includes feature film (*Star Wars*), interactive (SimCity 4), and award-winning short animated films (*Bunkie & Booboo*). He also single-handedly developed the CG pipeline for *South Park*. Terrence consults with major production studios on creative development and pipeline efficiency, and is a member of the Producers Guild of America, the Visual Effects Society and active in SIGGRAPH since 1988, including 2006 Computer Animation Festival Chair and currently as SIGGRAPH 2010 Conference Chair. He is the author of *CG101: A Computer Graphics Industry Reference (Second Edition)*.

CEMRE OZKURT

Senior Character Modeler, Electronic Arts   WWW.FISTIK.COM

Cemre Ozkurt was born and educated in Istanbul. He started creating short animations on his brother's Amiga computer when he was seven years old. He studied at the Graphic Design Academy at Mimar Sinan University. His work was published in many magazines, and won several awards in international competitions. Cemre worked on several different games and movies like *Spiderman 2*, Disney's *Mickey's Twice Upon a Christmas*, *Unreal Tournament*, *Sims 3* and Oscar-nominee short film *Gopher Broke*. He currently lives in San Francisco and works at Electronic Arts.

CYNTHIA RABUN

Senior Director, Human Resources, Dolby Laboratories, Inc.

Cynthia Rabun has over 20 years experience recruiting creative and marketing professionals for companies as diverse as Sony Music Entertainment Inc., Levi Strauss, and Landor Associates. Currently, she heads up the recruitment function for Dolby in San Francisco, CA. Cynthia has a bachelor's degree from U.C. Berkeley's Business Administration, where she studied marketing.

KYLE RAFFILE

Animator   WWW.COMFORTKYLE.COM

Kyle Raffile is a lighting artist and generalist animator who was a dual major in Multimedia Studies and Animation at Northeastern University.

STAN RICHARDS

Principal, The Richards Group   RICHARDS.COM

Stan Richards founded The Richards Group, now one of the nation's premier creative resources, after graduating from New York's Pratt Institute. His work has received awards in virtually every major competition in the world. The company was named *Adweek*'s Agency of the Year five times between 1988 and 2002. In 1997, *Graphis* magazine named The Richards Group one of the 10 best agencies in the world. Stan received the AIGA Gold Medal for career achievement in design in 1996, and in 1999, he received the highest honor available to a creative with his election to the Art Directors Hall of Fame, joining such luminaries as Walt Disney, Norman Rockwell, and Andy Warhol.

JASON RING

Creative Director, AKQA   JASONRING.COM

Jason Ring is a creative director at AKQA's San Francisco office and has over 15 years of design experience. His work includes digital and traditional solutions for iconic brands and cultural institutions like Brooklyn Academy of Music, McDonald's, Motorola, New Museum, Sprite, Target, and Yale. Ring holds a master's degree from the Institute of Design in Chicago. His work has been featured in *AdWeek, Artnews, Communication Arts, I.D., The New York Times* and *The Wall Street Journal*. Jason is a practitioner of traditional Chinese martial arts and a student of 34th-generation Shaolin Temple fighting monk Shi Yan Ming. He has participated in numerous martial arts performances in the U.S.l.

ELLEN SANDOR

Director, (art)n   ARTN.COM

Ellen Sandor is an internationally recognized multimedia artist, with works in the permanent collection of the International Center of Photography, Fred Jones Jr. Museum of Art, University of Oklahoma, Santa Barbara Museum of Art, and The Smithsonian. Ellen is an Affiliate of eDream, National Center for Supercomputing Applications, University of Illinois at Urbana-Champaign. She is a board member of the Lawyers for the Creative Arts, INTUIT, OXBOW, Board of Governors of The School of the Art Institute of Chicago, and chair of the Gene Siskel Film Center Advisory Board at SAIC, member of the Committee on Photography at the Art Institute of Chicago and an advisory board member of the Fred Jones Jr. Museum of Art, University of Oklahoma.

WILL SCOBIE

Illustrator   WWW.REVERIECREATE.CO.UK

An illustrator based in the south of England, Will Scobie produces illustration for clients such as MTV, Kanoti, Radford Wallis, Tullo Marshall Warren, Modern Creatives, and They Create. He is a member of the Coloured In collective. When he is not drawing, he creates electronic music and drinks cups of green tea.

EMIN SINANI

Web Designer, Noa Studios   WWW.NOASTUDIOS.COM

Emin Sinani is a student of industrial design at the University of Technology in Rotterdam, Eindhoven in The Netherlands. He has been designing websites using Flash and After Effects as a freelancer, and now for Noa Studios, for several years, and has recently become interested in animation and videos. Together, he and Paşcal Verstegen won the May 1st Reboot '08 for the Noa Studios v.8 site.

GUNNAR SWANSON

Principal, Gunnar Swanson Design Office   GUNNARSWANSON.COM

Gunnar Swanson's design has won over 100 awards for trademark, publication, type, packaging, and graphic design from the AIGA, *Print, Graphis, How*, the American Corporate Identity series, and other graphic design organizations, books, and magazines. He has written dozens of articles that have appeared in trade press and academic journals, and that were included in three major graphic design anthologies, and published internationally. He is the editor and designer of the Allworth Press book, *Graphic Design & Reading*. He has taught at the Otis College of Art and Design and the University of California Davis, headed the graphic design program at the University of Minnesota Duluth, has directed the multimedia program at California Lutheran University, and now teaches at East Carolina University.

WIP VERNOOIJ

Character Animator   WIPVERNOOIJ.COM

Wip Vernooij is a Dutch animator and cartoonist, based in London. After graduating from The Utrecht School of the Arts (HKU) in Image & Media technology, he continued to study traditional animation at Central St. Martin's College of Art and Design. In the years since then he has worked on various award-winning commercials, independent shorts, and interactive productions for studios like Unit9, PassionPictures, and Tandem Films.

PASCAL VERSTEGEN

Project Director, Noa Studios   WWW.NOASTUDIOS.COM

Pascal "Enkera" Verstegen is studying at the Grafisch Lyceum Rotterdam, The Netherlands. In 2007 he founded Noa Studios with Archan Nair, and was soon joined by Emin Sinani. Every year since 2005 he has spent one month working on a piece to document his current abilities. His graphic work has been recognized with Daily Deviations on the website www.deviantart.com, and with magazine features in the Japanese magazine *Windows100%*, as well as featured on MacThemes.net. Together, he and Sinani won the May 1st Reboot '08 for the Noa Studios v.8 site.

MITCH WEISS

Photographer   MITCHWEISS.COM

Mitch Weiss is a Boston-based photographer who specializes in studio and environmental portraiture. Since childhood he's had a fascination with the concept of stopping time, which has made photography a natural and intuitive format. He received his bachelor's degree in Art from Northeastern University, where he studied process and creative thinking through graphic design. Mitch is an active member of the American Society of Media Photographers in New England and the National Association of Photoshop Professionals.

LUKE WILLIAMS

Graphic Designer, Leo Burnett Advertising   LUKELUKELUKE.COM

Graduated from Maryland Institute College of Art with a BFA in Graphic Design, Luke Williams specializes in print design, with extensive practice in digital photography. He has worked among top professionals in the field including Pentagram partner Abbott Miller, acclaimed design writer Ellen Lupton, founder of Project M John Bielenberg, and renowned lettering enthusiast Marian Bantjes. Luke invested himself in an internship with Pentagram, and spent a year designing apparel graphics for youth clothing collections at Under Armour. Luke continues to evolve as an artist, and is always ready to explore new directions in design.

Index

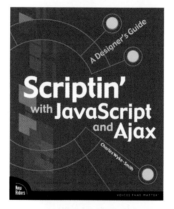